Unhomely Rooms

The Bucknell Studies in Latin American Literature and Theory

Series Editor: Aníbal González, *Pennsylvania State University*

The literature of Latin America, with its intensely critical, self-questioning, and experimental impulses, is currently one of the most influential in the world. In its earlier phases, this literary tradition produced major writers, such as Bartolomé de las Casas, Bernal Díaz del Castillo, the Inca Garcilaso, Sor Juana Inés de la Cruz, Andrés Bello, Gertrudis Gómez de Avellaneda, Domingo F. Sarmiento, José Martí, and Rubén Darío. More recently, writers from the U.S. to China, from Britain to Africa and India, and of course from the Iberian Peninsula, have felt the impact of the fiction and the poetry of such contemporary Latin American writers as Borges, Cortázar, García Márquez, Guimarães Rosa, Lezama Lima, Neruda, Vargas Llosa, Paz, Poniatowska, and Lispector, among many others. Dealing with far-reaching questions of history and modernity, language and selfhood, and power and ethics, Latin American literature sheds light on the many-faceted nature of Latin American life, as well as on the human condition as a whole.

The aim of this series of books is to provide a forum for the best criticism on Latin American literature in a wide range of critical approaches, with an emphasis on works that productively combine scholarship with theory. Acknowledging the historical links and cultural affinities between Latin American and Iberian literatures, the series welcomes consideration of Spanish and Portuguese texts and topics, while also providing a space of convergence for scholars working in Romance studies, comparative literature, cultural studies, and literary theory.

Titles in this Series

César Salgado, *From Modernism to Neo-Baroque: Joyce and Lezama Lima*
Roberto Ignacio Díaz, *Unhomely Rooms: Foreign Tongues and Spanish American Literature*
Mario Santana, *Foreigners in the Homeland: The Latin American New Novel in Spain, 1962–1974*

http://www.departments.bucknell.edu/univ_press

Unhomely Rooms

Foreign Tongues
and Spanish American Literature

Roberto Ignacio Díaz

Lewisburg
Bucknell University Press
London: Associated University Presses

Associated University Presses
440 Forsgate Drive
Cranbury, NJ 08512

Associated University Presses
16 Barter Street
London WC1A 2AH, England

Associated University Presses
P.O. Box 338, Port Credit
Mississauga, Ontario
Canada L5G 4L8

The paper used in this publication meets the requirements of the American National Standard for Permanence of Paper for Printed Library Materials Z39.48-1984.

Library of Congress Cataloging-in-Publication Data

Díaz, Roberto Ignacio, 1960–
    Unhomely rooms : foreign tongues and Spanish American literature / Roberto Ignacio Díaz.
        p.   cm. — (The Bucknell studies in Latin American literature and theory)
    Includes bibliographical references and index.
    ISBN 0-8387-5489-9 (alk. paper)
    1. Spanish American literature—History and criticism.   2. Authors, Spanish American—Language.   3. Latin America in literature.   I. Series.
PQ7081 .D485   2002
860.9'98—dc21   2001035475

In memory of
Carmen de Granda Vidaud
1904–2000

Este viento del sur . . . ¡ay! me devora
Si pudiera dormir . . .

   —José María Heredia (1821)

Heureux qui peut dormir sans peur et sans remords
Dans le lit paternel, massif et vénérable

   —José-Maria de Heredia (1887)

Contents

Acknowledgments

FROM ITS ORIGIN AND THROUGH ITS VARIOUS REBIRTHS, THIS BOOK HAS gained much from the generosity of people and institutions. A Whiting Fellowship in the Humanities allowed me to visit the Library of Congress and devote an entire year solely to writing, while a summer grant from Bates College helped finance a trip to the Bibliothèque nationale in Paris. More recently, the Zumberge Faculty Research and Innovation Fund at the University of Southern California provided substantial support for a full revision of this project, and my colleagues in the Departments of Spanish and Portuguese and of Comparative Literature at USC encouraged me with their goodwill. Peter Starr, specifically, helped me design a place in our curriculum where my research could thrive, while Lucille Kerr, with just a few discreet words of critical wisdom, revealed a new framework for this book's ideas, thereby becoming my most valuable implied reader. I also want to thank the students in my courses and seminars at USC for patiently accompanying me into those very remote provinces of Spanish American literature where my research often conducted me.

Several friends read drafts of this study in whole or in part, or attended lectures I gave on the subject; my gratitude to Roberto Castillo Sandoval, María Luisa Fischer, Efraín Kristal, Adriana Méndez Rodenas, Jorge Olivares, Claudia Parodi, and Enrico Mario Santí for their insightful and enthusiastic responses, and to Aníbal González for having welcomed my manuscript into a new and exciting publishing venture. If this book happily traverses linguistic and literary confines, it is due greatly to the examples of Claudio Guillén and Gustavo Pérez Firmat, each in his own way a veritable scholar *sans frontières*. I am also fortunate to count on Héctor Febles as a devoted reader and friend, one who transposes my words into keys far more imaginative than I could ever suspect. Beyond academia, friends in Los Angeles and San Francisco patiently listened to my tales of writing and rewriting; my thanks to Steve Boehm, Peter Hammond, Michael Landmann-Karny, Colin

Ormsby, Michael Puig and Jeffrey Saadeh for their loyal friendship and support.

The main ideas in this book were first rehearsed publicly at a meeting of the Institute for Cuban Studies in Cambridge, Massachusetts; I am indebted to María Cristina Herrera for opening that door, and also for upholding so lovingly the memory of places and persons. In the audience that afternoon was Verónica Cortínez, and I am most thankful that our forking paths continue to intersect to this day, no matter how far we may be from the original Yard.

When homelands are elusive, houses and even rooms may appear like diminutive republics or kingdoms of one's own, and this is the case with the various spaces that members of my family have inhabited at different times in different parts of the world. My mother, Ana María Esteve, has created homes in unlikely places— most memorably, perhaps, a minuscule room many winters ago in Madrid—and to this day she makes my long flights between Los Angeles and Miami seem like mere passageways in a vast house— our own private country, if you will, one that we share with Juan, Guegui and Joel, and where Claudia María de Lourdes reigns with absolute charm. A prince in his own right, Mitch Karasov maneuvered the *unheimlich* into a new realm—a comical place no doubt, but one where I feel strangely at home. To all of them, my love and gratitude.

An earlier version of chapter 3 first appeared in the article "Merlin's Foreign House: The Genres of *La Havane*," *Cuban Studies* 24 (1994): 57–82. My thanks to the publisher for permission to reprint.

Unhomely Rooms

Introduction: The Unhoused

This book starts with a bit of personal archaeology: my accidental find, at a library, of the three volumes of *La Havane*, by one Comtesse Merlin. Printed in Paris in the 1840s, almost out of sight on a darkened shelf, those dusty old tomes seemed untouched, the virtually forgotten text of an author with a mere handful of readers. Was this a Cuban book, as Merlin suggested on the first page, in a language that was not Spanish? Until then, my knowledge of the writer had been circumscribed to a few critical platitudes. Born in Havana at the end of the eighteenth century and a longtime resident of Paris, Merlin had written a lengthy travel narrative in French about Cuba, the book that I now saw for the first time. I recalled a mention of her name somewhere, no doubt in a footnote—for margins of all sorts have been the literal and metaphorical space habitually reserved for authors from Spanish America who write in languages other than Spanish. In the discourse about literature in this part of the world, like almost everywhere, language and nation are tightly intertwined. The Romantic alliance of *Volksgeist* and native tongue still informs much thinking about nationhood and cultural community, so to write in another language, as Merlin does, often results in critical and literary-historical elision.

As one excavates its various layers, *La Havane* reveals a peculiar form of in-betweenness. If at first the text resembles conventional travelogues in the European mold, it soon displays significant quirks of language and structure. Its French is strewn with numerous words and phrases in local forms of Spanish, while its strategies at times mimic the writing practices of Cuba's incipient national literature, such as *costumbrismo*, the scrupulous delineation of the country's particular mores and patterns of speech. Merlin, then, surfaces not merely as another exoticist traveler in Caribbean waters, but as an uncanny voyager in the interlingual and in what may be termed the interliterary. Here is a writer obviously well versed in French letters, but many passages in her text make sense only if read and evaluated also within the systems, or coherent clusters, of Cuban (or, more generally, Spanish American) literature. This is not a matter of thematics or intertextuality alone, but of exegesis and even intelligibility; *La Havane* invokes an interpretive act that engages the literatures of both France and Spanish America. Moreover, certain decisive meanings of the text—its shifting loyalties to Europe and the New World, for instance—hinge on the tenuous equilibrium established among these systems. The workings of these interliterary links, even as they allow Merlin's name to enter into the house of Cuban writing, signal the necessity of rethinking the traditional bonds between language and national (or continental) literary culture.

Merlin's heterolingualism—the certainty that her French, when viewed from the normative terrain of Spanish, *is* a different tongue—emerges as a strange, even disturbing, presence in countries where identity-thinking has traditionally willed one language to equal one people, and vice versa. But the fact that this author's French is another tongue does not mean that one must view it necessarily as an "other" tongue. If some exclude her prima facie from the national corpus, and if still others underscore only her perceived alterity, a close reading of Merlin's œuvre will reveal it as a fully valid, if perplexing, form of Cuban writing.[1] Moreover, Merlin's case is hardly unique. In virtually every period of Spanish America's history, one can find writers biographically linked with the continent (a term that I employ not only as a geographical, but as a cultural concept) who compose works in languages other than Spanish, or in a mixture of languages. The acknowledgment of these practices depends largely upon the various spatial and temporal parameters along which literary criticism and history construct the bodies of Spanish American literature and its variously intersecting national formations.[2] If some critics and literary historians go back to the pre-Hispanic period and endorse works in the continent's indigenous languages as valid elements in these bodies, and if others look north with favorable eyes to the linguistic heterogeneity of texts by Hispanic authors in the United States, the fact remains that the institutions guiding the study of Spanish American literature traditionally tend to focus solely on writing in Spanish. They have also tended to stress reading in that language, because, often, even those who do view heterolingual authors as possible elements within Spanish American literature tend critically to privilege translations into Spanish over the foreign-tongue originals.

The central positioning of Spanish in the imagination of Spanish America as a cultural and literary community is certainly justified, for Spanish, regardless of its imperial past or its regional differences, is one of the best tokens of, and arguments for, the continent's unity and identity. Beyond tautologies, Spanish is both Spanish America's lingua franca and its universally acknowledged vehicle for literature. If *La Havane* occupies a marginal shelf, Guillermo Cabrera Infante's *La Habana para un infante difunto,* another piece of writing about Merlin's birthplace but one written in Spanish, is visible in bookstores and libraries, curricula and scholarly discussions, from Tijuana to Ushuaia, if not, for other reasons, in Havana itself. But even in the five centuries after Columbus's first landfall, and even within the boundaries of Spanish America, there is ample evidence to suggest the expedience of reading critically beyond the officialdom of monolingualism. As it retrieves Merlin and other such authors from their peripheral sites, this study seeks to redesign the house of Spanish American literature as a multilingual archive: a polyglot location for authors, texts, and readers that may be seen as further evidence of the continent's hybrid makeup. If this heterogeneous library may at first seem to invoke the perils of Babel, the books it contains, when read closely, should reveal themselves as meaningful, if strange and slippery, elements in Spanish America's literary and cultural systems.

A plurality of tongues marks the act of writing in Spanish America as early as the colonial period. The multilingual body—mostly in Spanish, but open to the indigenous languages as well as other tongues—that emerges from even a cursory glance at these five centuries of Spanish rule and political independence is diverse and even bewildering. If welcoming written and oral texts in several languages unsettles the established discussion of Spanish American literature by introducing what seem to be centrifugal elements, heterolingualism itself is difficult to conceptualize as one coherent critical category. It is a forest whose various trees, as if springing from different climates and ages, seem to tell a perplexing story of incongruities. Besides eschewing Spanish, the authors and texts whose linguistic plurality is examined here under the heterolingual umbrella may have little in common among themselves; in fact, they often appear to exemplify altogether dissimilar processes of writing and reading, as even a partial list reveals. Fray Bernardino de Sahagún, for instance, and his native collaborators at the Colegio de Santa Cruz de Tlatelolco, transcribe oral Nahuatl texts using the Latin alphabet, while in Peru, Felipe Guaman Poma de Ayala (whatever his true ethnicity may have been) composes *Nueva corónica y buen gobierno* (1612–15) in Spanish, with notable interpolations in Quechua.[3] Departure from Spanish, then, may be regarded as either an instrument of empire or as an assertion of cultural resistance and continuity. Or one may also view it as Baroque fascination with New World cultural differences, as in Sor Juana Inés de la Cruz, who, situated at the heart of the viceregal court, writes *villancicos* in Latin and Nahuatl.[4] Or perhaps it is a matter of erudite self-affirmation in an international community, as in the case of Rafael Landívar, a native of Guatemala who, as a Jesuit exiled in Bologna, authors *Rusticatio mexicana* (1781), a vast chronicle about New Spain in outlandish—from the viewpoint of Spanish monolingualism—Latin verses: "Salve, cara parens, dulcis Guatimala, salve, / Delicium vitae, fons et origo meae" [Hail, dear fatherland, sweet Guatemala, hail, / Pleasure of life, source and origin of mine].[5] The dominant voices in colonial letters may negotiate several languages, but transactions outside of Spanish do not always favor an author's ulterior reception. Sor Juana is a canonical figure because she also writes, masterfully, in Spanish; but Landívar and others who wrote in Latin, regardless of their possible literary worth, often remain exiled from the discussion for linguistic reasons alone.[6] Texts and oral traditions in the indigenous languages, meanwhile, are often still mostly considered as worthy of anthropological and historical studies, but not of literary scholarship.[7]

Within this putative Spanish American multilingual library, the most salient distinction concerns texts in the continent's original languages and those in non-Spanish European tongues. Long the object of deletions, the New World's original languages have recently, and justly, achieved a more prominent role in the increasingly interdisciplinary history of Spanish American literature. In "Cultures in Contact" (and elsewhere), Rolena Adorno argues convincingly that unless native languages are considered, "there can be no full history of colonial Spanish American culture in the spoken and written word."[8] That this essay is a chapter in the 1996 *Cambridge History of Latin American Literature* suggests the increasing acceptance of Adorno's postulate; also, it reflects the permutations allowed by this particular history's focus not on Spanish

America, but Latin America, a multilingual construct that is often defined to encompass not only Brazil, but also even nations where the Romance languages are not spoken. The influence of configurations cannot be exaggerated; if Merlin is mostly absent from the discussion of Cuban literature, she was to be included in a history of writing in the Caribbean, a multilingual region, projected by Alejo Carpentier and Robert Desnos.[9] Yet, even as it stresses linguistic plurality, my study seeks to show why Spanish American literature remains an indispensable concept for literary scholarship and, quite specifically, for reading the continent's heterolingual texts. As we shall see, Merlin's *La Havane* and other such works reveal their meanings most clearly when viewed within, or against, the dominance of Spanish-language practices of writing.

If anthologies and critical studies confirm how the native tongues are now seen naturally by many as an integral part of Spanish American culture, a similar critical and literary-historical gesture for texts composed in European languages other than Spanish, which is my focus here, may seem at first more difficult to justify and accomplish. Writing in such languages—with the exception, perhaps, of English, or of interlingual forms of English and Spanish, within U.S. Hispanic literature[10]—may still often be perceived as the contrived artifice of certain elites: six or seven authors, perhaps, arrogantly seeking a select, possibly foreign, readership. The idea of snobbery, or at least eccentricity, is often implied; José Donoso humorously reports having read in Buenos Aires "novelas escritas en inglés por elegantes señoras con sombrero" [novels written in English by elegant ladies who wore hats].[11] The continent's indigenous languages, on the other hand, are spoken by millions and call this side of the Atlantic their only home; this is clearly where they appear in the world's linguistic atlases. Survivors of the Spanish conquest, Nahuatl, Quechua, and other tongues, are domestic, not foreign, languages. But English and French, or Italian and Latin and other tongues, are easily regarded as alien elements in these lands, and its authors are banished to other literary traditions. The risk of being branded an "extraterritorial," to use George Steiner's term, is sensed by many of these non-Spanish authors, hence the act in their writings of recording, explicitly and repeatedly, their filial ties with Spanish America.[12] Landívar's invocation in Latin of Guatemala as his "cara parens" is echoed decades later in Merlin's French text, where, from the outset, she clearly positions herself as a "fille de la

Havane" (1:2) [daughter of Havana]. As we shall see in the chapters that follow, it is often not vanity, but longing, that lies at the heart of writings by Spanish America's heterolinguals.

The critical quandary, however, is difficult to escape, for if Landívar's and Merlin's opening words denote the will to assert kinship and reclaim their absent birthplace in and through writing, the language in which they express themselves implies a more profound separation: a seemingly irreversible linguistic exile, often self-imposed, that gainsays not only the monolingual premises of the tradition, but also certain key relations between authors and readers at work in Spanish American literary culture. Even if by definition few writers can achieve their canonical status, authors such as José Martí and Pablo Neruda remain paradigmatic figures, great communicators with devoted national and continental audiences; even Jorge Luis Borges's cosmopolitan meanderings fit well into the monolingual equation, despite Steiner's insightful reading to the contrary, because Borges wrote almost exclusively in Spanish. In this context, one must question whether attempts at self-inclusion, when couched in a foreign language, can be taken simply at face value: even if one is critically receptive to the heterolinguals, it is unclear who their readers can be, or what type of reading community they are able to sustain. The normal lack of mutual comprehension between heterolingual authors and the continent's readers is the most obvious impasse that this study will try to resolve. Despite the fact that many readers in Spanish America do know other languages, Spanish American literature itself has been constructed as a monolingual tradition. Only through a conceptual shift will we be able to house within the tradition the authors of heterolingualism as well as the practice of reading and evaluating their works in the languages in which they were written.

If the previous sentences—like, indeed, the title of this study and its various chapters—contain words that recall the realm of architecture, such as "to construct," "houses," "rooms," and "habitations," it is because I seek to underscore the artificial nature of thinking about culture. This might be especially true in the cases of Spanish America and its nations, whose strands are nothing if not heterogeneous and where acts of imagination take place regularly in order to underscore similarities and assuage differences. In this context, chapters 1 and 2 investigate various textual strategies through which authors as well as literary critics and historians, despite the evidence of multilingualism, have elevated one tongue as the natural form of writing and reading in the continent. In various figurations of what José Martí called "our America," literary culture, directly or implicitly, has traditionally built Spanish America on the exclusion of the foreign: a house, as it were, whose touchstone is Spanish, and where indigenous languages may sometimes be heard, but not other European tongues. Yet, some of these texts (fiction, poetry, essay, literary scholarship), which in conjunction seem at first to constitute a discourse for Spanish monolingualism, may also be read to show how even they can make a case for creating a critical space—rooms, if you will, strange yet familiar—for the heterolinguals. (In this conjunction of the strange and the familiar, which I treat in detail in the chapters that follow, I am persuaded by Freud's "Das Unheimliche" [1919] and its implications in Julia Kristeva's discussion of nations and the foreign in *Étrangers à nous-mêmes* [1988]). Haunted by doubts about the autonomous status of Spanish American literature, or of Spanish America itself, it is understandable that part of the critical discussion should have concealed that which could be read as an attempt against the tradition's semblance of unity and coherence, like texts in other languages. In the reconceptualization that I propose, the seemingly foreign rejoins the obviously domestic in forming a new house of Spanish American literature—an uncanny or unhomely edifice for sure, with new problems concerning authors, readers, and literary history, but one that shelters more amply the vast range of writing in Spanish and other tongues by authors from the continent.

In chapters 3 and 4, I explore this idea of Spanish America's possible unhomeliness through the close reading of three heterolingual texts: Merlin's *La Havane* (1844), in which the author's foreign craft, the genre of the travel narrative, adopts forms linked with Cuban writing; *The Purple Land* (1885), by the Anglo-Argentine W. H. Hudson, whose tentative rapprochement to *literatura gauchesca* becomes evident to those who read between the lines of the English text; and María Luisa Bombal's *House of Mist* (1947), an English "version" of her novel *La última niebla* (1935), in which an exoticist romance, so different from the Modernist "original," obliquely tells the story of Bombal's own permutation to English. Resonant with the modalities and intimations of Spanish American literature, these texts yield their meanings most clearly when read not only as French, English, or U.S. American works, but as elements within the systems of Spanish American writing. Merlin, for instance, seems torn between her role as a French author writing to Europeans (the various recipients of the text's "letters") about an exotic island and, on the other hand, the paradoxical assumption—the real possibility—that she can also become a Cuban author through and despite her foreign tongue. In the cases of Hudson and Bombal, my focus shifts to the reader: each text, consciously or not, invokes a recipient familiar with two languages and two literary cultures. Influenced by Freud, I call this figure the unhomely reader, not only due to its bilingual or "biliterary" condition, but because its horizon of expectations can also encompass the uncanny space between languages and literatures that Spanish American heterolinguals create. In the end, these authors, texts, and readers show that the notions of "home" and "abroad," or "domestic" and "foreign," are spurious opposites that do not fully account for their interstitial habitation—unless, following Freud's discovery in his linguistic probe of *unheimlich* ("uncanny") and *heimlich* ("homely," but also "secret"), the two conceptual poles may be seen to contain a common ground.

Finally, chapter 5 retakes the issues of writing and reading in a foreign tongue, but now from the viewpoint of the Spanish American "boom" of narrative fiction. The international recognition achieved by this group of authors in the 1960s has arguably resulted in a sense of cultural self-confidence that allows more easily than before a benevolent reconsideration of the tradition's heterolingual margins. A canonical author in Spanish, Guillermo Cabrera Infante writes *Holy Smoke* (1985) and some short fiction in English, mirroring the unhomely practices of Cuban heterolingual writers, specifically Merlin: a fragment of *La Havane* is woven into Cabrera Infante's English-language text. Carlos Fuentes, in his novel *Una familia lejana* (1980), tells a story of translingual migration in which the Spanish American origins of several French-language poets play a crucial role: José-Maria de Heredia, born near Santiago de Cuba; and the Comte de Lautréamont (Isidore Ducasse), Jules Laforgue, and Jules Supervielle, all three natives of Montevideo. By writing in another language, or by writing about those who do, Cabrera Infante and Fuentes tell a story of Spanish American literature that literary history often forgets or suppresses. They, I shall argue, achieve through literature a retrieval of and a meditation on heterolingualism that in literary history has often been tentative at best.

But why should one read and preoccupy oneself with these heterolinguals? First, I believe, because they are there, even if this sounds banal, or even if the location of *there*—what library, what country, what history?—is not always altogether clear. Specifically, writing in English and French is not a rare practice among Spanish Americans in the nineteenth and twentieth centuries. In fact, some of the authors who eschew Spanish for another tongue occupy important places in those literary traditions wherein because of linguistic reasons they are more easily included. Heredia, the Parnassian poet, becomes a member of the Académie française, while Lautréamont, Laforgue, and Supervielle are also part of the canon of French poetry. But there are many other cases. Foreshadowing Merlin's return to Cuba, Flora Tristan travels to her father's native Peru and writes *Les Pérégrinations d'une paria* (1838); also the result of a journey is Ramón Páez's *Wild Scenes in South America; or, Life in the Llanos of Venezuela* (1862). In Argentina, the best-known case is that of Hudson, both a naturalist and a fiction writer; but there is also Eduarda Mansilla de García, author of *Pablo ou la vie dans les pampas* (1869), as well as Lucas Bridges, whose autobiographical *Uttermost Part of the Earth* (1948) chronicles the first English settlement on Tierra del Fuego. Born in Chile, Santiago Arcos composes *La Plata: Étude historique* (1865), while the Peruvians Ventura and Francisco García Calderón are the authors of fictional and political works, respectively, written in French. Two natives of Venezuela also write foreign-language memoirs: Reynaldo Hahn, in French; and T. R. Ybarra, in English. Born in Britain but a longtime resident of Buenos Aires, William Shand writes in English and Spanish; while, in reverse trans-Atlantic journies, Eduardo Manet leaves Cuba and Silvia Baron Supervielle emigrates from Argentina, both becoming authors in French, like Mariano Brull from Cuba and César Moro from Peru, both bilingual poets, and like Héctor Bianciotti, the Argentine novelist who also moved from Spanish to French. In recent years, there has been a growing critical interest among scholars of Spanish American literature in some of these figures, even if the theoretical implications of heterolingualism still remain, for the most part, unexplored.[13]

Interestingly, heterolingualism also concerns several of the continent's "representative" authors. If some of the writers mentioned above are little known outside of their local contexts, several of Spanish America's best-known literary figures—besides Bombal and Cabrera Infante, as well as Fuentes—occasionally write works in other languages, engage in the practice of self-translation, or both: Rubén Darío, José Martí, Vicente Huidobro, Victoria

Ocampo, Jorge Luis Borges, Alejo Carpentier, José Donoso, Manuel Puig, Edmundo Desnoes, Rosario Ferré, and Ariel Dorfman, among others. But if Darío and Martí, for instance, are securely anchored at the center of the Spanish American literary canon, one must still investigate whether Darío's poems in French, such as "Pensée" and "Chanson crepusculaire," or Martí's essays published, if not directly written, in English—"The French Water-Colorists," "The Bull Fight," and others—make any sense, literally and literarily, to readers of Spanish American literature.[14]

A direct consequence of the author's long residence in New York, Martí's publications in English signal *avant la lettre* a major fork in the issue of linguistic alterity and literary community: the writing of Hispanic authors in the United States, often in English or in the openly interlingual forms of Spanglish (or, in Martí's case, English versions, by someone else, of essays that Martí wrote originally in French). Several questions emerge. Can works by U.S.-identified authors such Cristina Garcia and Junot Diaz be read as Spanish American texts as well? If so, what does this double habitation mean for Spanish American—and, for that matter, also U.S. American—literary criticism and history? And what about Elena Poniatowska's translation of Sandra Cisneros's *The House on Mango Street* (1989) into Spanish—should this act be read as a welcoming gesture that shelters the author also in the house of Mexican fiction? And beyond the United States and Spanish American borderlands, beyond English and French, is it justified to read, say, Witold Gombrowicz's Polish œuvre, as some have suggested, in the context of Argentine literature?[15] And what is the literary expression of the Welsh in Argentina and the Germans in Chile, or of Chileans in Swedish and Argentines in Italian? And what, if any, is the significance of Wallace Stevens's and José Rodríguez Feo's cross-cultural dialogue in *Secretaries of the Moon* (1944–55; publ. 1956), their novel-like correspondence in English?[16] Or what about Octavio Paz's work with three other poets in *Renga* (1971), a tetralingual volume? Or Cabrera Infante's collaboration with his translators—can those altered texts change how we think about the limits of Cuban literature? And how should one read *Revelations on the Paraguayan War* (1866), a pamphlet whose missing Spanish original is attributed to Domingo F. Sarmiento by Enrique Anderson Imbert?[17]

These questions may seem to undermine the essentialist arguments on the autonomous character of the Spanish American canon as well as some deeply held views on the production and reception of literature in the Spanish American context. When confronted with this possible sequel of blurred critical categories, it is easy to understand why heterolingualism is for many best left alone. But this motley crew of authors bespeaks the fact that writing in another language is not an exceptional occurrence in the Spanish American realm of letters. Yet, as I said, the acute differences among them—and among their texts and the readers they invoke—also underscore the difficult challenge of designing orderly paradigms for the study of heterolingualism. One may start by arguing, first of all, whether "Spanish American" accurately describes many of these writers, whose biographical circumstances, such as birth, lineage, and residence, constitute a possible link with the continent, but not necessarily a site of literary-historical filiation. Mansilla de García is in every way an Argentine, even if she writes in French, but Tristan arrives in Peru only at age thirty, and remains there for little over a year's time. The riddle that heterolingualism posits is intricate, moreover, because writing in another language may signify little for an author's status, as in the cases of Darío and Martí, or it may be seen to imply a significant estrangement from Spanish American literature, as it happens with Landívar and Merlin. In all of these instances, however, heterolingualism involves a central dilemma in literary history: determining who and what should be "in" or "out" when it comes to drawing the virtually official portraits of national and continental letters. Biography and thematics are important criteria, but they cannot function as a litmus test. To cite one example, one would be hard-pressed to include *The Old Man and the Sea* (1952) within Cuban or Spanish American literature, despite the novel's Cuban protagonist or Hemingway's long residence near Havana. I will argue, however, that in the case of Merlin and others, the facts of biography, especially when underscored by a textual engagement with the native land, should at least be seen to call for a suspension of disbelief, a delayed judgment, until a critical act of reading has taken place that may reveal, or not, the text's possible meanings in the context of Spanish American literature.

Nevertheless, summary exclusions, often of an arbitrary ontological nature, have been the rule when confronting the heterolinguals and their works. Merlin, again, is a good example. Seeking to settle the thorny question of Merlin's "essence" for good, Gastón Baquero states, "una cubana escritora no es siempre una escritora cubana" [a Cuban who writes is not always a Cuban writer].[18] Cleverly concise, Baquero's bon mot exemplifies how rhetoric serves the intertwining prejudices of nationalism and literary evaluation, but it fails to explain the mazelike threads of *La Havane* and the true complexity of its interliterary relations. Regardless of critical pronouncements, the text still happens to exist, and its linguistic alterity, though perplexing, may say as much about culture in the author's native land—marked by literal and figurative translation[19]—as the most traditional sketches of manners and customs by Merlin's Hispanophone contemporaries.

But to declare the writings of Merlin and others as elements in Spanish American literature, as I do here, should be not only an act of will—although I am not ashamed to describe my critical gesture, initially, as willful, *voluntarioso*—but a demonstrable necessity in the search for sense and signification. These, I believe, are still valuable, perhaps indispensable, factors in the lives of nations and cultural communities, where thinking about local identity continues even in the face of globalization. Literary archaeology's objets trouvés are not for mere exhibit alone, but ought to be engaged in a process of meaningful relations with other works in the literary tradition to which they purport to belong. Although it eschews the notion of national literature, Claudio Guillén's conceptualization of literary system suggests a possible critical method for reading and thinking about heterolingual texts. In Guillén's discussion of literary history, "a system is operative when no single element can be comprehended or evaluated correctly in isolation from the historical whole (or 'conjuncture'—in Spanish, *conjunto* or *coyuntura*) of which it is a part."[20] Guillén describes this view of literary system as "relatively open, loose, disjointed,"[21] and this theoretical flexibility matters, for the picture that ultimately emerges from reading heterolingualism should not mimic the unwieldy taxonomies of much previous literary criticism and history. In the exemplary case of Merlin, as the conceptual rigidity of literary borders starts to vanish, new meanings come forth that point to the long reach not only of French, but also of Spanish American literature. What matters is not whether Merlin is a Cuban or French author (she is arguably both), but that her text's complexity should not be concealed for the sake of narrow nationalisms or neat literary classifications.

If the figure of Merlin speaks dissonantly with respect to the continent's established literary-historical narratives, it cannot be erased without misrepresenting the possible limits of writing by Cubans and other Spanish Americans. For, if *La Havane* undergoes a permutation when read as a Spanish American text, Spanish American literature, too, as non-Spanish elements become meaningful under its sway, emerges as a more complex and influential category than monolingualism would allow. Literary-historical representation, of course, can never be absolute and whole; as David Perkins states in *Is Literary History Possible?* "the only complete literary history would be the past itself,"[22] and such total recall would be as cumbersome as the all-recording memory of Borges's protagonist in "Funes el memorioso." What I propose, then, is not mere augmentation (although this will occur), but rather a critical opening that will be fine-tuned enough to retrieve and incorporate seemingly discordant, but ultimately meaningful, voices and inflections. In summary, then, the objective of this study is twofold. First, by reading English and French works by Spanish Americans within Spanish American literature, I seek to demonstrate how this heterolingual assembly of writings reveals a range of signifying notes that would remain unperformed, as it were, if read solely as part of the tradition to which language alone seems to point. Second, if these texts are indeed meaningful within this literary culture, then certain paradigms of Spanish American literature—the linguistic premises of the tradition, but also the concepts of author and reader—must be revised in order to account for the quirks of heterolingualism. Beyond literary studies, my insertion of foreign languages within the continent's systems should also modify how one defines and discusses Spanish American culture in general, which is, after all, what other disciplines have already done. That the heterolinguals are there is not just a fact, but a call for interpretation. If anthropology, history, and linguistics fully recognize Spanish America's multilingual condition, the field of literary studies, by examining its own axioms and broadening its concepts, may well opt to do the same in the future.

I am aware that promulgating a non-Spanish Spanish American literature engages an apparent oximoron, one that portends disorientation and instability, two related ills that have long plagued the continent's cultural self-perception. But the linguistic decentering proposed here (I am reminded of Paz's "Centro móvil," his preface to *Renga*) does not affect Spanish America alone, nor does it entail any radical cracks in its literature's conceptual edifice. Heterolingualism, the interlingual, and the interliterary boast, after all, an

ancient lineage in the Hispanic traditions. The origins of Spanish
poetry itself are often constructed on the Mozarabic *jarchas,* the
short interlingual verses—Romance and Semitic—attached to Arabic and Hebrew poems, while the use of another script also marks
the strange texts of *literatura aljamiada* with a literal sense of unhomeliness. (The literature of Spain itself is at least tetralingual,
given the country's linguistic plurality; in addition, one may consider authors such as José María Blanco White and texts such as
Felipe Alfau's *Locos: A Comedy of Gestures* [1936] or Pablo Pi-
casso's play, *Les quatre petites filles* [1948]). Garcilaso de la Vega,
like other Renaissance authors, wrote not only in his vernacular
Spanish, but also in Latin, while the Inca Garcilaso, his namesake
born in the New World, infused his *Comentarios reales* with words
and metaphors from Quechua, as we shall see in chapter 2. Similarly, the imprint of other tongues also defines the novels of José
María Arguedas, Miguel Ángel Asturias, and Augusto Roa Bastos.
    The conjunction of several languages in one author, text, or tra-
dition is also, of course, an ancient phenomenon in Western writing, from the Middle Ages through the twentieth-century avant-
garde, as Leonard Forster shows in *The Poet's Tongues.* In *Extraterritorial,* as he explores the writings of Borges, Samuel Beckett, and
Vladimir Nabokov, George Steiner speaks of these authors' linguistic plurality and "unhousedness" as emblematic of "a lost center"
(viii); this recognition, if disturbing, in fact contributes to a better
understanding of works by these writers and, more generally, of
writing in the twentieth century. If this study, too, ventures to re-
configure Spanish American literature as an entity with no fixed
linguistic midpoint, it does so expecting a better understanding of
Spanish America's hybridity, for a new critical stance receptive to
heterolingualism will allow us to retrieve and gain insight into other
authors and texts that have long been concealed, but who speak,
in their own way, to the kaleidoscopic nature of Spanish America.
Oddly enough, if at first it may seem that the acknowledgment of
heterolingual practices unhinges Spanish from its customary central position in literary studies, it will become apparent that the
practices of writing in Spanish are still a major signifying element
even in those works that shun the language. Consequently, this
study does not seek to deauthorize the long tradition of literary history for which Spanish is the sine qua non of Spanish American
literature; rather, the chapters that follow are meant first and foremost, if I may borrow the Inca Garcilaso's words, as a *comento y*

glosa, commentary and gloss. It is also a kind of translation, not in the literal, but in the etymological sense: a carrying across of authors and texts for other readers to estimate and, it is hoped, esteem.

What may lead someone to write in another language is often a matter for speculation. Seeking various forms of vertigo, one may argue, the parachuting speaker in Huidobro's *Altazor* (1931) proclaims, "Se debe escribir en una lengua que no sea materna" [One must write in a tongue that is not a mother tongue].[23] Heeding his own advice, Huidobro was himself a bilingual author who wrote in French as well as Spanish. Also a bilingual poet, Joseph Brodsky states, "When a writer resorts to a language other than his mother tongue, he does so either out of necessity, like Conrad, or because of burning ambition, like Nabokov, or for the sake of greater estrangement, like Beckett."[24] Brodsky's own reason for transiting from Russian to English, he confesses, is his love for W. H. Auden and his poetry. Reading the authors mentioned by Brodsky, one can also think of similar motivations in the Spanish American heterolinguals. But regardless of what the causes may be, the textual outcome—these adventures and misadventures in the interlingual and the interliterary—is where the focus of this study will be. If the walls that separate languages and literatures are permeable, as these works show, there is no reason then why the critical discourse should not be equally open. Significantly, a sense of greater estrangement will result, as it does in Brodsky's reading of Beckett, but estrangement itself, I hope to show, is also a valid cornerstone upon which to build a national, or a continental, literary tradition.

The title of this study was first suggested by Supervielle's "La Chambre voisine" (1930), a poem functioning as an intertext in *Una familia lejana,* Fuentes's restoration, through fiction's partial magic, of writing in French by authors from Spanish America. Rooms and houses—there is a villa in Fuentes's novel where France and Spanish America mysteriously coinhabit—are also a bridge to Freud's essay and etymologies. Metaphorically and inherently, Freud's notion of the *unheimlich,* in its eventual convergence with its opposite *heimlich,* lies at the heart of what heterolingual authors create: textual spaces that are familiar, yet strange; strange, yet familiar. As they traverse and confound linguistic and literary codes, the heterolinguals show distinctly how some elements in the culture of Spanish America (in other cultures, too) may emerge, perhaps, as startlingly alien even to those readers who think they know the literary culture as well as they know themselves. But, then again, how well does one know oneself? In this context, culture no longer needs to be viewed as a set of commonly shared connotations, as some would have it, but may re-emerge as an unhomely site where the sense of strangeness that Freud locates in the individual extends to national, or continental, communities as well.[25] Despite the semblance of fragmentation, one should not regard this with fear. If this study strives to construct a critical house with a few odd rooms, it also attempts to prove how the strange inhabits in a natural, not menacing, way even those cultural locations whose original blueprints had stressed the familiar intimacy of linguistic homogeneity. Moreover, when brought to light, the unhomeliness of heterolingualism should reveal its own kind of strange beauty. If one of the tenets of verbal art is defamiliarization, these writings in other tongues will provide readers with new lenses through which to see the continent's practice of literature beyond the most evident corpus written in Spanish.

1

The House of Spanish, I:
Maskings of Our America

IN DECEMBER 1945, THE CHILEAN POET GABRIELA MISTRAL BECAME THE first Spanish American author to receive the Nobel Prize for literature. The ceremony at Stockholm's Stadshuset, filled with pageantry, is lovingly chronicled by Manuel Mujica Lainez in an article for Buenos Aires's *La Nación,* later reprinted in *Placeres y fatigas de los viajes* (1986), a collection of travel pieces on Europe. Written mostly in the 1940s and 1950s, Mujica Lainez's fifty-some essays in that book reveal what some may perceive as an upper-class Argentine's inevitable passion for the Old World's established cultural forms: Shakespeare at Stratford-on-Avon; the Gothic heights of León and Chartres; opera at La Scala and La Fenice; even the mythic oracle at Delphi. If in Spain the traveler feels at home "por razones que se vinculan con las viejas raíces de la sangre" [for reasons linked to the ancient sources of my blood],[1] but remains identified as a foreigner because he does not sound like a Spaniard when he speaks, his selective affinities with Europe are virtually complete once he arrives in France: "en París, los que hemos aprendido el francés de pequeños logramos, si operamos con fortuna, pasar por franceses" (209), [in Paris, those of us who learned French as children, if we operate with good fortune, are able to pass for French]. For Mujica Lainez, as for other Argentine figures of his generation and upbringing—the names of Victoria Ocampo and Jorge Luis Borges readily come to mind—language proficiency goes hand in hand with deep cultural liaisons that transcend the strict limits of nation and continent. English and French (other tongues, too, but to a lesser extent) become languages of reading, if not also, at times, of writing. Mujica Lainez's invocation of "fortuna" to describe his talent in French is interesting, for it signals not only the pleasures inherent in a tourist's sojourn, but also

29

one Spanish American man's skill in camouflaging his origin and masking himself, perhaps, in another self. That heterolingualism should then be associated by some with a certain measure of cultural elitism hardly comes as a surprise.

In Sweden, however, the very cosmopolitan Mujica Lainez, as he affectionately greets Mistral after the ceremony, vehemently invokes their common cultural roots, predicated, as we shall see, on the language that Spanish Americans share. Approaching her, he tells Mistral, "Señora, considere usted que es el abrazo de nuestra América" [Madam, please realize that this is our America that embraces you].[2] One must note the phrase "our America," for it reverberates with specific meanings in the Spanish American context. "Nuestra América" (1891) is the title of the best-known essay by José Martí, who, of all nineteenth-century intellectual figures, perhaps most clearly incarnates Spanish America's attempt for self-affirmation vis-à-vis the rest of the world, specifically Europe and the United States. First published in 1891 in a Mexico City newspaper and later reprinted in numerous anthologies of Spanish American literature, "Nuestra América" is traditionally read as Martí's cultural and political manifesto, an outcry against the imperial designs of the United States and a call to Spanish America to forge a cultural platform of its own by turning inwards: "La universidad europea ha de ceder a la universidad americana. La historia de América, de los incas acá, ha de enseñarse al dedillo, aunque no se enseñe la de los arcontes de Grecia. Nuestra Grecia es preferible a la Grecia que no es nuestra" [The European university must bow to the American university. The history of America, from the Incas to the present, must be taught in clear detail and to the letter, even if the archons of Greece are overlooked. Our Greece must take priority over the Greece which is not ours].[3] That Mujica Lainez should recall Martí's phrase when speaking with, and writing about, Mistral bespeaks a collective imagination beyond national borders that fits well into Martí's vision of Spanish America as one community with a cultural core of its own. But what I seek to explore here is how various literal and oblique invocations of "nuestra América"—not just Martí's essay, but a number of other texts dealing with issues of culture in the continent—create, perhaps unwittingly, a discourse in which English and French heterolingualism is often disregarded, or even branded as negative, in favor of the homogenizing role of Spanish. This discourse encompasses a multiplicity of texts belonging to various genres: fiction, poetry, literary criticism, history, journalism, and cultural theory. But monolingualism, with all its benefits for identity-thinking, is often a mirage; even as it elevates the dominance of Spanish, the discourse of "nuestra América" at times also exposes significant cracks through which foreign tongues come back to haunt the critical edifice. If one listens and reads closely, our America emerges then as an unhomely America, but this, I suggest, is also an America we can, and should, call our own.

In discussions of nineteenth-century Spanish America, Martí is often placed in opposition to Domingo Faustino Sarmiento, the Argentine author who later became president of his nation. If Sarmiento's call for European settlers to civilize the vast expanses of Argentina is often viewed as an impediment to New World cultural independence, Martí's apology for native forms leads, inversely, to his virtual consecration in much of the critical discussion, including literary history. In Jean Franco's *Spanish American Literature since Independence* (1973), for instance, an insightful analysis of the various incarnations of "civilización y barbarie" in nineteenth-century Argentine writing ends with a caveat. Sarmiento and other Romantic authors such as Esteban Echeverría and José Mármol "still had a colonised imagination," but Martí, before the turn of the century, would achieve, according to Franco, a radical shift grounded on the autochthonous: "It was not until José Martí that a Spanish American writer attempted to find virtues in the barbarism that European civilisation utterly condemned."[4] Franco's words—her use of "still" and "until"—imply a linear literary-historical process and narrative wherein that which is perceived as foreign, or even foreign-influenced, is often regarded as a defect or detour.[5] Indeed, in *Facundo* (1845), Sarmiento's ambivalence regarding the indigenous and absolute love of things European reaches at times an extreme level, as when he extols the industriousness of certain immigrants: "ningún gaucho alemán ha abandonado su trabajo, su lechería o su fábrica de quesos para ir a corretear por la Pampa" [No German gaucho has ever left his work, his dairy farm, or his cheese factory just to run around the pampas].[6] Combining the signs of "civilization" and "barbarism," the uncanny *gaucho alemán* bespeaks Sarmiento's racial preferences.[7] In this context, one can sympathize with Franco's argument for progress; moreover, one can easily see why European languages besides Spanish—which also mark the text of *Facundo*, especially the epigraphs—are viewed by some as alien, even alienating, vehicles of expression.

Yet, colonized or not, the fact remains that Sarmiento is as much a Spanish American author as Martí, whose texts in French and English, incidentally, may tell a more complex story of the native and the foreign in Spanish American literary culture than one would initially suspect. Still, the Martí one knows best is the potent Spanish-language voice in "Nuestra América" who salutes the indigenous and African strands in the continent's culture even as he decries imitations of Europe and the United States:

> Éramos una máscara, con los calzones de Inglaterra, el chaleco parisiense, el chaquetón de Norteamérica y la montera de España. El indio, mudo, nos daba vueltas alrededor, y se iba al monte, a la cumbre del monte, a bautizar sus hijos. El negro, oteado, cantaba en la noche la música de su corazón, solo y desconocido, entre las olas y las fieras. (6:20)

> [We were a masquerader in English breeches, Parisian vest, North American jacket, and Spanish cap. The Indian hovered near us in silence, and went off to the hills to baptize his children. The Negro was seen pouring out the songs of his heart at night, alone and unrecognized among the rivers [waves] and wild animals. (91)]

What strikes me in this passage is first and foremost the image of the mask in relation with the foreign—a metaphor suggesting a preposterous form of mimicry, and one that will reemerge in other contexts that will concern indirectly the reading of heterolingual authors. Martí's use of the imperfect tense is curious. The negative conditions that he enumerates are seen as things of the past; suddenly, in the middle of this long paragraph, a switch to the present tense signals the rise of a better Spanish America. One of his first statements concerns mutual knowledge among the peoples of Spanish America: "Se ponen en pie los pueblos, y se saludan. '¿Cómo somos?' se preguntan; y unos a otros se van diciendo cómo son" (6:20) [Nations stand up and greet one another. 'What are we?' is the mutual question, and little by little they furnish answers] (93). In this text that seeks a shared continental imagination, Martí uses his mighty rhetoric to will "nuestra América" into being, but he camouflages the foreign, still easily detectable everywhere: deeming it dangerous—and rightly so, from the viewpoint of politics—he masks the foreign by labeling it an illegitimate mask. One may interject that the cultural ties that bind Spanish America with Europe and the United States can be imagined as indispensable

threads in the continent's history of hybridity, but Martí's conceal-
ings show easily their own fissures, even within the essay: "Las lev-
itas son todavía de Francia, pero el pensamiento empieza a ser de
América" (6) [The frockcoats are still French, but thought begins to
be American] (91). Again, one notes the sartorial metaphor to
speak about the foreign, but there is a modification: what was first
decried as a mask is now simply a form—a foreign-looking artifact,
indeed, but one beneath which it is possible to read the presence
of Spanish America.[8] It is in these openings that "Nuestra
América" best reveals the complexity of Martí's œuvre and, I believe, of Spanish America as a whole, including its eccentric tradition of heterolingualism.

Traveling from Martí's text, the phrase "nuestra América"—with
its elevation of such words as "nuestro" and "nosotros"—may be
traced almost as a leitmotif in the Spanish American cultural discourse, especially, for obvious reasons, where continental forms
are stressed over national ones. It resurfaces clearly in the subtitle
of Roberto Fernández Retamar's essay, *Calibán: Apuntes sobre la
cultura en nuestra América* (1972), a text linked with the Cuban
Revolution's project of cultural self-definition for Latin America
and the Caribbean.[9] It is also the phrase that María Pilar Donoso
employs, almost conversationally, to describe the continent on the
occasion of the symposium of writers and artists at Chichén Itzá, a
major event in the rise and consolidation of a Spanish American
sense of literary unity: "El viaje a Chichén fue en avión, que es el
único medio posible en nuestra América tan ancha y extensa" [We
travelled to Chichén Itzá by plane, the only possible way to travel
in our America, which is so large and spread out].[10] Years before,
in praise of María Luisa Bombal's *La amortajada*, Borges writes:
"libro que no olvidará nunca nuestra América" [a book that our
America will never forget].[11] It comes as no surprise, then, that
Mujica Lainez, celebrating the achievements of a fellow Spanish
American author, should quote the memorable title of Martí's pivotal essay. In these citations and reconfigurations of "nuestra
América," Spanish plays a decisive role, as authors—and, one
must assume, readers as well—tacitly or explicitly situate the lan-
guage at the very core of, and as the common ground for, Spanish
American culture.

If the continent's perceived monolingualism were not such an in-
grained tautology, there would be little need to underscore the fact
that Spanish America lacks a true linguistic center, that it is clearly

a polyglot region. Although the authors whom I study here would be hard to classify among any linguistic minority groups—even the Anglo-Argentine Hudson becomes a writer in England—the general status of other languages in Spanish America still affects their reception. For various reasons, only a handful of nations—Bolivia, Paraguay, Peru, Puerto Rico—have legally recognized at different times the existence of more than one language within their borders, but the fact remains that Spanish is only one of many tongues, indigenous and foreign, that have been or are now spoken in each and every country.[12] If governments obviously exert significant power in the various constructions of nationhood, they are certainly not the only parties responsible for the official elevation of Spanish throughout the continent. The institutions of literature—authors as well as literary historians and critics—have also kindled the language's virtual consecration, not only as lingua franca (which it is, faute de mieux), but as the innate and only feasible instrument for a united Spanish American literary tradition. Given the absence of strong supranational political entities and the limited roles of such cultural agencies as the national academies of the Spanish language, the peerless primacy of Spanish from Mexico and Cuba to Chile and Argentina has come about unofficially. In this chapter, I intend to show how the blueprints for what one may call the house of Spanish are traced by a diversity of texts from various periods and regions. They are but a limited sample of a cultural discourse that exalts Spanish as the continent's truest form of expression, and as the one location of culture where all Spanish Americans may feel more or less at home even outside of their countries. Although I shall take into account historical circumstances, the texts I examine here should not be viewed as a history of literary Spanish in the region. Instead, my brief readings are intended to be synchronic, by which I mean that I view these texts as sections of the construct we now call Spanish American literature. Some of these pieces speak with a magnificent forked tongue: even as they elevate Spanish, they underscore its problematic status and open the door to other languages.

Crucial for this survey are the writings of two figures who lie at the very heart of the continent's literary establishment: Rubén Darío, arguably Spanish America's major poet of all time, and Enrique Anderson Imbert, who may well be is its most accomplished literary historian. Darío's monumental œuvre and Anderson Imbert's vast critical project have directly contributed to a general view

of linguistic homogeneity, yet in some of these authors' writings—
arguably, and significantly, in minor texts—not only do they open
the way for what may turn into a full acknowledgment of heterolingualism, but they also conceive a kind of critical locus—peripheral
and unofficial, yet quite revealing—that can shelter, or even mirror,
the practices of heterolingual writing and reading in Spanish American literature. As they write about Spanish America or about its
literature, Darío and Anderson Imbert take readers along intricate
routes—not linear trails, but veritable gardens of forking paths—
leading up to unforeseen spaces that one, after Freud's "Das
Unheimliche," may describe as uncanny: strange, yet familiar, territories. Heterolingual writings, which the cultural discourse often
does not see, now enter the house of Spanish through a back door,
or through cracks in the wall, invoking the need to rethink the linguistic parameters of Spanish America's literary culture.

Freud's notion of the uncanny emerges here as a valuable concept for thinking about Spanish America's heterolingualism. The
seemingly negative connotations—suggested in such Spanish
words as *sospechoso* and *siniestro,* which Freud, in a brief interlingual gesture, quotes in his essay as translations of *unheimlich*
(196)—may give way, as Julia Kristeva proposes, to a less lugubri-
ous conceptualization of the nation, one that houses the foreign
through a calm admittance of everything, the familiar as well as the
strange. Variously translated into Spanish as "lo siniestro" and "lo
ominoso," Freud's concept has also been rendered as "lo extraño
familiar," and this interplay between the strange and the familiar
best captures the relations between *heimlich* and *unheimlich* that
Freud writes about.

When Spanish American authors speak of their continent, they
often showcase the Spanish language not only as home, but sometimes even as a splendid mansion. That Spanish was the language
of imperial domination—as Antonio de Nebrija's 1492 grammar
had unwittingly foreseen—does not truly matter, as Pablo Neruda
declares in his autobiography, *Confieso que he vivido* (1974): "Qué
buen idioma el mío, qué buena lengua heredamos de los conquistadores torvos" [What a great language I have, it's a fine language
we inherited from the fierce conquistadors].[13] Mujica Lainez's sentiment of cultural pride at the Nobel banquet is also clearly related
to the recognition of Spanish sounds at a prestigious international
gathering: "Por su sencilla dignidad, que todo el mundo calificó in-

mediatamente de ser real en esta monarquía, Gabriela Mistral hizo honor esta tarde a los pueblos de lengua española" (121) [Because of her simple dignity, which everyone in this monarchy described as regal, Gabriela Mistral honored this evening the Spanish-speaking peoples]. What clearly establishes Spanish America at this world institution is its proud assumption of the language of empire, and Mujica Lainez's record of Mistral's triumph possesses a clearly audible linguistic sign: "las bóvedas policromas resonaron con los idiomas diversos: el inglés, el finlandés, el noruego, el español" (124) [the polychrome vaults resounded with the various languages: English, Finnish, Norwegian, Spanish]. Panglobal sympathies are evident here—the Second World War has ended and the United Nations charter has just been signed in November—but each country or region must still boast its own ethnic signs at the international concert of nations. For Spanish Americans, even for a multilingual person such as Mujica Lainez, a common tongue is the ultimate emblem of cultural bonds. If the continent inherits its language from Spain—and Mujica Lainez does not exclude the *madre patria* from sharing in Mistral's victory—it is the manifold nations in the New World that give Spanish its overarching plurality and the sense of supranational community that stems from the existence of numerous Spanish-speaking peoples, all united in reverence of their linguistic patrimony. To George Bernard Shaw's quip that the United States and Great Britain are divided by a common tongue, one may contrast Miguel de Unamuno's sonnet "La sangre del espíritu" (1910): "La sangre de mi espíritu es mi lengua / y mi patria es allí donde resuene / soberano su verbo" [The blood of my spirit is my tongue, and my fatherland is wherever its sovereign word may resound].[14] If these lines may be read as elements in Spain's attempt at cultural self-assertion beyond the military defeat of 1898, Unamuno's poem also underscores the commonality of Spanish that permits the countries of multiethnic Spanish America—"legión de razas" [legion of races]—not only to see Spain as the *madre patria,* but also each other as *repúblicas hermanas.* A Spanish American commonwealth of nations has not yet, and possibly never will, come about, but Spanish as the continent's common wealth—as the keystone of its cultural edifice—is viewed as a virtual truism in the discussion of identity, especially that surrounding literature.

Written upon the fifth centennial of Columbus's first voyage to the New World, and almost five decades after Mistral's journey to

Stockholm, Carlos Fuentes's *The Buried Mirror* (1992) also listens to the unifying role of Spain and its language in a continent whose self-conceptions might otherwise be altogether fragmentary: "We might have a more powerful Indian tradition in Mexico, Guatemala, Ecuador, Peru, and Bolivia; or a stronger European presence in Argentina or Chile; or a stronger black tradition in the Caribbean, Venezuela, and Colombia. . . . But Spain embraces all of us: she is, in a way, our common place, our common ground."[15] Fuentes's book (on which the BBC series was based) accomplishes for a wide international audience what *Terra nostra* (1975) did for a smaller number of readers; both are a vertiginous tour—an astounding tour de force, in the case of the novel—through several centuries of Spanish and Spanish American history and art, with a special emphasis on the cultural diversity of the Hispanic world: the coexistence of Christians, Jews, and Muslims on the Iberian Peninsula, as well as the emergence of new cultural forms and values stemming from the encounter of indigenous Americans, Europeans, and Africans in the New World.

But there is one more link in the Hispanic chain. For Fuentes, the growing visibility of Chicanos and Mexican-Americans and other people of Spanish American descent in the United States is an element in the story of migrations and transculturation that originated with the outward push of Spain. If "Hispanic U.S.A.," the last chapter in *The Buried Mirror,* acknowledges the English-language writing of several Chicano and Puerto Rican authors (344), Fuentes's vision stresses first and foremost the ascendant and defining role of Spanish: "Los Angeles is now the second largest Spanish-speaking city in the world. . . . You can prosper in southern Florida even if you speak only Spanish. . . . By the middle of the coming century, almost half the population of the United States will be Spanish-speaking" (343). It would be difficult to argue with the statement that "multilingualism, then, appears as the harbinger of a multicultural world, of which Los Angeles is the prime example" (347), but one wonders to what extent this city—and the rest of the nation, for that matter—would be relevant to Fuentes's reflections on Spain and the New World if the number of U.S. Hispanics who spoke Spanish were drastically reduced. The dominance of Spanish simplifies the telling of a story that, as Fuentes the novelist reveals in *Una familia lejana,* is vastly more dissonant and complex. In *The Buried Mirror,* Fuentes also urges his readers to "consider the definitive statements of Rosario Ferré or

Luis Rafael Sánchez, who simply decided to write in Spanish from
the island of Puerto Rico" (344). Regardless of the fact that Spanish is Puerto Rico's majority language, and therefore the language
one would normally expect its authors to employ, one still wonders, in the context of Fuentes's apology for Spanish, about the
possible significance of Ferré's habitual practice of self-translation
into English, or, moreover, about the fact that her latest novels, *The
House on the Lagoon* (1995) and *Eccentric Neighborhoods* (1998),
were originally written in English.[16] In this context, one must also
mention Fuentes's own practice of writing in English, as in *Myself
with Others* (1988), a collection of essays.

Ideological proclivities, which often play a major role in the written culture of Spanish America, seem to make little or no difference
when it comes to the elevation of Spanish. Many literary figures
associated with different viewpoints—the right and the left, and
various configurations thereof—become strange bedfellows of sorts
when it comes to the defense of Spanish. Since the rise of nationhood in nineteenth-century Spanish America, as we shall see, the
literary uses of Spanish around the continent have been altogether
heterogeneous—the language's various permutations signifying
aesthetic as well as ideological choices that will also concern heterolingualism. But either as a loyal relation of Spain's Castilian, as
Mujica Lainez and others would have it, or in mercurial metamorphoses, such as one can ascertain in Nicolás Guillén's *poesía afroantillana* and in various literary experiments by other authors, only
Spanish, no matter how extremely its lexicon and syntax are
twisted or bent, is commonly construed as the proper center of nation and literature. Showing its linguistic origins across the Atlantic, Mujica Lainez's first book is entitled *Glosas castellanas* (1935),
while one of Guillén's best-known early poems, radically different
from anything written in Spain, is predicated on the fact of not
knowing another tongue: "Tú no sabe inglé" [You Know No En-
glish]. By choice or by default, the virtues of Spanish monolingualism seem to prevail.

Roughly contemporaries, Mujica Lainez and Guillén may easily
be seen as antipodean figures, situated as they are at opposite ends
of Spanish America and the political spectrum. If Mujica Lainez, a
self-styled linguistic chameleon, can pass for a native in bourgeois
Paris, Guillén, as one of the most visible poets linked with the
Cuban Revolution, rises as a "Third World" voice who serves for a
time as Cuba's ambassador in Moscow. Several of Guillén's now

canonical poems celebrate what seems to be the triumph of Spanish—Cuba's Spanish—in the cultural landscape of Cuba. Featured
in numerous anthologies, Guillén's "Canta el sinsonte en el Turquino" (1964) features a speaker who, returning by airplane to
Cuba upon the revolution's triumph, asserts to a fellow passenger
his own monolingualism: "—¿Inglés, no habla el inglés? / —No,
monsieur; no señor, / nunca lo pude hablar" ['English, don't you
speak English?' 'No, monsieur; no, sir, I was never able to speak
it'].[17] In the poem, the erasure of English from revolutionary Cuba
is part and parcel of other social victories, such the elimination of
racism: "Una cabeza negra y una cabeza rubia juntas van por el
mismo camino" (2:103); [A black head and a blonde head walk together along the same path]. Yet, in a paradoxical gesture that several texts by Guillén and other authors repeat, the interlingual
nature of "Canta el sinsonte en el Turquino" belies its seeming apo-
logia for Spanish monolingualism. After saying farewell to a number
of real-world personalities—"Mr. Wood, Mr. Taft, / adiós. . . . Mr.
Nixon, adiós" (2:102)—the speaker resorts to an allegorical usage
of English that reveals his own significant, if minimal, knowledge of
the language: "Mr. Night, Mr. Shadow, ¡adiós!" (2:102). Even as its
repression is declared, English, or interlingual forms thereof, breaks
into the monolingual spaces of Guillén's text. If the linguistic pos-
tures of Mujica Lainez in the essays in *Placeres y fatigas de los viajes*
and that of the speaker in this poem by Guillén are ultimately dissimilar—the former is proud of his uninflected French, while the latter happily proclaims his ignorance of other languages, especially
the one most clearly resounding with neocolonial overtones—their
oblique apologias for Spanish constitute a strong common bond,
one that sheds some light on the widespread denial of heterolingualism as a possibility of Spanish American literature. Guillén's symbolic valedictory to English, specifically, is particularly significant
in the context of Cuba's literature of exile, which, from the writings
of the Comtesse Merlin in the mid-nineteenth century to the latest
texts by Cuban-American authors in Miami and elsewhere, has
often bid its own literary adieux to Spanish.[18]

But what interests me most in Guillén's own interlingual English,
however, is the possibility of mapping out a territory marked by the
conflict between monolingual nationalism and literary aesthetics.
If English rises as a new sign of empire, it is also one language
upon which Guillén's art often rests: English may be broken in his
poetry, but its residues serve as the bricks that codify new Cuban

texts. The poet's ambivalent use of English—Guillén's unspoken English—is already evident in the early "Tú no sabe inglé," first published in 1930 in Havana's *Diario de la Marina* together with seven other poems under the collective title of *Motivos de son*. "Tú no sabe inglé" poignantly depicts in a nonstandard form of Cuban Spanish what happens to, and with, English in the social and literary battlefields of the nation's culture. Justly regarded by critics as a watershed in the literatures of Cuba and the Caribbean, *Motivos de son* is, as Luis Iñigo Madrigal states, "la adecuación poética de un ritmo folklórico cubano que, a más de ser acabada expresión de la doble raíz étnica y cultural de la isla del Caribe, era una de las formas de la música popular más antigua y difundida en el país" [the poetic adaptation of a Cuban folkloric rhythm that, besides being a well-finished expression of this Caribbean island's double ethnic and cultural roots, was one of the oldest and most widespread forms of popular music in the country].[19] Iñigo Madrigal's words matter because they summarize some of the major concepts upon which the discourse of Cuban culture, including literature, is traditionally built: the dual African and Spanish legacy; the workings of transculturation (a concept, in effect, created by the Cuban anthropologist Fernando Ortiz); and the elevation of the folkloric, especially music, as the ancient and privileged matrix of national art.

Indeed, by transposing the rhythms of the autochthonous *son* into an idiosyncratic verse, one may argue that Guillén creates an essentially Cuban, or even Caribbean, poetic diction. But, in some of these poems, the shadow of English (and, more generally, American culture) reveals itself as a central signifying element in the Afro-Hispanic house of Cuban writing. In "Tú no sabe inglé," the speaker addresses one Víctor Manuel—spelled "Bito Manué," signaling the phonetics of a Cuban dialect—whose Spanish monolingualism has apparently impeded a relation with an American woman:

> La mericana te buca,
> y tú le tiene que huí:
> tu inglé era de etrái guan
> de etrái guan y guan tu tri.

> [The American woman is looking for you,
> and you have to avoid her,
> for your English was just strike one,
> strike one, and one two three.][20]

The text, like others by Guillén, underscores the power of the United States over Cuba, so overwhelming that even love (unless one knows English) may be painful: "No te namore ma nunca, / Bito Manué, / si no sabe inglé, / si no sabe inglé" (1:110) [Don't fall in love again, Víctor Manuel, if [because] you don't know English, you don't!]. In the general context of Guillén's poetic work, Víctor Manuel's exemplum, then, may be interpreted as an oblique call for U.S. American exclusion—as well as that of English—from Cuban affairs, romantic and otherwise.[21] This, achieved decades later, is what the speaker of "Canta el sinsonte en el Turquino" in fact celebrates.

But, beyond the constraints of ideology, the linguistic fabric of this poem demonstrates the extent to which much Cuban literature constitutes an uncanny experiment in the interlingual. The short stanza quoted above may be read as the strange remnants of a Spanish *romance*, a kind of verse that migrated early from Spain to the New World, becoming in the nineteenth century a preferred site for viewing the Hispanic core of Spanish America. As in that traditional poetic form, there is in Guillén's poem a narrative that starts in medias res, and each line may be made to read, albeit awkwardly, as an octosyllable; moreover, the second and fourth lines have a kind of *rima asonante,* as in the *romance* form. Elsewhere, Guillén proves himself a master of classical Spanish meters, but here the poet's art lies in the residues of those forms and, prominently, in the shattered morsels of English found therein. The lexicons of baseball and arithmetic are curiously intertwined here: one is reminded of schoolchildren learning to count in English. As "strike one" becomes "etrái guan", and "one, two, three" an emphatic "guan tu tri," one can see how Guillén's involvement with English is not only a matter of politics, but of poetics.[22] The poem's interlingualism emerges, then, less as an act of eviction than as a testament to accomodation: the foreign is admitted into, or appropriated by, Cuban phonetics, literature, and culture. Even as Guillén reshapes English, the foreign tongue enters into the nation's literature, making the eventual rise of bilingual Cuban-American writing, or even Guillermo Cabrera Infante's decision to write in English from his London exile, not a complete rupture with Cuban cultural forms, but rather an intensification, north of Cuban territorial waters, of practices that were already conspicuous on the island.

But code-switching, which in U.S. Hispanic literature is often read as a liberating break with the literary practices of the monolingual English-speaking mainstream, often retains in the Spanish American tradition the negative ideological underpinnings evident in Guillén's texts. A more recent case in point—one that also concerns possible neocolonial relations—is that of Ana Lydia Vega's "Pollito chicken" (1977). In this story, Suzie Bermiúdez [*sic*], a Puerto Rican woman living in New York, speaks and thinks in both English and Spanish, although, as a reflection of her low cultural self-esteem, she prefers the former. Her interlingual forms of speech are mirrored in the narrator's language, an ironical, if empathic, voice, as when it describes Suzie's impressions on a return visit to Puerto Rico: "Le pareció very encouraging aquella proliferación de urbanizaciones, fábricas, condominios, carreteras y shopping centers. Y todavía esos filthy, no-good Communist terrorists se atrevían a hablar de independencia" [The proliferation of tract housing, factories, condos, roads, and *shopping centers* seemed *very encouraging* to her. And those *filthy, no-good Communist terrorists* still dared to speak of independence {emphasis indicates English in the original}].[23] English, then, as in Guillén's "Canción puertorriqueña" (see note 22), is linked here to native assimilation and the island's colonial status. It is significant that Suzie switches to a non-English Puerto Rican diction only through sexual passion; feeling uninhibited, she proudly proclaims: "VIVA PUELTO RICO LIBREEEEEEEEEEEEEEE!" (79). That colonial Suzie's return to her native language occurs through the mediation of sex seems to invoke certain cultural stereotypes surrounding carnality and the tropics, but the ironic workings of "Pollito chicken" nevertheless underscore the ties that bind language and nationhood, which in Puerto Rican literature are at times expressed by deriding English.[24] In this context, it is not surprising that writing in English—and, as a corollary, the works of Puerto Rican authors in the United States—should have been viewed not as another form of Puerto Rican writing, but as a foreign development, another tongue that threatens the cultural unity of the nation's literature.[25]

It may indeed be a sign of immoderate political or cultural influence from the north that traces of U.S. American speech should be so abundant in Spanish American literature, especially in the Caribbean. This situation, of course, has parallels in other historic and geographic contexts; suffice it to recall the condemnation of the so-called *afrancesados* in eighteenth-century Spain, or the laws against the use of *franglais* on the airwaves of France. In Spanish

America, however, some texts have engaged in the interlingual not as a sign of cultural resistance, but as a vehicle for revealing—and at times even reveling in—a less official side of the nation, one that some would like to remain concealed. Also an unconventional text linguistically, Cabrera Infante's *Tres tristes tigres* (1967) could be read as one more locus for viewing U.S. hegemony in the Caribbean, as in the initial scene at the fabled Tropicana nightclub: "*Showtime!* Señoras y señores. *Ladies and gentlemen*" (emphasis in original); [Showtime! *Señoras y señores.* Ladies and gentlemen].[26] Unlike Guillén's Víctor Manuel, the master of ceremonies who speaks here is also a master of the interlingual, and, given the text's fond attachment to the quirks of Cuban Spanish, one may regard the fluctuation between one tongue and the other as one more natural element in "los diferentes dialectos del español que se hablan en Cuba" (9) [the different dialects of Spanish that are spoken in Cuba], which is how the language of the novel is described in the ironically titled "Advertencia" [Warning], the author's opening remarks to the reader, which are omitted in the novel's English version.

One sentence on this first page of the text is especially suggestive of this embrace of linguistic fracture: "predomina como un acento el habla de los habaneros y en particular la jerga nocturna, que, como en todas las grandes ciudades, tiende a ser un idioma secreto" (9) [the speech of the residents of Havana prevails like an accent, especially the jargon of the night, which, as in every great city, tends to be a secret language]. The intersection of the secret and the nocturnal implies the possible role of literature in uncovering and welcoming languages that may threaten the nation's unity. In its nonjudgmental posture, this voice differs from that which tells Suzie Bermiúdez's story in "Pollito chicken" or that which speaks to Víctor Manuel in "Tú no sabe ingle"; we are also a long way from Mujica Lainez's very proper salutation to Mistral's pristine Spanish words in Stockholm. Just as the story told in Hoffmann's "Der Sandmann" (1817) allows Freud to corroborate the haunting links between the strange and the familiar, the impure tongues spoken by the inhabitants of *Tres tristes tigres* disclose a space whose linguistic fabric is hardly as predictable as one would expect in a nation whose official language is Spanish. Cuban literature itself, as the parodies of several authors in the text's various tellings of Trotsky's death reveal, is hardly monolingual: Martí's and José Lezama Lima's dictions may be rooted in the Spanish

Golden Age, but that of Lydia Cabrera requires a glossary of African terms, while Alejo Carpentier's style abounds in Gallicisms and even citations in "perfecto toscano arcaizante" (244) [perfectly archaized Tuscan dialect (258)], plus a footnote in French to a future translator: "Avis au traducteur: Monsieur, Vous pouvez traduire le titre—'Chasse au Vieil Homme'. S.V.P.—L'Auteur" (241).[27] The irony recalls the manner in which Suzie is viewed in "Pollito chicken," but in this text there is no final redemption through a more native form of speech: all authors, including one *auteur*, are clearly presented as Cuban writers. The markedly interlingual heteroglossia of Cuban literature, which Cabrera Infante mimics and creates in his text, is echoed years later by the author's own writings in English, which I discuss in chapter 5, as one more sign of the nation's unhomely condition.

In Freud's Greek dictionary—which he consults, among other lexicons, as he investigates the linguistic peculiarities of the concept at hand—*unheimlich* is translated simply as "*xénos* (i.e. strange, foreign)" (196). Indeed, the elision of other languages from the established discussion of Spanish American literature often displays a certain measure of xenophobia, a fear of losing one's home to foreigners, of having one's house taken over by strangers or the strange. Many Spanish American nations may be considered multilingual because of the indigenous languages spoken by their populations, but others—Argentina, Cuba, and Puerto Rico are cases in point—have witnessed the emergence of other tongues mainly as the direct result of migratory waves, such as immigration, exile, or residence abroad. If in Guillén's poetry or Vega's fiction linguistic alterity is associated with intrusions by an external power, in many Argentine texts the interlingual results from the nation's open-door policy to citizens of many other countries. This is, after all, the land where Sarmiento blooms as author and president. The European influx into the River Plate region is one of the truisms of the Spanish American cultural discourse, as Fuentes reminds the reader in *La nueva novela hispanoamericana* (1969): "Una vieja *boutade* dice que los mexicanos descienden de los aztecas, los peruanos de los incas y los rioplatenses de los barcos" [An old quip claims that Mexicans descend from the Aztecs, Peruvians from the Incas, and River Plate people from the ships].[28]

Indeed, by 1914, 50 percent of the population of Buenos Aires was estimated to have been born in another country, mostly Spain,

Italy, and other European nations.[29] From multilingual immigration in Argentina and elsewhere, there often ensues a hierarchical view of language and dialect differences, one that concerns not only Spanish and other tongues, but also "purer" dialects of Spanish over those marked by a foreign element. The patrician character in Borges's "La señora mayor" (1970), who descends from a hero of South America's wars of independence, views the speech of a Spanish royal visitor with trepidation because it reminds her of an immigrant group: the infanta speaks like a *gallega* (slang for a Spanish woman), not an Argentine lady.[30] This attitude, of course, is often also a matter of class. If other languages—Italian, Russian, Yiddish—are naturally tied to the nation's immigrant groups, Spanish reigns as the tongue of the old landowning class, whose prejudices Mujica Lainez mordantly exposes, toward the end of his career, in *El gran teatro* (1979). In this novel, members of Buenos Aires's upper class attend a performance of Wagner's *Parsifal* at the Teatro Colón and comment derogatorily on those whose speech denotes not foreign origin, but simply a lower social status; when someone exclaims, "¡Cuánta gente ha venido al Colón!" [So many people have come to the Colón], he is quickly chastised: "*Nosotros* decimos *a* Colón" (emphasis in the original); [*We* say *to* Colón].[31] Scenes of social and cultural struggle are enacted in, or around, Buenos Aires's temple of the high arts, and they possess a linguistic sign. Likewise, in Ernesto Schóó's *El placer desbocado* (1988), also a novel, the Teatro Colón is depicted as fallen into immigrant hands: "¿Sabés que dan en el Colón, querida? *I puritani*, ¿entendés? *I puri tani*" [Do you know what's playing at the Colón, dear? *I puritani*, you get it? Pure *Tani* (Italians)].[32] Most telling, however, is the fact that at least a modicum of Italian is needed in order to hear an interlingual sarcasm in the title of Bellini's opera—just as one must also know a little English to understand Guillén's "Tú no sabe inglé," or a substantial amount to follow the plot of Vega's "Pollito chicken." Only those societies that speak more than one language can produce a kind of discourse whose ironical twists and serious judgments rely upon unimpeded circulation across linguistic boundaries. Nevertheless, that one is at home in a foreign tongue does not mean that native speakers of it will be welcome in one's national houses of culture, literal as well as figurative.

Perceptions of linguistic oddity affect others besides immigrant groups. Born into an old Argentine family, Victoria Ocampo was trilingual (Spanish, French, and English), but felt most comfortable writing in French. In two lectures collected in the second volume of her *Testimonios,* published in the early stages of the Second World War (1941), Ocampo, a staunch supporter of the Allies, situates her beginnings as both reader and writer in the languages of France and Britain. Speaking in French before a PEN Club banquet in Paris in 1938, Ocampo recounts her early bilingualism: "Je passai assez vite de l'alphabet à *L'auberge de l'ange gardien* et de l'espagnol au français. J'y passai même si complètement qu'en rentrant à Buenos Aires j'avais déjà attrapé une passion pour la lecture et un besoin de mots français qui durent encore. En fait, j'avais presque oublié mon espagnol" [I progressed quite rapidly from the alphabet to *L'Auberge de l'ange gardien,* and from Spanish to French. My progress was so complete that, by the time I returned to Buenos Aires, I had developed a passion for reading and a need for French words that still endure. In fact, I had almost forgotten my Spanish].[33] If Ocampo locates the origins of her practice of reading in French, the first memorable act of writing occurs in yet another tongue, English, after a childhood incident with her British governess. As she confesses in 1940 to the members of the "Olivos and Vicente López Monthly Get-Together" near Buenos Aires, "One day I was feeling so injured about some punishment inflicted upon me that I wrote an article in English against the British Empire. Miss Ellis never saw it though she inspired it. I was ten years old and it was my first essay or pamphlet; that is why I owe to her the beginning of my literary career."[34] Indeed, her first publications were two poems in French, and her first book, *De Francesca à Beatrice* (1924), was also written in that language and translated into Spanish; the French original was published later, in 1926. If foreign tongues served Ocampo as useful tools for corresponding with André Malraux or Virginia Woolf, achieving the status of an Argentine author and reaching a national audience required a switch to Spanish. This often meant writing first in French and then translating her own texts or having someone else translate them into the language of most Argentine readers. As founder and editor of *Sur,* arguably Spanish America's most influential literary journal of the twentieth century, Ocampo thrived on cultural exchanges across national and linguistic borders, but as an author in her own right, as others have shown, she was hindered by the fact that her best language for writing was a foreign tongue.[35]

If heterolingualism—specifically, the absence of Spanish—often

turns an author into an awkwardly self-conscious figure, it is somewhat ironic to remember that the conceptual beginnings of Spanish
America's national literatures in the nineteenth century occured at
a time when writers were equally unsure about their relationship
with the language (and culture) of Spain.[36] Throughout Spanish
America, in a deliberate search for a national expression, the texts
of Romanticism and *costumbrismo* often stress the linguistic indi-
viduality of the nations they represent, especially vis-à-vis neigh-
boring countries and Spain. That Borges's protagonist in "La
señora mayor" should have a linguistic memory of the Spanish infanta who visited Argentina on the centennial of its independence
reveals a New World pride in its own forms of speech, but this was
hardly a natural development in the realm of literature. Since
Spaniards have been known to negatively judge the dialects of
Spanish Americans, Borges's tale may be read as one more retort
to such pronouncements as Américo Castro's *La peculiaridad lingüística rioplatense y su sentido histórico* (1941), in which the
speech of Argentines is depicted as flawed. In Borges's angry, ironical review of that book, "Las alarmas del doctor Américo Castro,"
it is Spain's Spanish that is presented as markedly quirky: "confun-
den acusativo y dativo, dicen *le mató* por *lo mató,* suelen ser inca-
paces de pronunciar *Atlántico* o *Madrid"* [they confuse the
accusative and the dative, they say *le mató* for *lo mató,* they are
usually incapable of pronouncing *Atlántico* or *Madrid*].[37] But beyond Borges's quarrel with the scholar, the Spanish American anxiety about establishing a national language of its own, especially in
the nineteenth century, is all too real, and that this search happens
mostly in the spaces of writing only underscores the artifice involved in the process. In Juan de Valdés's *Diálogo de la lengua* (c.
1535), an inspired treatise on the uses and values of Spanish, the
main speaker defends the correspondence between speech and
written style: "el estilo que tengo me es natural, y sin afetación ninguna escrivo como hablo, . . . porque a mi parecer en ninguna lengua stá bien el afetación" [the style I have is natural to me, and,
without any affectation, I write like I speak, . . . because, in my
opinion, affectation is not a good thing in any language].[38] In much
of Spanish American literature, however, authors often do not write
like they speak, but instead copy the ways others express themselves, usually the rural or "lower" urban classes, and these forms,
as we shall see, become important elements in the foundation of
national literatures. In this regard, the presence of artifice, even af-

fectation, in Hispanophone literature will constitute an important angle from which to read and evaluate heterolingual authors and texts.

One of the major thrusts of Spanish American literary practice after political separation from Spain (or even before, as is the case with Cuba and Puerto Rico) is the project of creating national literatures: a clearly identifiable corpus of writing for each country in which differences (geographical, social, linguistic) are underscored as signs of literary independence. A classic locus to view this effort is the work of Esteban Echeverría, whose "La cautiva" (1837) and "El matadero" (1838–40) are now rightly considered foundational texts of both the Argentine and the Spanish American traditions. Characters, themes, settings, styles, and even issues of genre appear in these works that will become pivotal elements in the systems of Spanish American literature, including those of heterolingualism. In the prologue to his *Rimas* (1837), a book whose opening text is "La cautiva," Echeverría privileges the nation's spatial distinctiveness as the source of Argentine literature: "El Desierto es *nuestro,* es *nuestro* más pingüe patrimonio, y debemos poner *nuestro* conato en sacar de su seno, no sólo riqueza para *nuestro* engrandecimiento y bienestar, sino también poesía para *nuestro* deleite moral y fomento de *nuestra* literatura nacional" (my emphases) [The Desert is *ours,* it is *our* richest patrimony, and we must exert *ourselves* to draw from its depths not only wealth for *our* growth and welfare, but also poetry for *our* moral delight and promotion of *our* national literature].[39] Beyond space, what emerges as most clearly distinct in "El matadero" is not the silent desert, which is not featured here, but the speech of lower-class characters, the workers and hangers-on at the slaughterhouse: "¡Che!, negra bruja, salí de aquí antes que te pegue un tajo" (101) [Hey there black witch, get out of there before I cut you open].[40] As in the poems by Guillén, there seems to be an aesthetic and ideological split in Echeverría's fiction. Noé Jitrik has argued that the author cannot reconcile his moral option for the noble *unitario* character, whose bookish diction is audibly detached from the most patently native sociolects of Argentina, with the artistic need for those characters who virtually rape and murder his protagonist, but whose oral style achieves a sense of linguistic autonomy.[41] Because the lofty forms that Echeverría's *unitario* employs are not obviously recognized as signs of a nascent Argentine literary tradition, the author must resort to the speech of others. In heterolingual texts, one can observe a comparable, yet more perplexing, problematics: how can one sound Spanish American in English or French?

Echeverría's minute representation of local forms of Spanish is in a sense nothing new in Spanish American letters. Sor Juana Inés de la Cruz, to quote just one example from the colonial period, had already depicted African- and Basque-inflected forms of Spanish in her *villancicos* and employed Latin and Nahuatl in her works, as if to document the linguistic complexity of society in New Spain. But in the nineteenth century, with the rise of nationalism, the multiple practitioners of *costumbrismo* and other trends throughout the continent, including Echeverría in "El matadero," will devote special attention to registering their countries' linguistic quirks. This practice has lasted through the twentieth century, and it is still ongoing under other forms. The glossaries that usually follow the editions of many regional novels, such as José Eustasio Rivera's *La vorágine* (1924) and Rómulo Gallegos's *Doña Bárbara* (1929) as well as the dialectal specificity of *literatura gauchesca* (which I treat in my reading of Hudson in chapter 4) and *poesía afroantillana,* are all part and parcel of this focus on some kind of national speech. Even recent works of fiction by authors linked with the panglobal culture and affinities of the McOndo group, such as Alberto Fuguet's *Mala onda* (1991) and Jaime Bayly's *La noche es virgen* (1997), prolong this search by carefully depicting, as New Age *costumbristas,* the sociolects of the young in cities like Santiago de Chile and Lima.[42] Grounded at first on local dialects, but eventually codified into literary styles, these homespun forms of Spanish still function as identifiable signs of national literary traditions. Heterolinguals such as Merlin and Hudson will also adopt and adapt some of these conventions, as if to naturalize, at least in some minimal form, the salient foreignness of their writings.

The fetish of local speech is certainly not exclusive to the Spanish American domain, but surfaces regularly in texts by authors from new nations and emergent bodies of literature; and these practices, of course, are not the only possibility of Spanish American writing, even if at times various versions thereof have been critically elevated as such. The privileging of the autochthonous has caused some authors to openly question its aesthetic validity, as in José Donoso's *Historia personal del "boom"* (1972), where regional novelists of a previous generation are ironically outfitted with "lupas de entomólogos" [entomologists' magnifying glasses], which they deploy as they go about each country cataloguing "la flora y la fauna, las razas y los dichos inconfundiblemente *nuestros*" (my emphasis); [flora, fauna, race, and sayings that are unmistakably ours].[43] But perhaps the most eloquent precursor of Donoso's critique is Borges's essay, "El escritor argentino y la tradición." Here, there is yet another turn of the screw to the matter of national literature and the local, one whose final image—a mask, as in Martí's "Nuestra América"—will concern heterolingualism in a particular way. Underscoring the artificial speech of *literatura gauchesca* as city imitations of folk poetry—which, unlike its urban copies, tends to eschew regionalisms—and stressing the fact that neither Shakespeare nor Racine felt obliged to write about their own countries, Borges comments ironically on the Romantic coupling of literature and nation: "El culto argentino del color local es un reciente culto europeo que los nacionalistas deberían rechazar por foráneo" (156) [The Argentine cult of local color is a recent European cult which the nationalists ought to reject as foreign] (181). Citing Gibbon's authority that there are no camels in the Koran, Borges concludes that it is precisely this absence that signals the book's authenticity; as a true Arab, Muhammad took camels for granted, and therefore felt no compulsion to represent them textually: "eran para él parte de la realidad, no tenía porque distinguirlos; en cambio, un falsario, un turista, un nacionalista árabe, lo primero que hubiera hecho es prodigar camellos, caravanas de camellos en cada página" (156) [for him they were a part of reality, he had no reason to emphasize them; on the other hand, the first thing a falsifier, a tourist, an Arab nationalist would do is to have a surfeit of camels, caravans of camels, on every page] (181).[44]

Obliquely, Borges's passionate reasoning points to the literary quandaries of those Spanish Americans who write in other languages. As we shall see in the chapters that follow, Merlin's *La Havane* adopts the practices of Cuban *costumbrismo* within its French text, while W. H. Hudson's *The Purple Land* approximates, in English, certain patterns of *literatura gauchesca*. In both texts, local words and color abound, and the question rises whether one should, therefore, regard Merlin and Hudson as falsifiers, tourists, or nationalists. Merlin's text follows the protocols of travel writing, while Hudson, born and raised in Argentina, is often listed among the "English travelers" who wrote about the country, and in this context, where the reality of their birthplaces is no longer a part of their lives, one may tentatively read their adoption of certain nativist conventions as willful signs of journeys back "home." This is an absence whose most obvious literary-historical counterpart is the nonexistence of Argentine literature in Echeverría's eyes when he writes "La cautiva" and "El matadero." The textual relevance of the local is especially significant when one compares *La Havane* and *The Purple Land* with other heterolingual texts, such as Merlin's *Les Lionnes de Paris* (1845), a romance of contemporary Parisian society, or Hudson's *Afoot in England* (1909), on the English countryside, where one would be hard-pressed to find any elements that signal the need of reading these works within the systems of Spanish American literature, or, consequently, the appropriateness of viewing Merlin and Hudson as Cuban and Argentine authors respectively. A conflict, then, becomes evident. If their imitations of Spanish American forms emerge as somehow suspect and may turn these authors into Borges's poseurs, the elision of nativist elements from their writings is also problematic, for it may be interpreted as absolute detachment and self-exclusion—unless, of course, one were to accept nonengagement with country or continent as a legitimate form of being a Spanish American author.

The writings of Borges himself, as is well known, have often been critiqued for their apparent uninvolvement with Argentina and, more generally, with the discourse of "nuestra América." Regardless of its relevance, this accusation is easily dismissed if one reads any number of Borges's works, from the intimate poems of *Fervor de Buenos Aires* (1923) to the globetrotting texts of *Atlas* (1984), with an open mind. Moreover, even if Steiner readily identifies him as an extraterritorial, Borges, unlike Beckett and Nabokov, or Merlin and Hudson, wrote almost exclusively in his country's majority language. If arguments for his exclusion from the corpora of Argentine and Spanish American literatures are easily disputed, as even Fernández Retamar in the context of a negative reading admits,[45] the texts of the heterolinguals may face an uphill struggle not only due to their language, but because the antidote to that foreign sign may be perceived as an overly artificial, even affected, self-insertion into the national literature. The central issue of literary-historical taxonomy—who belongs and who does not—may ultimately involve what seems to be a kind of double standard for heterolingualism. At the end of "El escritor argentino y la tradición," Borges urges Argentine writers to treat "universal" themes because "o ser argentino es una fatalidad y en ese caso lo seremos de cualquier modo, o ser argentino es una mera afectación, una máscara" (162) [either being Argentine is an inescapable act of fate—and in that case we shall be so in all events—or being Argentine is a mere affectation, a mask] (185). Indeed, one may safely assume that even if Echeverría and his contemporaries had not willfully created a national literature through their anxious focus on the local, they would still be regarded today as Argentine authors.[46] Some heterolinguals, however, as they attempt to conceal their foreignness with the local mask, may expose their own extraterritorial condition even more plainly.

Fraught with danger, the mask is also relevant in reading the works of Alejo Carpentier, whose literary career began in French and who sensed, as Roberto González Echevarría explains, that only by developing a native form would he avoid the risk of not being a Spanish American writer: "Carpentier's literary enterprise is a search for that *pied-à-terre* that he felt he was losing in 1939."[47] But that search, which results in the canonical *El reino de este mundo* (1949), is followed by the realization that his theories of Spanish American fiction may be altogether artificial. A change, therefore, is detectable in *Los pasos perdidos* (1953), his next novel, in which, in the words of González Echevarría, "Carpentier's only possibility is to turn himself into the object, unfolding and fragmenting the self of his prologue—interrogating his own mask."[48] Masks, then, I would argue, stand as an ambivalent metaphor in Spanish American identity-thinking. If in Borges they appear as dispensable or deceitful signs of nationhood, in Carpentier the act of donning a mask triggers a literary reflection not only on his own authorial condition, but on the practice of writing in Spanish America. Moreover, if masks themselves are an artifice, the act of masking and unmasking—oneself as well as others—may well be the most natural practice in Spanish American literary culture. In the thorny case of the heterolinguals, as we shall see, the mask will function also as a valuable metaphor—not so much as a tool to determine whether these writers should be described as "in" or "out" vis-à-vis Spanish American literature, but as a site in which to view the various workings of their unhomeliness.

One strange mask is the one worn occasionally by none other than Martí, who, situated at the center of both the Cuban and Spanish American literary traditions, sometimes forsakes his native Spanish and publishes in French and English instead. In the author's incomplete *Obras completas,* the corpus of heterolingual writings is minimal, yet its very existence serves to foreground a leitmotif of Cuban literary culture: once abroad, the tongue of the Cuban condition is not always the official language of Cuba.[49] That Martí, the Cuban author par excellence, whose verses and essays are treasured by all, should occasionally exist only in another tongue cannot be overestimated. If somewhere in his writings, at the very heart of the national literature and of Spanish America's literary culture, one can hear words in the languages of foreign empires that are not Spain, then, arguably, the house of "nuestra América" may yet open its doors to those whose linguistic alterity is often read to signify alienation. One may argue that these essays were written years before he critiqued the continent's European masks in "Nuestra América," but the fact remains that Martí, in the richness of his discourse, has more than one face—indeed, more than one mask. If at times Martí wears his Anglophone persona quite naturally, at times he casts himself as an outlandish creature for a reader whose expectations seem to include a benign, if predictable, form of exoticism: the colorful mask of distant locations and cultures.

A Cuban in the United States—a proto-Cuban-American of sorts—Martí lived for over fifteen years in New York, traveling frequently to places with large Cuban populations, like Key West and Tampa, where he pronounced those splendid orations that are today, for Cubans, veritable *lieux de mémoire*. Although it is not common to envision Martí as a life on the hyphen—to use Gustavo Pérez Firmat's metaphor for Cuban-American culture—there are instances where his biographical journey shows him to be equally at home and out of place in both cultures. Martí was banished from Cuba in 1879 and, after a sojourn in Spain and France, arrived in New York in January 1880. Within a few weeks, he began to write essays for *The Hour*, a weekly publication, and, later that year, also for *The Sun*. As Jorge Mañach recounts in his classic biography, *Martí el apóstol* (1942), the editors of *The Hour* wanted their contributors to limit themselves to writing about what might be considered their specializations; Martí had just arrived from France, therefore he was entrusted, at first, with art criticism.[50] The titles of the essays he would eventually write for both journals reflect the vast range of his knowledge of European arts and letters: "The French Water-Colorists"; "Pushkin"; "Flaubert's Last Work: Bouvard and Pécuchet"; "Sarah Bernhardt." That Martí wrote enthusiastically about Europe's culture, not unlike Mujica Lainez years later, shows how "Nuestra América" is only one aspect of a broader, more complex vision of imperial and colonial relations. That Europe and the United States may have much to be admired becomes evident also in his Hispanophone works. By the late 1880s, more than twenty newspapers throughout Spanish America were reprinting the texts he wrote for Mexico City's *El Partido Liberal* and Buenos Aires's *La Nación;* despite his eventual warnings to the continent's readers about U.S. American expansionism, many of these writings show Martí as an author for whom these United States were more than a menacing foreign country.

For a U.S. American readership, Martí, besides publishing serious essays on the arts, occasionally composes texts in which he contrasts the country in which he now resides and the cultural milieu from which he comes, all in an ironic vein. There emerges an authorial voice that critiques the United States, whose citizens are mechanical and materialistic, while it commends the organic vitality of the Hispanic world, specifically Spain, whose cultural forms are the subject of four essays dating from 1880: "Modern Spanish Poets"; "Raimundo Madrazo"; "Fortuny"; and, perhaps predictably, "The Bull Fight." Also from the same year are three essays, collected under the title "Impressions of America," that focus on life in the United States. This last group bears an enigmatic signature: "By a very fresh Spaniard." That the leader of Cuba's struggle for independence should call himself a Spaniard may come as a bit of a shock, but not in the context of Martí's entire biography and other works. Born of Spanish parents who had settled in Cuba, Martí writes several poems in which aspects of Spain are praised; "Poema X" in *Versos sencillos* (1891), lovingly depicts the art of a Spanish dancer, while "Poema VII," about Aragon, stresses the love of freedom that may bind Spaniards and Cubans. Also, one can imagine, a Spaniard's signature might make the seemingly treacherous use of "America" as a synonym of the United States somehow more palatable to Spanish American sensibilities.

Writing as a "fresh Spaniard" (which, as the editors of the *Obras completas* correctly point out, may be interpreted either as "newly arrived" or "insolent"), Martí, from the start, judges sternly what he sees: "I am, at last, in a country where every one looks like his own master. One can breathe freely, freedom being here the foundation, the shield, the essence of life. One can be proud of his species here. Every one works, every one reads. Only does everyone feel in the same degree that they read and work?"[51] The lack of real sentiment is linked with the search for material possessions, which in turn leads to an absence of intellectual pleasure and good taste. Martí in New York strikes the pose of the flâneur and, as he walks down Fifth Avenue or Fourteenth Street, perceives "many non-senses, many high deeds" (19:105); he concludes rather severely: "Size and number; these are the elements of greatness" (19:105). The third and last essay ends with a somber note on the city's destitute population: "They moved painfully, as if they wished to blot out of their minds their sorrowful thoughts—and were all lying down on the grass or seated on the benches, shoeless, foodless, concealing their anguish under their dilapidated hats" (19:123).

Much of the thematics revealed in these passages duplicates Martí's concerns in his works in Spanish, specifically on issues of liberty and social justice. That he is writing for Americans as a "fresh Spaniard" does not dissipate entirely certain echoes that allow the reader of Spanish American literature to recognize Martí's voice and vision. Yet, a permutation occurs in those essays in which the focus falls directly on Spain. This becomes already evident when one compares Martí's depictions of American and Hispanic women. If women in the United States are censured for "their calculated coldness, their contempt of passions, their dry practical notions of life" (19:114), the author extols "the chaste abandon, the savory languor, . . . and gentle grace of our Southern women" (19:113). The descriptions of both groups are, of course, simplistic, and might appear also in works written by Spanish American authors in Spanish for Spanish American readers.

But Martí's English-language essays go further, as this stereotypical depiction of Spain from "Modern Spanish Poets" reveals: "In the land of Spain, warmed with sunlight and shaded with orange trees, where women glow like burning lava, where flowers perfume the air, where even ruins smile, and the dawn sparkles, where poppy-laden fields look like lakes of blood, where cosy little cottages nesting in rose-dotted foliage seem to burn their immates in happiness . . ."[52] The exotic image of Spain as a burning, passionate country is in direct contrast to Martí's other descriptions of it, not only in the poems from *Versos sencillos* mentioned above, but also in essays such as "Centenario de Calderón," published in Caracas's *La Opinión Nacional* in 1881, not long after "Modern Spanish Poets" appeared in *The Sun*. In a short vignette of life in Madrid that is part of "Centenario de Calderón," Martí sketches an altogether different portrait of Spain. First, the land's coloring is more subdued: oranges, roses, lava, and blood fade away, and in their place one sees pale mornings, white milk, black umbrellas, and a metaphorical golden dust. There is one Don Juan, but, instead of pursuing señoritas, he is simply portrayed carrying a harmless basket; although there are donkeys, they are not just picturesque animals, but elements in an enterprising city, with bookstores, parks, and metropolitan angles of vision. There is also the non-Mediterranean prospect of changing seasons. In English, Martí describes England as a "land of fog" and Spain as a "land of flowers" (15:16), but, in Spanish, Spain is no longer the land of endless summer: it also has its "nieblas autumnales" [autumnal mists].[53]

Why is Martí's Spain so different in English and Spanish? One may speculate quite rightly about the author's skills in each language, but part of the answer must also lie in two figures of the reader, quite distinguishable, that each of the author's two tongues seems to invoke. In his preview of a rare bullfight in New York, Martí resorts to a negative syntax to signal the ways in which the audience's expectations of a certain Spain will likely be foiled: "The boxes today will not be filled with ladies in black mantillas, each with a red rose in her hair and a red rose pinned to her left breast."[54] Regardless of whether women in Spain really attended bullfights dressed in this fashion, Martí's exotic image may be interpreted as an ironic nod to those tourist-like readers who, to paraphrase Borges's essay, would also expect many camels in the horizons of the Koran. Martí's self-exoticism is, in that sense, a mask, for he does not indulge in these quaint portrayals when he addresses a Spanish-speaking reader. Then again, it is a mask that Martí wears quite self-consciously; through irony and hyperbole, one can detect a measure of impatience in the author's voice.

To relate what Martí scribbled in a foreign tongue to what he wrote in Spanish, as I have done here, is somehow unfair, almost like comparing the brief French passages in *Henry V* with the rest of Shakespeare's œuvre. Yet, reading Martí's English publications—or his French prose, for that matter, travel pieces such as "L'Amérique Centrale" and "Un Voyage à Venezuela"—from the viewpoint of Spanish American literary culture may serve as a point of departure for understanding the quandaries of heterolingual authors. If they need the national thematic as a first step into the systems of Spanish American literature, to write about their native lands in English and French often implies considering the demands of another reader, one who knows and expects specific signs of the foreign. The mask has now two faces: one's reader's *costumbrismo* is another's exoticism, and in both cases the author speaks for Spanish Americans with an outsider's voice.

A century after Martí's English-language articles, another Cuban in America—a Cuban-American from New York—wrote a novel dealing with the United States and her native land. In Cristina Garcia's *Dreaming in Cuban* (1992), the United States is also the land of material wealth, while Cuba is enshrouded in magic, spirituality, and romance: a strange space filled with seashells, mangoes, and birds. The text's English prose is crisscrossed by words in Spanish, specifically Cuban Spanish. Their semantic field is often Cuban music ("danzón", "guaracha") or Afro-Cuban religions ("santero," "orisha," "babalawo," "botánica," "yerba buena"); culinary terms as well are especially abundant ("arroz con pollo," "carne asada," "palomilla," "yuca," "natilla," "café con leche").[55] But if many of these words seem directed at a U.S. American audience in search of ethnic color, there are still other terms that seem to invoke another reader. Repeatedly, characters in *Dreaming in Cuban* address each other in Spanish or, given the local specificity of many of these phrases, one should perhaps say "Cuban": "hija," "mi hija," "mi hijita,;" "hombre," "chico," "chiquitico," "caballero," "mi amor," "mi cielo" (*passim*). That these terms of endearment appear as elements of oral speech implies a conversation of sorts with readers who may be Cuban or, more precisely, Cuban-American. In the context of this novel in English, one can sense a dream of writing in Cuban, of making the foreign tongue speak the familiar language of home: neither the United States nor Cuba, but an interstitial location or—why not?—both countries.

Garcia's Cuban lexicon—so exotic, perhaps, to the so-called mainstream reader, but so strangely domestic in the spaces of Cuban-American unhomeliness—has a precursor in Martí's last work, the majestically intimate *Diario de campaña* (1895), with which the author rounds up his writer's life upon his return to Cuba to join the War of Independence. On 9 May 1895, only days before his death, Martí beholds the Cauto, the island's largest river, and, "ante el vasto paisaje del río amado" [facing the vast landscape of the beloved river], he captures the strange nature of his native land by listing, one by one, the species of the island's vegetation: "curujey," "guásima," "jatía," "ateje," "caguarán," "júcaro," "jubabán," "yamagua." One may regard this linguistic expedition through Cuban botany as yet another Spanish American catalogue of the local flora, but Martí's act is contextually different. After years of exile, the author's inventory implies an ultimate recovery of the spaces of home: Cuba no longer as a dreamland, but as a prodigious, if poignantly brief, reality. All the trappings of the mask—a "Cuban" mask, now—may be there, but how can one fault Martí's eyes for focusing so intently on what for him had been for so long invisible?

Regardless of exile, however, Martí's English and French publications are only brief outings. Martí, like Borges and Carpentier, usually writes under the same roof that also shelters his readers: men and women from his nation and continent with whom he shares a common tongue and literary culture. Masks may be donned at will, but masks may also be removed without peril. However, in the case of the heterolinguals, as we shall see, the mask may emerge as an indispensable form of the author's face. Borges writes about being an Argentine as either an act of fate or an affectation, but for those who write in other languages, who risk becoming authors doomed to a foreign tradition, the mask reveals what otherwise might remain concealed. With this in mind, these unhomely masquerades, foreign yet familiar, may allow the Spanish American reader to look the heterolinguals plainly in the eye and recognize them, despite their strangeness, as their own.

2

The House of Spanish, II:
America the Unhomely

Almost three decades after Gabriela Mistral's triumphant reception in Stockholm, Pablo Neruda traveled to that city to become the second Nobel Laureate in Literature from Chile and, after Miguel Ángel Asturias, the third from Spanish America. Born in 1904 like Neruda, Alejo Carpentier may well have become the fourth author to receive the prize; some speculate that the year in which he died, 1980, the Swedish Academy had already decided to confer on him, a resident of Paris, that distinction. Had it happened, Carpentier would have become the first Cuban author so honored. But was he a Cuban author? In Neruda's posthumous *Confieso que he vivido* (1974), the poet recounts his acquaintance with Carpentier in Paris in the period just before the Second World War. As he reminisces about the Place Dauphine, "nervaliana, con olor a follaje y restaurant" [Nerval's Place Dauphine, with its smell of leaves and restaurants], Neruda states, "Allí vivía el escritor francés Alejo Carpentier, uno de los hombres más neutrales que he conocido. No se atrevía a opinar sobre nada, ni siquiera sobre los nazis que ya se le echaban encima a París como lobos hambrientos" [The 'French' writer Alejo Carpentier, one of the most uncommitted men I know, lived there. He didn't dare voice an opinion on anything, not even the Nazis, who were about to fall upon Paris like famished wolves].[1] If the English translation of Neruda's memoirs qualifies Carpentier's alleged French condition with quotation marks, the original is brutally ironic. Long the object of jests and witticisms about his French accent, last name, and even tastes, Carpentier's maskings and unmaskings, which Roberto González Echevarría analyzes, manifest the difficult path towards Spanish American authorship for those writers caught between languages and cultures.[2] The source of Neruda's quip is more personal and political than it is linguistic; also in his memoirs, he refers affectionately to one heterolingual, Jules Supervielle, as "el viejo y noble poeta uruguayo" (266) [the aging and noble Uruguayan poet] (190), and calls another, Lautréamont, "joven uruguayo" (365) [young Uruguayan] (262). He also speaks of collecting the first editions of Lautréamont's works, together with those of Jules Laforgue, the third French-language poet from Montevideo.

But if Neruda is able to imagine a continental literary community in which a poet's foreign tongue is not necessarily a token for exclusion, others have held opposite views. Denying Lautréamont, Laforgue, and Supervielle the status of Uruguayan authors, Ángel Rama, also a Uruguayan, privileges language as the defining property of one Spanish American literature: "Si existen orígenes comunes, historia en buena parte común, nutridos problemas comunes, aquello que con mayor inmediatez y tangibilidad estatuye la aproximación, instaura la comunidad, no está en ninguno de esos elementos, sino en el uso de la lengua y en la comprobación que es la misma, idéntica, en todas partes" [If common origins, a mostly common history, and manifold common problems exist, that which establishes a rapprochement and enacts a community with greatest immediacy and tangibility is not those elements, but the use of one language, verifiably the same everywhere].[3]

Beyond the adjective "common," which he employs three times, and the appeal to "community," Rama's citation also reveals, if only obliquely, the possibility of viewing Spanish America from a different angle. Specifically, the words "inmediatez" and "intangibilidad," because they are qualified with the adjective "mayor," suggest that much in this discussion may be regarded as a matter of degree rather than absolute substance. By stretching one's imagination, one may conceivably reach authors and texts whose proximity to Spanish American literature is not patently evident, but whose relevance within it becomes obvious once they are read with benign eyes. Rama goes on to say that only language can set a literature's precise limits ("sólo la lengua es capaz de fijarle un límite preciso"),[4] but, in more practical terms, it is critics and literary historians, anthologists and editors, as well as authors who engage in speaking and writing about literature, who actually define the boundaries of literary bodies.[5] When Carlos Fuentes incorporates Spanish American heterolingual authors into the fabric of *Una familia lejana*, as we shall see in chapter 5, there is a focus on less tangible and immediate, but still significant elements of Spanish American literature. Indeed, authors and critics have variously underscored the role of the discourse about literature in the formation of corpora and canons, which suggests that even the monolingual criterium could be modified to accommodate writing in other tongues. This chapter investigates how some very visible writings, specifically Enrique Anderson Imbert's *Historia de la literatura hispanoamericana* and Rubén Darío's "A Roosevelt," have contributed to the commonly held view of a monolingual Spanish American literary tradition. Yet these two authors, in margins or less well-known contexts—such as Anderson Imbert's *Los domingos del profesor* and Darío's *Los raros*—have also written to suggest the possibility of reading heterolingualism as a part of Spanish American literature. As it turns out, the less official a critical site is, the more favorable a reception may be afforded to the continent's heterolinguals. Unwittingly, as far as one can tell, Darío and Anderson Imbert point to a possible conceptualization of Spanish America and its nations on the basis of unhomeliness, a feeling or condition already suggested by such authors as Garcilaso de la Vega, Sor Juana Inés de la Cruz, Lucio V. Mansilla, and others, on whose works I shall also briefly stop before moving to the heterolinguals.

For a critic with a vast knowledge of foreign literatures and tongues, Enrique Anderson Imbert is surprisingly resolute about excluding works in languages other than Spanish, native as well as European, from his *Historia de la literatura hispanoamericana* (1954, first edition), arguably one of the continent's best and most complete literary histories.[6] With his habitual forthrightness, Anderson Imbert includes the following clarification in the prologue of the 1967 edition:

La literatura que vamos a estudiar es la que, en América, se escribió en español. No ignoramos la importancia de las masas de indios. Pero, en una historia de los usos expresivos de la lengua española en América, corresponde escuchar a quienes se expresaron en español. Por la misma razón no nos referiremos a los escritores que nacieron en Hispanoamérica pero escribieron en latín (como Rafael Landívar), en francés (como Jules Supervielle) o en inglés (como W. H. Hudson). Tampoco a los que escribieron, sí, en español, pero sin experiencia americana (como Ventura de la Vega). En cambio, incorporaremos a

nuestra historia a los extranjeros que vivieron entre *nosotros* y em-
plearon *nuestra* lengua (como Paul Groussac). (my emphasis)

[The literature of the Americas we are going to study is the one that was
written in Spanish. We do not ignore the importance of the masses of
Indians; however, in a history of the expressive uses of the Spanish
language in America, it behooves us to listen only to those who expressed themselves in Spanish. For this same reason we will not refer
to the writers who were born in Spanish America, but who wrote in
Latin (like Rafael Landívar), in French (like Jules Supervielle) or in English (like W. H. Hudson). Nor will we consider those authors who,
although they wrote in Spanish, {had no American experience}. On the
other hand, we will include in our history those foreigners who lived
among us and used our language (like Paul Groussac.)][7]

These parameters for the study and definition of Spanish American
literature signal the unbreakable linkage between language and
cultural systems that informs much identity-thinking in the continent and its various nations. For Anderson Imbert, the coherence
of a continental literary history rests first and foremost on the bedrock Spanish American principle of linguistic unity.[8] The phrase
"las masas de indios," even as it confirms the existence of native
strands in Spanish America's cultural fabric, underscores through
its nameless generalization the essential alterity of these ethnic
groups, while, in addition, it disregards the fact that many authors
of indigenous origin have written in Spanish. When authors who
write in other European languages are mentioned, Anderson Imbert emphasizes what sounds like a breached promise. Given their
biographies, which he calls "experiencia americana," these writers
could very well have been a part of this tradition—unlike, say, the
Spaniard Ramón del Valle Inclán, who wrote about Spanish
America in *Tirano Banderas* (1926), but was no Spanish American
himself. Yet, by composing their works in another language, whatever their particular reasons may have been, Landívar, Hudson,
and Supervielle unwittingly provoke their own exclusion from one
of the most influential documents in the institutions of Spanish
American literature.[9]

  In Anderson Imbert's tightly conceived scholarly project, one
can understand how heterolingual authors, writing in either native
or European tongues, could only serve as destabilizing elements.
To welcome other languages would be to open innumerable doors
into other literary habitations. These authors and texts would con-

stitute detours from a narrative that, even if it carefully avoids the linear thrust of progress favored by other historians,[10] nevertheless gathers, reads, evaluates, and classifies a vast array of literature within very specific parameters. There is in Anderson Imbert's astoundingly detailed history a self-conscious search for completeness. If the protagonist of Borges's "Funes el memorioso" was unable to forget anything, Anderson Imbert's *Historia* wants to remember and record everyone, even if the outcome is, at times, only a monotonous listing of names and dates: "Cerremos por ahora esta exposición de poetas peruanos con una línea de puntos suspensivos: PABLO ABRIL (1895), ALFREDO GONZÁLEZ PRADA (1891–1943), CÉSAR A. RODRÍGUEZ (1891), FEDERICO MORE (1889), FEDERICO BOLAÑOS (1896), DANIEL RUZO (1900)" (2:44) [For the time being, we close this exposition of Peruvian poets with a few names as suspension points].[11] Anderson Imbert's ironic stance—the historian is also a masterful storyteller—is a self-reflecting comment on his historiographical method. The scholar's meticulous mind seeks to catalogue the totality of Spanish-language literature in Spanish America, and he recognizes his work's mushroom-like growth with a flurry of humor: "concebimos nuestra *Historia* como un cuerpo desnudo, vivo y voraz: ¡El peligro está en haber creado un Frankenstein!" (9) [we conceived our *Historia* as a naked, living, and voracious body: the danger lies in having created a Frankenstein!].

But even as it critiques itself, Anderson Imbert's project also underscores its lofty goals, expressed in terms reminiscent of Martí's "Nuestra América": "Nuestra voluntad ha sido rendir un servicio público: juntar lo disperso, clasificar el fárrago, iluminar con una única luz los rincones oscuros de una América rota por dentro y, por tanto, poner en manos del lector una Summa" (13) [Our wish has been to offer a public service: to put together that which was scattered; to classify the jumble; to illuminate with one light the dark corners of this fractured America, and, thus, to place a Summa in the hands of readers]. One can only speculate about the historian's relief upon deciding that this project, at least from the viewpoint of language, ought to have some limits; one can only imagine the magnitude of a literary history, researched with Anderson Imbert's superior standards, that remained open to still other concerns, such as heterolingualism. But beyond practical considerations, there is also a sense of mission not unlike Martí's: this Summa, one feels, must focus on Spanish—"nuestra lengua"—so that it can emphasize the possible unity of Spanish American nations.[12] Yet, it is with a certain measure of wistfulness that the historian arrives, now and then, at the linguistic terminus that he himself has set. This happens when he discusses César Moro—"por el lado de sus escritos en francés se nos escapa de esta historia" (2:184) [on the side of his writings in French he escapes from our history]—or Vicente Huidobro's heterolingual phase: "Huidobro publicó poemas en francés que escapan a esta historia si bien en muchos de ellos se perfila definitivamente su creacionismo" (2:55) [Huidobro published poems in French that escape this history even if in many of them one can definitely view his creacionism]. Both poets are the actors of their own literary-historical flight, but one can also see Anderson Imbert wanting to pursue them; the use of *si bien* is a clear sign of his translingual intelligence and, moreover, an acknowledgement of his own project's artifice.

In "A Brief History of the History of Spanish American Literature," which opens the *Cambridge History of Latin American Literature,* Roberto González Echevarría credits Anderson Imbert's *Historia* as being "the most authoritative of all the histories, by far the most inclusive and detailed, and the one written by the best literary critic" (26). One can only agree with this evaluation. A clear, yet unacknowledged, virtue of Anderson Imbert's profoundly erudite investigation of the Spanish American archive is his masterful readings of some critical margins, such as the writing of women authors. These are analyses that predate the rise of feminist literary criticism and the reevaluation of some virtually forgotten women writers. Years before Dulce María Loynaz reemerged from virtual oblivion by receiving the Premio Cervantes (1992), Anderson Imbert had included in his *Historia* an insightful reading of Loynaz's *Jardín* (1951), a novel whose withdrawal from Spanish American fiction's explicit concern with social issues likely contributed to its critical elision. Today, some of his remarks on the text appear rather dated, and have, in fact, been omitted from later editions of the *Historia*: "Si el estilo tuviera sexo, femenino sería éste, en el sentido en el que se habla de la feminidad del estilo de Virginia Woolf" (2:252, 1974 edition) [If style had a gender, this would be feminine, in the sense that one speaks of the femininity of Virginia Woolf's style]. Other observations, however, remain extremely perceptive. Imbued by formalist principles, Anderson Imbert's readings focus primarily on the works themselves, rejecting the extraliterary concerns, often political, of much Spanish American literary criticism. His analysis of *Jardín*, for instance, even as it situates the novel at the center of an emergent Spanish American modern canon, still underscores the historian's own high aesthetic standards: "Las debilidades de la novela en cuanto novela no disminuyen el valor del libro, ópimo, de los más granados en toda su generación por el decoro de sus formas y por el constante acierto de las imágenes poéticas" (2:230) [The novel's shortcomings as a novel do not diminish the book's worth, which is most high; it is an an outstanding book, one of the most exquisite of its generation for its formal beauty and the sustained merit of its poetic images]. Loynaz's style—her splendid use of Spanish—redeems other defects her book may have.

Anderson Imbert's readings, as one can see here, are often informed by stylistics, arguably the privileged critical method among Hispanists of the mid-twentieth century. This focus on an author's mastery of language—instead of thematics, structure, or ideology—may also shed some light on Anderson Imbert's refusal to admit heterolingual works into Spanish American literature. By working only with Hispanophone texts, the historian feels very much at home in his perusal of *Jardín*: he can gauge the value of Loynaz's images and forms by comparing the novel to other works written in Spanish. Stylistics, as Anderson Imbert describes it in *La crítica literaria*, allows a natural identification among language, society, author, and critic, one that, in a sense, justifies the historian's option for monolingualism: "El método estudiará, pues, la tradición lingüística de la sociedad de donde procede el escritor que le interesa; estudiará la actitud que el escritor tiene ante esa lengua y los ideales de expresión personal que lo animan" (80) [The method will study, then, the linguistic tradition of the society from which comes the writer in which it is interested; it will study the writer's attitude vis-à-vis that language and the ideals of personal expression that animate him]. In a sense, everything and everyone remain within the house of Spanish. In his reading of *Jardín*, Anderson Imbert relates Loynaz's style to that of Virginia Woolf, but regarding Woolf's style, however, the historian specifically writes "se habla," "one speaks," which is best understood as "they say," suggesting that the description and evaluation of Woolf's language falls outside of the linguistic realm whose limits he has circumscribed. Anderson Imbert, then, seems to underscore not only the bounds between language and the national and continental literatures, but also the close ties between an author's tongue and the critic's literary-historical evaluations.

In actual practice, however, Anderson Imbert's own writings on works in other languages—"El cuervo de Poe" (1949) and "El taller de Marcel Proust" (1952), to name just two—demonstrate the critic's superb talents as a reader of literature in English and French. Yet, such essays are collected in a volume modestly entitled *Los domingos del profesor* (1972), which Anderson Imbert introduces with this caveat: "Como profesor he publicado libros, estudios y artículos más académicos que estas páginas. Las que aquí agavillo son ligeras, conversacionales y ajenas a mi actividad profesional" [As a professor, I have published books, studies, and articles that are more scholarly than these pages. These sheaves of papers are lightweight, conversational, and alien to my professional activity].[13] Most interesting here is the gradation of academic labor that the critic's writings do not support: if the professor has two hats—one to be worn when he enters the formal institutions of literature, such as the *Historia,* and one for freer wanderings in other territories—he never goes around quite hatless; indeed, the authoritative critic and the self-proclaimed amateur are equally apt and insightful readers. Predictably, Anderson Imbert's rapprochement to Spanish American heterolingualism takes place in the less official context of *Los domingos del profesor.*[14] Yet, the peripheral status of these writings constitutes a useful angle from which to view the *Historia* and its margins—its tentative approximation to works in other tongues as a possibility of Spanish American literature.

One essay, specifically, seems to reveal a measure of strife within Anderson Imbert's monolingual construction of Spanish American literature in the *Historia.* Written in 1941, shortly after he became a professor—"Hasta 1940 fui periodista; después, profesor" (7) [I was a journalist until 1940, and later a professor], reads the opening sentence in *Los domingos del profesor*—the essay "El nacionalismo literario" ought to be read against the exacerbated backdrop of the Second World War, but it is also, arguably, Anderson Imbert's early *ars critica,* an apology for those professional readers who seek to achieve an equilibrium between the claims of two seemingly opposite poles in literary studies. One extreme, that of comparative literature, underscores supranational concepts such as "Romanticism" and "European literature," while the other, termed "literary nationalism," values each work for its capacity to represent "una micronación" [a micronation].[15] Anderson Imbert proposes that literature is more complex than either one of these critical approaches seems willing to admit. If literary internationalism neglects "la historicidad del hombre" (16) [man's historicism], and if its nationalist counterpart ignores "la originalidad del hombre" (16) [man's originality], both critical currents in the end obscure the essence of verbal art:

> El poeta puede expresarse a condición de que el universo resuene en él; y el universo no despierta en la obra como abstracción, sino como experiencia concreta y personal, revestida con los rasgos inmediatos del hogar, de la aldea, de la región, del país, de la civilización, del Ser en cuyo centro el poeta está produciendo. Una obra literaria no es ni internacional ni nacional: es, simplemente. (16; emphasis in original)

> [The poet can express himself provided that the universe resounds in him; and the universe does not waken in the work as an abstraction, but as a concrete, personal experience, sheathed with the immediate traits of home, village, region, country, civilization, and of the Being in whose center the poet is producing. A literary work is neither international nor national: it is, quite simply.]

This ending, which some may be tempted to dismiss as simply a rhetorical flourish, obliquely engages a possible vision of Spanish American literature, a hybrid construction that is both international, as it involves at least nineteen countries, and somehow national, since these countries may not form a single state, but may still be seen as united through their writings as one cultural community. But this is not Anderson Imbert's concern yet; he is more than a decade away from composing his *Historia*. A preoccupation of this essay, at least in passing, is those authors or groups whose linguistic alterity would constitute in effect reason enough for exclusion from the *Historia de la literatura hispanoamericana*. Underscoring the problematic nature of *genio nacional* as a valid concept for the evaluation of literature, he observes, first, that "la óptica interior de cada idioma no es más poderosa que el ojo vivo del escritor, por lo que quien se asome a través de los lentes de la prosa inglesa de W. H. Hudson verá muchas perspectivas del argentino W. H. Hudson" (16) [the internal optics of each language is not more powerful than a writer's living eye, so that whoever may look through the lenses of W. H. Hudson's English prose will see many perspectives of the Argentine W. H. Hudson]. Secondly, he states, "la raza no obliga a ningún comportamiento literario previsible" (16) [race does not force anyone into any predictable literary behavior]. If the latter observation, with its ethnological overtones, may be read as a sign of the critic's belief in one "nuestra América" composed of various races, Anderson Imbert's remarks on Hudson imply at least the possibility of constructing Argentine and Spanish American literatures beyond the narrow constraints of language.

Anderson Imbert's choice of an extended ocular metaphor— "optics," "eyes," "lenses," "seeing"—to speak about Hudson's writing is telling in two regards. First, it elevates an author's individual perspective over that of the tradition into which language seems to consign him or her. Nation and continent, in a sense, may be seen outside one language's styles and stylistics. Hudson is no longer viewed as an English traveler; now, at least to a degree, he is an element in the nation's literature: his eyes are those of an Argentine author, even if he looks at his native land through the dark glasses of English. But Anderson Imbert's figurative lenses, secondly, engage not so much the author as it does Hudson's reader, the performer of the verb "asomarse," the onlooker who "looks in" or "leans out" and ultimately ascertains the ties that might bind Hudson's writing to Argentina. This reader—which I define as an unhomely reader in chapter 4—is a figure whose outlook takes in the strange familiarity, or familiar strangeness, of heterolingual texts. Its existence, which Anderson Imbert implies here, suggests the possibility of another kind of Spanish American literary history, one that, after all, the *Historia* comes close to revealing. There, the historian's choices—the lenses he opts to wear—are openly displayed, and if heterolingualism is denied an active role in this narrative, its existence is at least recognized in the prologue and several other brief instances. This *Historia* stresses the literary uses of Spanish in the Americas, but one might also envision another account founded on the principles of unhomeliness, a study that would allow, or at least make allowances, for the incorporation of writing and reading in other languages.

Indeed, as we saw with Huidobro and Moro, Anderson Imbert's *Historia* itself does at times come tantalizingly close to incorporating heterolingual texts, even as it proclaims that it ought not to go *there*. Works in other tongues occupy little nooks and crannies, as it were, in Anderson Imbert's house of Spanish American literature, through which the historian can see them escaping—repeatedly— into other literary traditions. Yet, in these peripheral sites, they also manage to escape the historian's acts of eviction, a paradox through which the *Historia* becomes a more complex document than its prologue reveals. Thus, in this double movement, the heterolinguals are both housed and unhoused. At the end of chapter 5, for instance, one reads a deletion and a return: "En 1780 se representó en Perú la anónima pieza *Ollantay*, pero no nos concierne porque estaba en quechua: basada en una leyenda incaica, la estructura y las convenciones son, sin embargo, hispánicas; su importancia es histórica, por coincidir con la rebelión de Tupac Amaru II" (1:180) [In 1780, the anonymous play, *Ollantay*, was performed in Peru, but it does not concern us because it was in Quechua; based upon an Inca legend, its structure and conventions are nevertheless Hispanic; its importance is historic, as it coincides with Tupac Amaru II's rebellion]. This recognition of the interlingual and the interliterary as forms of writing in Spanish America is in effect more substantial, at least judging from the space devoted to it, than what Anderson Imbert says about many of the Spanish-language authors and texts mentioned in the *Historia*. Still, *Ollantay* is not officially integrated in Spanish American literature. Included almost as an afterthought, it is relegated to another discipline—history—as often happens with texts in the continent's indigenous tongues.[16] Heterolingualism, then, is only a brief excursion: a glimpse into Hudson's Anglo-Argentine eyes retrieves an author who will remain ultimately out of focus, if not invisible.

This literary-historical impediment to heterolingualism is ultimately a mixture of theoretical and aesthetic considerations. In the *Historia*'s prologue, Anderson Imbert refers with sadness to the "mil obstáculos" (1:7) [thousand obstacles] that literary creation has routinely encountered, and still does, in Spanish America. In his estimate, in over four centuries of writing, one may find only about twenty-five authors "que honrarían cualquier literatura" (1:7) [would honor any body of literature], and this explains why the *Historia* is forced to include "a mucho escritor malogrado" (1:8) [many writers gone to waste]. What prevails among Spanish American writers is "la improvisación, el desorden, el fragmentarismo, la impureza" (1:7–8) [improvisation, disorder, fragmentation, impurity]. But that the continent's writing is described in these terms denotes not only the historian's anxiety about the tradition, but also about the task at hand. Unless one carefully lays out a design, the house of Spanish American literature that emerges here may turn out to be as defective and fragmentary as Spanish American literature itself. In this context, a multilingual archive—even if certain texts in Quechua depend upon Hispanic forms, even if one author who writes in English may still appear to be an Argentine author—would constitute an additional threat to the project's search for coherence. In the last editions of the *Historia,* Anderson Imbert himself recognizes the shortcomings of his own method. The "Apéndice 1970–1981" is mostly a series of lists, prefaced by a melancholy note: "Edición tras edición he tratado de actualizar mi *Historia* pero, por mucho que añada, la estructura interna del libro es la de 1954. Hoy, con una nueva visión crítica, yo organizaría la materia de otro modo" (2:428) [I have tried to update my *Historia* one edition after the other, but no matter how much I add, the book's internal structure remains that of 1954. Today, with a new critical vision, I would organize the subject differently]. One wonders whether a new critical eye, born after the international rise of Spanish American literature in the 1960s, could have created new rooms for the heterolinguals, even if this had meant drawing a more fragmentary set of blueprints for the continent's literature.[17]

Reading Anderson Imbert's *Historia,* one notices how its delineation of Spanish America often coincides with Martí's vision in "Nuestra América." Its overall plan seeks to create a continental corpus out of whatever materials are available, a gesture reminiscent of Martí's dictum in his essay: "El vino, de plátano; y si sale agrio ¡es nuestro vino!" [The wine is made from plantain, but even if it turns sour, it is our own wine!][18] The adjective *nuestro* in its various forms is usually employed by Anderson Imbert to refer to himself, but on occasion it is meant literally to encompass, with a measure of pride, the entire continent. In the "Apéndice," for instance, he speaks of "la producción literaria en nuestros países" (2:428) [the literary output of our countries]. If most chapters in the *Historia* are internally organized by regions or countries, the principal storyline focuses on literary evolution and periods in a wide continental context: "Agrupar a los escritores por países hubiera roto la unidad cultural de Hispanoamérica en diecinueve ilusorias literaturas nacionales" (1:10) [Grouping the writers by country would have broken the cultural unity of Spanish America into nineteen illusory national literatures].[19] It is interesting that national literatures should be presented as the figment of some critical dreamland, while Spanish America, which lacks political unity, is in its turn construed as a solid historical fact, even if Anderson

Imbert, like Martí, is aware that a truly continental mindset remains very much a work in progress, a community still in the process of being imagined.[20] Martí travels in several countries, and writes, from his home in New York, numerous essays for newspapers in Mexico City, Caracas, and Buenos Aires, thus creating the sense of a Spanish American literary culture. Similarly, Anderson Imbert's *Historia* seeks to function as a critical space where Spanish America can take an inventory of its various elements. This endeavor, in effect, is as much a literary as it is a literal roll call. The long listings of authors' names are justified in this project where nineteen nations, whose authors and readers hardly know each other, are assembled into one critical category: "La abundancia de nombres llama la atención sobre el hecho de que los países hispanoamericanos están tan incomunicados entre sí que los valores se cotizan en mercados locales: renunciar a ellos ofendería los orgullos nacionales" (1:11) [The abundance of names calls attention to the fact that Spanish American countries are so poorly linked that stocks are traded in local markets: forswearing them would offend national sensibilities]. The task of writing a history of Spanish American literature constitutes, then, a kind of mission, wherein the historian, as a great communicator between various countries, rises over national or nationalist concerns, yet remains responsive to them; ultimately, the *Historia* creates a supranational discourse that builds what it purports merely to reflect.

One author in particular, the poet Rubén Darío, stands in Anderson Imbert's *Historia* not as a national, but as a truly continental literary figure. In the *Historia,* the chapters devoted to writing in the colonial period are mostly organized outside of regional classifications, but the names of nations, as concepts around which to structure the historian's analysis of literature, begin to appear in chapter 8, with the post-Independence generations. National literatures may be illusory formations, as Anderson Imbert claims, but nations, politically speaking, are not. More problematic is the status of "Spanish America" in the decades following the dissolution of viceregal institutions, which had created a semblance of continental unity. In chapter 11, which is devoted to the period 1895–1910 (the first date being, perhaps not coincidentally, the year of Martí's death), Anderson Imbert begins his argument with a direct citation of Martí's famous locution for the continent: "En el capítulo anterior se vio cómo nuestra América, que después de 1880 ya había

pasado lo peor de la anarquía, entraba en una era de prosperidad"
(1:397) [In the last chapter it was seen how our America, which
after 1880 had suffered the worst anarchy, was entering an age of
prosperity]. The first author discussed in this chapter is Darío, and,
significantly, he is placed outside of any national category. In fact,
an analysis of Darío's poetry actually precedes the section entitled
"Centroamérica," which is where the poet, on the basis of birth,
would naturally belong. As he traces Darío's journey from his native Nicaragua to Chile, where *Azul* (1888) is published, and then
to Spain and Argentina, Anderson Imbert carefully sketches the
portrait of a poet who not only has lived and traveled around Spanish America, but also knows that his writings, and those of his New
World contemporaries, will be instrumental in the creation of a
continental Spanish American literary tradition. Anderson Imbert's
exact words are important, because they dramatize the rise of a living society of poets, with Darío as captain, in the Spanish-speaking
nations of the New World:

> Más talentoso que los poetas jóvenes de Buenos Aires ya iniciados en
> el parnaso francés, Darío se dejó rodear y pronto fue aclamado como
> cabecilla. . . . Rubén Darío había observado desde sus años de Centro-
> américa que nuevos poetas estaban haciéndose oír. Después sospechó
> que esas voces americanas se alzaban sobre el coro de poetas de Es-
> paña; y empezó a sentir el orgullo de una generación americana inde-
> pendiente. (1:402)

> [More talented than the young poets of Buenos Aires already initiated
> in the French Parnassus, Darío let others surround him and was soon
> proclaimed leader. . . . Rubén Darío had observed since his years in
> Central America that new poets were being heard; he then surmised
> that those American voices were rising over the choir of poets from
> Spain; and he started to feel the pride of an independent American gen-
> eration.]

It is clear from these meditations on the poet, here as well as in his
La originalidad de Rubén Darío (1967), that this Nicaraguan
author's wine—to use Martí's image—is not at all bitter in Anderson Imbert's critical mind. If some, in Darío's time and later, fault
the poet for his immersion in French themes and forms, there is
also a virtual critical consensus that *modernismo*, the new aesthetics, is Spanish America's first major contribution to the world of
literature. This is not a matter of poetic language alone, but of lan-

guage politics. That Darío's revolution is marked by an adoption of French meters is important, but so is Spanish America's newly perceived capacity to transform the tongue of Spain at will, to treat and improve Spanish with an owner's rights. If regionalist practices had been instrumental in the construction of national literatures, Darío and his confreres emerge as tokens of the rise of a continental tradition, one whose banner is the renovated house of Spanish.

A commonplace of Spanish American literary studies concerns Darío's volte-face in *Cantos de vida y esperanza* (1905): the frivolous or decadent undertones of the earlier poetry give way to new philosophical and political concerns. What is somewhat less evident, perhaps because its validity is almost universally acknowledged, is the manner in which Darío's new focus on politics foregrounds Spanish, more than almost anything else, as the defining element of Spanish American culture and unity.[21] The symbolic officialdom of Spanish is clearly manifest in "A Roosevelt," a sharp censure of the rising influence of the United States in the Western hemisphere. Like "Nuestra América," the poem exemplifies the Spanish American fear, at the turn of the century, that its Protestant, English-speaking neighbor to the north was becoming overly powerful. As it constructs Spanish America for its foreign foe, a soldier in the United States's "splendid little war" against Spain, Darío's speaker stresses the continent's pre-Hispanic past. There are allusions to Moctezuma, Cuauhtemoc, and the Incas, as well as a heartfelt mention of Netzahualcoyotl, the poet-king of the Aztecs, all of which reveal a proud willingness to admit non-Hispanic elements as an integral part of Spanish America's cultural legacy: "la América nuestra, que tenía poetas / desde los viejos tiempos de Netzahualcoyotl" [our own America, which had poets / since the ancient times of Netzahualcóyotl].[22] But in this "América nuestra," as in those figurations of "nuestra América" examined in chapter 1, the tongue of choice must be Spanish. The prevailing vision is that of "la América española" (39) [Spanish America] (39), "la América ingenua que tiene sangre indígena, / que aún reza a Jesucristo y aún habla en español" (38) [our naive America / with its Indian blood, an America / that still prays to Christ and still speaks Spanish] (38). This depiction of Spanish America in terms of race, religion, and language speaks to its perceived differences vis-à-vis the United States, but also to the cultural values on which the continent's various nations traditionally represent themselves for national audiences, who are, after all, the poem's true recipients. If the discourse of *mestizaje* lies at the core of many of Spanish America's attempts at self-definition, the realities of multilingualism (or religious plurality, for that matter) do not. Reprinted numerous times in anthologies and textbooks, Darío's poem conjures Spanish America as a multiracial society predicated on the homogenizing voice of monolingualism: like the poem itself, Spanish America assertively speaks Spanish even to the president of the United States. The discord between north and south has a clear linguistic accent in other writings as well. In an essay devoted to Edgar Allan Poe, Darío describes his arrival for the first time at New York's harbor, where he can hear "el ladrante *slang* yanqui" (emphasis in the original) [the barking Yankee slang]; if he admires the works of Poe and other American authors, the speech of ordinary people strikes him as animalistic: "gritan, mugen, resuenan, braman" [they scream, moo, resound, bellow].[23]

But there is in Darío's œuvre a more complex message about foreign tongues and, therefore, the prospects of heterolingualism among Spanish American authors. If English is the tongue of an ungodly empire to the north, French, due northeast, is the tool through which Darío approaches a revered cultural milieu. In the poet's first books, France itself, from misty visions of Versailles to sensual depictions of the Parisian *bohème,* emerges as a kind of spiritual home. One sonnet in *Azul,* "De invierno," wistfully portrays the rich interior of a French bourgeois household in winter, an environment far removed from the author's provincial hometown in Nicaragua, and even from Valparaíso, the more worldly Chilean port city where the book was first published. When Darío composes "De invierno," he has not visited France yet, so this invention of Paris insinuates an intimacy that reflects mostly the emotional workings of Darío's readings. The poem is written in Spanish, but its *versos alejandrinos,* adapted from the French sonnet, may be interpreted as a formal hommage, as so many other things in Darío, to the cultural symbols of France. But Darío's affinity for French literature, especially poetry, is most explicitly revealed in the essays of *Los raros* (1896; 1905), a series of portraits of writers inspired by Paul Verlaine's *Les Poètes maudits* (1884). Aptly entitled, *Los raros* is also the poet's open embrace of French writing by Spanish American authors. The book chronicles Darío's passionate reading of mostly French writers (Leconte de Lisle, Verlaine, and a host of minor figures) and a handful of figures from other countries (Poe, Ibsen). If most of the authors whom Darío discusses here write in French, not all who do so were born in France. Significantly, of the three writers with some degree of "American experience," as Anderson Imbert would put it, only one, Martí, wrote in Spanish; the other two are the Comte de Lautréamont, born Isidore Ducasse in Uruguay, and Augusto de Armas, a Cuban-born and -educated poet, who penned a collection entitled *Rimes byzantines* (1891).[24]

Ever the cultural leader portrayed by Anderson Imbert, Darío credits himself in *Los raros* for introducing Lautréamont to Spanish American readers: "Mas hoy mismo, en Francia y Bélgica, fuera de un reducidísimo grupo de iniciados, nadie conoce ese poema que se llama *Cantos de Maldoror,* en el que está vaciada la pavorosa angustia del infeliz y sublime montevideano, cuya obra me tocó hacer conocer a América en Montevideo" (183) [But right now, in France and Belgium, outside a minuscule group of initiates, nobody knows the poem entitled *Songs of Maldoror,* into which is cast the frightful anguish of this unhappy and sublime son of Montevideo, whose works it fell on me to make known to America in Montevideo]. It is through Darío, then, that Lautréamont achieves a metaphorical return to his birthplace and an introduction to a Spanish American readership. In the essay on de Armas, what matters most in Darío's eyes is the cultural links that exist among all "Latin" countries: France as well as the nations of Spanish America. That these associations had an imperial past—the notion of common cultural bonds between Latin Europe and Latin America having developed in France to justify Napoleon III's exploits in Mexico—does not carry much weight at this point.[25] Citing the authority of Théodore de Banville, Darío praises de Armas as the only foreigner capable of crafting a French verse, thus stressing de Armas's Cuban condition, while at the same time setting a few more bricks on the seductive edifice of a Latin spirit, a *Geist* perceived as different from that of northern Europe or the United States: "Augusto de Armas representaba una de las grandes manifestaciones de la unidad y la fuerza del alma latina, cuyo centro y foco es hoy la luminosa Francia" (142) [Augusto de Armas representaba una de las grandes manifestaciones de la unidad y la fuerza del alma latina, cuyo centro y foco es hoy la luminosa Francia" (142) [Augusto de Armas represented one of the greatest manifestations of the unity and strength of the Latin soul, whose center and focus today is luminous France].[26] No matter how much Darío's own writings may dwell on the metamorphosis of nature into art, de Armas's writing in French is not viewed as a willful artifice, but rather as a natural option for those raised under the aegis of the various Romance languages and literatures.

Darío's devoted reading of poetry in French written by Spanish Americans engages several conceptual problems, but three are particularly relevant to this analysis of the continent's heterolingualism. The first speaks to the possible role of language and biography within national or continental literary traditions. A writer's birthplace matters, Darío suggests, but not in every case does biography hold the key to an author's works, nor does it determine the literary tradition within which they will or should be read. To the figure of de Armas, Darío opposes that of José-Maria de Heredia, the Cuban-born author of *Les Trophées* (1893), a key text of the Parnassian school, but one, in Darío's eyes, not written by a Spanish American poet. Repeatedly using various forms of the adjective "nuestro," Darío explains that Heredia "llegó a París muy joven, apenas tiene de americano el color y la vida, que en sus sonetos surgen, de nuestros ponientes sangrientos, nuestras fuertes savias y nuestros calores tórridos; Heredia se ha educado en Francia; su lengua es la francesa *más* que la castellana" (141; my emphasis) [he arrived in Paris very young, and virtually the only American thing about him is the life and color which, in his sonnets, emerge from our blood-colored sunsets, our strong saps and our torrid heats; Heredia has been raised in France; his language is French *more* than it is Spanish]. Even as he suggests climatic criteria for the evaluation of literature, Darío dismisses them as trivial and focuses instead on the specifically textual issue of language: not only which tongue the poet chooses, but the degree ("more" or "less") to which one may perceive the imprint of another linguistic code— Spanish in French, for instance—in the written text. Darío does not elaborate any further, but there is at least an intuition in *Los raros* of the interlingual at work in the writings of those whose consciousness inhabits two languages.[27] Beyond the biographical, the discernible shadow of Spanish in the other tongue may be read as a meaningful tie between a heterolingual author and the culture of Spanish America. Indeed, the interlingual, as we shall see in the chapters that follow, is a pivotal element in the writings of Merlin, Hudson, Bombal, and Cabrera Infante, as it signals an intrinsic rapprochement to the systems of Spanish American literature: a first glimpse of unhomeliness.

The second question, to which I have already alluded, concerns the different values attached to English and French in the continent's cultural and political life. If English is tainted with the commercial, even imperial interests of the United States—which one sees in "Nuestra América" and other texts—French, despite France's own designs on Mexico, is the language of a nation that many in Spanish America have seen as the best antidote to the perceived dark legacy of Spain. Darío speaks of "la luminosa Francia" (142) in his essay on de Armas in *Los raros*, and the adjective, of course, invokes the notions of Reason and Enlightenment. (This image of France vis-à-vis Spanish American heterolingualism is one of the subjects of Fuentes's *Una familia lejana*, which I examine in chapter 5).

At different times and places, however, English and French have elicited other reactions. In Sarmiento's *Facundo*, which precedes *Los raros* by several decades, epigraphs in English and French head the book's chapters as equal tokens of European civilization. Britain, too, has at times functioned as Spain's foe in the service of Spanish America; Simón Bolívar and Andrés Bello travel to London seeking support for Spanish America's independence, and Bello remains in that city for almost twenty years.[28] In recent decades, English (or interlingual Spanglish) has also become the well-regarded literary vehicle of Hispanic authors in the United States, whose texts may often be read as one more instance of "the Empire writing back," if one takes into account the historic reasons behind this large minority presence north of the Mexico-U.S. border.[29] The United States has also served as a refuge for exiles and others with diverse motivations to live there. One precursor of U.S. Hispanic authors is Martí, whose well-established English-language career in *The Hour* and *The Sun* seems to offset the prevailing view that he regarded North America only with an exile's eyes. But in Martí and other heterolinguals, linguistic permutation may emerge as the clearest expression of absence from one's homeland. What some may read as renegade acts may also be interpreted as melancholy signs of the loss of home. Since Martí's engagement with the cause of Cuba is unequivocal, it is unlikely that his heterolingualism would be read as the act of a turncoat; given this fact, others who write in English may conceivably travel back to the house of Spanish American literature on Martí's unhomely coattails.

Engaging the works of Martí, but also those of de Armas, *Los raros* may be read today as a strange cultural journey around the notions of center and periphery. Indeed, the third challenge posited by Darío's book speaks to the construction of Spanish Ameri-

can literature itself and the relations among its possible
constitutive elements. In a certain way, heterolingualism such as
that of de Armas implies a complete forswearing of one's native
culture, but Darío's retrieval suggests a different presumption: one
can go home again. When Steiner speaks of the linguistic unhousedness of extraterritorials, he may be right, unless, of course, one
wills to erect a house where the foreign may be made to feel quite
at home. Darío's study, where Martí and de Armas rest side by
side, is a possible touchstone of this design. It would be a strange
house because it would have some rooms leading uncannily into
other habitations, and Darío's title for his book of literary portraits
is relevant here, for *Los raros*—the odd, the rare, or should one say
the unhappy few?—invokes a vision of literary culture in which the
cozy nooks and crannies of a structure deemed familiar are in-
vaded by a host of foreign signs that obfuscate established visions
of Spanish American literary culture.

In a sense, a feeling of strangeness or unhomeliness is nothing new
in New World writing—from colonial times to the present. As he
explores the viceregal culture at whose core Sor Juana Inés de la
Cruz flourished in the second half of the seventeenth century, Octavio Paz remarks on the acute consciousness among criollos of
their odd, even outlandish status, what one may describe as their
essential unhousedness in space and culture. If the indigenous
peoples of New Spain knew that the place in which they lived was
their land, Paz argues, and if Spaniards knew that old Spain was
home, the criollos are left to inhabit—both in America, where they
were born, or in Europe, whence their parents came—a place that
is never fully their own, yet never fully alien. The French in the
seventeenth century, as Paz explains, see themselves individually
confirming each human being's universality, but the criollos regard
themselves as exceptions. In this existential context, the aesthetic
of the Baroque emerges as a fortunate coincidence, for the Baroque
allows and thrives in the exploration of strangeness, so manifest in
the transcultural forms of New Spain.[30] In the process, this new
world stands as a strange location of culture: an unhomely habitation, indeed, but one in which, faute de mieux, these new beings
must make themselves feel at home. Literature, as it attempts to
speak about this familiar yet alien realm often adopts a strangely
contradictory language. In the *loa* preceding Sor Juana's "El divino
Narciso" (c. 1688), which deals with the theological implications

of the encounter between Europe and the New World, the character of América, an Indian woman, sees the Spaniards riding their horses in battle, and asks: "¿Qué Centauros monstrüosos / contra mis gentes militan?" [What are these Centaurs, man and horse, / that now my followers assail?].[31] How can one who has never seen a horse speak so knowingly of centaurs? That América is nonetheless familiar with the myth-ridden parlance of the invaders, without knowing their real-world entities, is an incongruity that may well be taken as an emblem of strangeness: horses are defamiliarized, but so is the logic of language, whose fault lines are not concealed. Uncannily, Sor Juana represents here the fractious interplay between the alien and the domestic that no overarching theory of Spanish American culture is completely able to dispel—unless, of course, as Sor Juana seems to do here, one focuses without fear on the possible unhomeliness of home.

Attempting to understand the semantic oddity of *heimlich*, which can mean its opposite, *unheimlich*, Freud concludes, "for this uncanny is in reality nothing new or alien, but something which is familiar and old-established in the mind and which has become alienated from it only through the process of repression" (217). Whatever the specific psychoanalytical underpinnings may be, culture in Spanish America, in its search for homogeneity and a perception of total self-understanding, has often constructed itself on elisions and erasures. Literary criticism and history often forget books in which the domestic is made alien, as, for instance, in Merlin's depiction of her childhood house in Havana using the language and conventions of a foreign literature. But if some conceal them, these seemingly alienated authors usually find a textual mechanism that allows them to return home, haunting the well-guarded corpus of national and continental literatures. Strangely, even paradoxically, Merlin takes up *costumbrismo* in French, and Hudson engages *literatura gauchesca* in English, asserting through the interlingual and the interliterary the ties that bind the strange and the familiar not only in the practices of heterolingualism, but, arguably, because of its multiple ethnic strands, through Spanish American culture as a whole.

Indeed, much of Spanish American literature may be read as an intersection of the domestic and the foreign, a place that is, in that sense, both homely and unhomely. Sarmiento's *Facundo* displays this condition in its interlingual epigraphs. Many chapters are preceded by citations from the French and English, and one can also find a French translation of a line by Shakespeare ("Un cheval! Vite un cheval!... Mon royaume pour un cheval"),[32] or a Spanish rendering of a passage by Hugo or Lamartine, or even a French phrase of undetermined origin, as in the book's initial epigraph, "On ne tue point les idées" [One does not kill ideas].[33] These paratexts seem to privilege the foreign tongue over Spanish, so one is able to understand Jean Franco's vision of Sarmiento as a colonized imagination, seen in chapter 1. The citations from the Orientalist archive—Alix's *Histoire de l'Empire Ottoman* (127), for instance, or Roussel's *Palestine* (145)—may also denote the need to support the text with the trappings of European authority. Still other epigraphs are internally interlingual, as in those taken from European travel narratives about South America; a Spanish word or toponymic appears within a passage in English and French, which introduces the larger text in Spanish: "Le Gaucho vit de privations, mais son luxe est la liberté" (95) [The Gaucho lives by depriving himself, but his luxury is freedom]. (That this citation is a French translation of an English original complicates the matter even further.) If Sarmiento's use of a foreign text seems to obey colonial hierarchies, one may also venture a different interpretation. In a reverse kind of exoticism, Sarmiento, writing from remote South America, showcases his multilingual library; from it, sentences and paragraphs come forth to be exhibited, like precious oddities, in the mostly Hispanophone text. But either as framers of authority or as items from a collection, or as both, these interlingual excursions are convoluted forms, invoking both the ancient etymology of the Greek *barbaros,* he who speaks a foreign tongue, but also the word's Spanish derivative, the concept against which Sarmiento writes: *barbarie,* or barbarism. If *Facundo* presents itself as an argument for civilization, its textual space is wrinkled by a Romantic, perhaps Baroque, multiplicity of tongues that seemingly contradicts the book's call for order in the Argentine Republic.

In his desire for European immigration to populate the vast expanses of Argentina, Sarmiento is paving the way for the nation to become even more culturally fragmented than it had been until then. Earlier I quoted the author's invocation, toward the end of *Facundo,* of a *gaucho alemán,* a German gaucho, who would prefer to labor at his cheese factory rather than roam about the pampas with the untamed spirit of Argentine gauchos. Regardless of the actual number of industrious German gauchos who may have been living in Argentina at the time, it is striking that the text of *Facundo* should approach its end on this note of in-betweenness: not simply a vision of Europeans civilizing the country's wild spaces, which is what Sarmiento explicitly wants, but one strange apparition of Germans and gauchos textually united as one. In a certain fashion, the interstitial gives way to the transcultural. Since European patterns and norms are to be mimicked as much as possible, this return of the reprehensible gaucho—the familiar figure in Argentine life that Sarmiento admires but also wants to repress—within a phrase that describes an immigrant is a kind of uncanny sighting, albeit now without the element of fear. Morphologically—if not, at first, semantically—the process whereby a *gaucho alemán* is born is not altogether different from the interplay between *heimlich* and *unheimlich* in Freud's text: the familiar noun *gaucho* becomes unfamiliar once the adjective *alemán* is added onto it to conceal or domesticate its original nature. But no anxiety is shown in front of the German gaucho because barbarism, which will not remain hidden in Sarmiento's text, has become better housed—that is, in the author's eyes, civilized—in the nation through the paradoxical act of opening the spaces of home to the alien. If Sarmiento is right, the foreign culture will transform—or restore—the nation into a truer home.

Sarmiento's sentence, however, is suspect, not only because of the violent history of Argentina (like that of most Spanish American countries) even after immigration, but because of its curious negative structure: "ningún gaucho alemán" (372). If no German gaucho has ever behaved like a wild gaucho, the reader is left to wonder whether there were *any* significant numbers of German gauchos around in the first place. One may also speculate about what sort of terror an equally probable inversion of terms would produce in the author: instead of a *gaucho alemán*, one can conceive the strange figure of an *alemán gaucho*, a character resembling the woman from Yorkshire in Borges's "Historia del guerrero y de la cautiva" (1949), who after living among the Indians for years, signals her decision to remain with them by drinking a sheep's blood in front of Borges's horrified English grandmother. If, in this fiction, the Germanic warrior, a barbarian, opts to become a citizen of Ravenna and is given a Latin epitaph upon his death, the captive Englishwoman, who now speaks "un inglés rústico, entreverado de araucano o de pampa" [a rustic English, interwoven with Araucanian or Pampan],[34] realizes that home is among those whom she has grown to love best. At the end of the text, the narrator ponders these two choices and concludes that, perhaps, they are one and the same: what matters is the "secret impulse" that both the warrior and the captive heed.

But can "civilization" and "barbarism" really be one and the same? Can a real-world country have the courage of Borges's decidedly fictional imagination and incorporate the strange on equal terms with the familiar? A different figuration of Argentina comes out of Lucio V. Mansilla's *Una excursión a los indios ranqueles* (1870), a travel narrative of sorts in which the author, a cosmopolitan citizen of Buenos Aires, ventures into Tierra Adentro, the little-known territory of the Ranquel Indians, to negotiate the last details of a peace treaty. Like other works in nineteenth-century Spanish American literature, Mansilla's *Excursión* is a hybrid text from the viewpoint of both genre and tone. The narrative starts on a playful note, with Mansilla telling his narratee, the Chilean Santiago Arcos, that he has been able not only to penetrate the Indian settlements, but also to eat, before Santiago ever could, an ostrich-egg omelette in those remote places. The sense of competition is sustained throughout the text, and it often concerns Mansilla's experience as a man who has seen the world, unlike the provincial soldiers and friars who accompany him on this expedition. Not only has he traveled the four corners of the earth, as he puts it, but he has done it, like a character out of Jules Verne, by every conceivable means of locomotion: "en buque de vela, en vapor, en ferrocarril, en carreta, a caballo, a pie, en coche, en palanquín, en elefante, en camello, en globo, en burro, en silla de manos, a lomo de mula y de hombre" [on a sailing ship, on a steamer and a locomotive, in a cart, on horseback, on foot, by coach, on a litter, on an elephant's back, by camel, in a balloon, on a donkey, on a sedan chair, on the back of a mule, and on the back of a man].[35]

An Orientalist of sorts—his first piece of writing is a text entitled "De Aden a Suez" (1855)—Mansilla engages in the common Spanish American practice of viewing one's own country as an exotic territory. In the case of Argentina, the ostrich-egg omelette, however, is a but a small thing compared with what is truly strange, even dangerous: the Ranquel Indians who, in the lands referred to as Tierra Adentro, are in conflict with the expansionist government of Sarmiento, now president of Argentina. Mansilla's use of the word *excursión* in his title is the text's first instance of irony, for the feat he must undertake is fraught with peril: a journey to a certain heart of darkness. That he will accomplish this with a group of soldiers and friars, a company reminiscent of other expeditions from the beginnings of the Spanish conquest of the New World, signals the book's ancient lineage in what we now read as Spanish American literature. But it soon becomes evident that Mansilla's narrative is different; a military man, the author does not espouse a Manichaean point of view. In effect, in its treatment of the Ranquels, the book constitutes a response to the monolithic ideologies of much discourse of empire; more specifically, the *Excursión* addresses and opposes *Facundo* and its formulaic notions of "civilization" and "barbarism."

One of the most dramatic passages in the text occurs before Mansilla's departure for the south, and it concerns his behavior toward Linconao, a young Indian afflicted with smallpox. Perhaps because the young man is the brother of Ramón, one of the Ranquel *caciques* whom he will soon visit, Mansilla decides to transport Linconao to his own house for medical attention. But in order to do so, he himself must lift Linconao's pestilent body onto a carriage. On touching the man's granulose skin, Mansilla is repulsed and frightened, but realizes that he must finish his act of charity, so he takes Linconao in his arms. Doing so, he declares theatrically, "Aquél fue un verdadero triunfo de la civilización sobre la barbarie; del cristianismo sobre la idolatría" (71) [Here was a true triumph of civilization over barbarism, of Christianity over idolatry] (10). Linconao eventually survives, and Ramón is deeply thankful to Mansilla, which should facilitate the latter's journey. Moreover, that this event could be considered a *true* triumph for civilization implies that other announcements of its victory, or definitions of the concept, were less credible. In the Argentine context, furthermore, the explicit mention of the term may easily be interpreted as a retort against the president's theories and practices vis-à-vis the Indians, and thus against the prevailing vision of Argentina as a nation.[36]

Although seductively self-serving, Mansilla's acts and words in this episode and others constitute a fissure in the discourse about the indigenous peoples in much of nineteenth-century Spanish American literature. On multiple occasions, the text of the *Excursión* invokes the same racist prejudices that inform other writings of the time. But, even as Mansilla shows his cultural filiations, he reveals a curious will to listen and understand the viewpoint and—at times quite literally—the language of the Ranquels. His description of the Indians' reaction to his solicitude for Linconao is particularly telling of the author's view of himself in relation to those about whom he writes: "Los indios quedaron profundamente impresionados; se hicieron lenguas alabando mi audacia y llamáronme su padre" (71) [The Indians were profoundly impressed: they fairly babbled in praise of my daring and called me their father] (10). To exhibit such pleasure in being called a father may be read as a predictable instance of Western paternalism, but the phrase "hacerse lenguas," literally, "to become tongues," is surprising. That these Indians are shown to be people who speak—even if they cannot be comprehended, even if the image turns them into mere bodies, like Linconao—is already a triumph of sorts, especially if one reads this portrait against others in contemporary texts by Argentine authors. In the second part of José Hernández's *Martín Fierro* (1879), for instance, the gaucho hero repeatedly stresses the senseless sounds made by the Indians:

> Y aquella voz de uno solo,
> que empieza por un gruñido,
> llega hasta ser alarido
> de toda la muchedumbre,
> y ansí alquieren la costumbre
> de pegar esos bramidos.
>
> (II, 325–30)

> [And that cry, from just one of them,
> starting as a groan,
> grows till it gets to be a howl
> coming from the entire horde—
> and that's how they get the custom
> of bellowing the way they do.][37]

If etymologically a barbarian is someone who cannot speak, these Indians are made to fit that definition. Moreover, in Martín Fierro's rudimentary theology, the sound of the Indians is a sign of their ungodly status: "dan cada alarido atroz / que hace erizar los cabellos; parece que a todos ellos / los ha maldecido Dios" (II, 579–82) [giving out the most hideous howling that sets your hair on end—it's as if the whole lot of them were damned by God] (219).[38]

Mansilla's "hacerse lenguas" is an ambiguous phrase not only because of its corporality, but because the tongue, as an organ, can help produce noises that do not constitute any form of speech. In the Spanish American context, however, *lengua* has other connotations. In colonial writings it means "interpreter," and if that archaic definition does not apply here (Mansilla calls his interpreter *lenguaraz*), the phrase still suggests a measure of dignity that *lengüeteo* (II, 223) [jabbering away] and *lengüetiar* (II, 266) [jabbering], the words employed by Martín Fierro to describe the speech of the Indians, contradicts. Furthermore, Mansilla, almost like a linguist, spends much time taking notes on Araucanian, the language of the Ranquels. In chapter 21, for instance, he provides a phrasebook-like list of numbers so that his narratee and readers can learn to count, as he puts it, in one more language (243; 113); more specifically, he describes their "three manners of conversation" (237; 109). Analyzing their numerical system, Mansilla observes that it resembles that of Germanic languages ("según se ve por el ejemplo de *queú-marí*, que vale tanto como cincuenta, pero que gramaticalmente es *cinco-diez*," [245] [as is seen for example in quehú-marí, which amounts to fifty but is grammatically five-ten] [114]), and that, by having such concepts as "one million," it is clear that these Indians possess abstract mathematical notions (243; 114). Through his philological investigation, Mansilla reaches a more favorable conclusion about Ranquel society: "estos bárbaros no son tan bárbaros ni tan obtusos como muchas personas creen" (243) [these barbarians are neither as barbaric nor as obtuse as many people think] (114). The statement, once again, may be paternalistic, but it unsettles the formulaic generalities of other authors and texts. With predictable irony directed at the official discourse of Argentina, Mansilla traces a parallel, again, between the customs and manners of the Ranquels and those of one European people dear to Sarmiento's heart: "Los alemanes, justamente orgullosos de ser paisanos de Schiller y de Goethe, se parecen también a ellos. Bismarck, el gran hombre de Estado, contaría las águilas de las legiones vencedoras en Sadowa, lo mismo que el indio Mariano Rosas cuenta sus lanzas al regresar del malón" (244) [The Germans, justifiably proud to be the compatriots of Schiller and Goethe, also resemble them. Bismarck, that great statesman, surely counted the eagles of the conquering legions of Sadowa in the same way that Mariano counts his lances on returning from a raid] (114). What matters is not so much Mansilla's beliefs—the Ranquels, like other ethnic or social groups, may be seen to be both civilized and barbarian—but his ironic, albeit inconsistent, sabotage of the nation's rules of inclusion and exclusion.

It is significant in this citation that Mansilla uses the word "malón" [raid] so lightly, for it is arguably one of the most feared terms in the lexicon of nineteenth-century Argentine literature. The plot of Echeverría's "La cautiva" and some episodes in *Martín Fierro* depict starkly the terrifying attacks by Indians on the European settlements of the pampas. Whatever the real-world brutality may have been, authors spare no rhetorical devices in their narrations of this act and the ensuing captivities. A woman in Hernández's poem, for instance, describes in detail how an Indian, after having slit her young son's throat, binds her hands with the boy's guts (II, 1113–16). Rewriting and compressing certain aspects of that literary tradition, Borges makes his captive from Yorkshire describe, in her vanishing English, what surviving a "malón" and living among the Indians could mean.[39] In Borges's fiction, the year of the encounter between his grandmother and the other Englishwoman is 1872. This is the time of Argentina's southward expansion in the coldblooded Campaña al Desierto, and visiting the Ranquels just before this all-out war, Mansilla writes when there is still hope that a kind of peaceful coexistence may be established.

Nevertheless, fear prevails when he travels into Tierra Adentro in search of the Ranquel Indians. Indeed, the first encounter on the desolate plain between the two groups starts on a note of trepidation. Mansilla's text first records a prolonged scream by the Indians (195; 83), who then surround his group of men: "Mi sangre se heló . . . Estos bárbaros van a sacrificarnos, me dije" (195) ["My blood froze . . . 'These barbarians are going to sacrifice us' "] (83). Another scream then follows, but after some moments of hesitation, it becomes evident that there will be no bloodshed. Mansilla's men greet the Ranquels—some 250 of them—in the Indian manner, a handshake followed by a shout, and then the author, as leader, salutes the Cacique Ramón, who is in his turn still visibly scared, with an embrace. Tension finally dissipates, Mansilla is cheered by all, and he responds with an uncanny proclamation: "¡Viva el Cacique Ramón! ¡Viva el Presidente de la República! ¡Vivan los indios argentinos!" (196) [Long live Chief Ramón! Long live the President of the Republic! Long live the Argentine Indians!] (84).

Signals of peace, Mansilla's vivas are uncanny because they seek to reimagine Argentina as a nation where men and women who are strangers—indeed, who may be terrified of each other—will live peacefully in the same domestic, or domesticated, space. That a cheer to Sarmiento is followed by one in which "Indians" are proclaimed "Argentines" is surely an unexpected turn of

events, because it implies that inimical loyalties and discourses
may be reconciled and sheltered within one nation. Argentina will
admit the Ranquels as Argentines, and these new Argentines will
still retain an identity as Indians.[40] Thus, Mansilla's text foresees
one community where the familiar and the strange may intersect
freely. The nation no longer needs to be conceived as a space of
sameness; strangers no longer need to fear each other. An *indio argentino* can be as much a part of the nation as a *gaucho alemán*.
Moreover, even if Mansilla does not say so explicitly, one can also
read the *Excursión* as a textual nod to the heterolingualism of nations. Among the Ranquels, he learns and employs the word
"yapaí," a kind of salutation, and describes how it is used when
drinking: "Se inicia con un *yapaí*, que es lo mismo que si dijéra-
mos: *the pleasure of a glass of wine with you?*, para que vean los de
la colonia inglesa que en algo se parecen a los ingleses" (281) [It
begins with a *yapaí*, which is as much as saying, 'The pleasure of
a glass of wine with you?' I wouldn't want our English colony to
think that it bears no resemblance to the Ranquels] (137). Like
Borges's captive, who is unafraid that Araucanian and Pampa have
filtered into her English, Mansilla's text makes room for tongues
previously regarded and overheard as foreign. What the *Excursión*
advances for all these languages may well serve as a model for a
literary history of Spanish America that would not mask the continent's linguistic unhomeliness. In Sarmiento's Argentina, indigenous languages may have been perceived as stranger than English,
but now, in the cultural constructions of Spanish America, a hierarchical reversal may be observed. Mansilla's lesson, as it were, may
now be extended to encompass all forms of nation and continent
expressed in any other tongue.

Departing from Freud's postulate that strangeness lives within
each individual, Kristeva weaves the theory of the uncanny into
her discussion of the foreign as an element of fear within communities. She observes that Freud mentions the Greek ξένος as a possible translation for *unheimlich*, but that there is really no discussion
of foreigners in "Das Unheimliche." Yet, by playing with that interlingual correspondence between "uncanny" and "foreign," and
with the related concepts of "foreigner" and "stranger" contained
in the French *étranger*, Kristeva reads in Freud an oblique defense
of the heterogeneity of cultures and nations: "Délicatement, ana-
lytiquement, Freud ne parle pas des étrangers: il nous apprend à
détecter l'étrangeté en nous" [Delicately, analytically, Freud does

not speak of foreigners: he teaches us how to detect foreignness in ourselves].⁴¹ Aware that the cultural homogeneity of France is now neither possible nor desirable, Kristeva proposes to extend Freud's lesson of insightfulness to a new conceptualization of community: "Une communauté paradoxale est en train de surgir, faite d'étrangers qui s'acceptent dans la mesure où ils se reconnaissent étrangers eux-mêmes" (290) [A paradoxical community is emerging, made up of foreigners who are reconciled with themselves to the extent that they recognize themselves as foreigners] (195).

In effect, Kristeva's paradoxical communities are nothing new in Spanish America, where a plurality of races and tongues are long-standing facts in the lives of nations. Thinking and writing about this essential diversity is not an untrodden path, either; in fact, one finds examples thereof even in colonial times. One may cite the works of the Inca Garcilaso, who seeks to reconcile his dual European and New World cultural legacy, with their corresponding languages, by means of a written discourse in which linguistic translation is also a bridge between cultures. As he compiles the stories told to him by his elders, Garcilaso cites linguistic alterity as a source of conflict in pre-Hispanic America, where groups who spoke different languages considered each other enemies and would engage in cannibalism.⁴² Seen against this ancient context, his act of translation emerges as a possible triumph of humanism and imagination.⁴³ Regarding his own indigenous tongue, Garcilaso seems to say two things; in his "Advertencias acerca de la lengua general de los indios" (Notes on the General Languages of the Indians of Peru), one of the prefaces to his *Comentarios reales* (1609), Quechua is mentioned among "las dicciones bárbaras" (5) [barbarous languages] (5), but it is also described as "una lengua muy galana" (6) [so elegant a language] (6) that Spanish speakers misunderstand and even corrupt. Beyond the merits of one language or the other, Garcilaso's own practice of writing has as its source the need for correct understanding across linguistic barriers, which he states in his famous evaluation of previous historical writers on the Incas: "Que mi intención no es contradecirles sino servirles de comento y glosa y de intérprete de muchos vocablos indios que, como extranjeros en aquella lengua, interpretaron fuera de la propiedad de ella según que largamente se verá en el discurso de la historia" (4) [For my purpose is not to gainsay them, but to furnish a commentary and gloss, and to interpret many Indian expressions which they, as strangers to that tongue, have rendered inappropriately. This will be fully seen in the course of my history] (4). A child of linguistic plurality, Garcilaso is aware that those who do not know Quechua in an intimate way will find many of its elements strange, such as the phrase "guardar en el corazón" [to keep in your heart], by which his great-uncle means what a Spaniard would call "guardar en la memoria" (40) [literally, "to keep in memory," meaning "to remember"]. But the author might also suspect that readers of his text can yet learn these alien expressions. In book 1, chapter 15, Garcilaso explains directly the meaning of "guardar en el corazón," but in chapter 23 he uses it himself freely in conjunction with the phrase's Spanish double: "Todo lo cual les mandaba guardasen en el corazón y en la memoria para corresponder con el servicio como leales vasallos" (57) [He bade them keep all this in their hearts and memories, and repay it with their service like loyal subjects] (58).

What strikes me here is the gracious coexistence of both metaphors: the text's *concordia,* but something else as well. True, readers can yet learn these alien expressions, but Garcilaso still chooses to follow the Quechua image with its Spanish counterpart. In this uncanny doubling, I believe, Garcilaso delicately teaches us to protect the notion of strangeness: to use only the Quechua phrase would mean that Spanish has totally assimilated it, but to have one phrase as the other's mirror reminds us that the Incas are still the speakers of another tongue. The unhomely coexistence of two languages is not concealed in *Comentarios reales,* and that such a text is considered a classic site of Spanish American writing bodes well for the future prospects of heterolingualism in the critical discussion. If the Renaissance, as some have argued, is a culture in which the communication of other cultures is paramount,[44] Spanish American literary studies in this new age of multiculturalism may yet follow Garcilaso's example and house the strange— authors and texts as well as practices of reading—while preserving the sense of unhomeliness.

The problem of comprehension, however, remains at the heart of the matter. Plainly put, it is obviously impossible to read a text in a language that one does not understand. Garcilaso writes in Spanish, but four out of the five works on which my study focuses in the following chapters are written in foreign tongues. If translations are no doubt a route that must be explored, one must consider to what extent even the best versions are faithful to the original's unhomeliness. This is not only an issue of language, but one that engages the more general problem of understanding other cultures, including those that one wills to house within one's nation or continent. In her preface to Rigoberta Menchú's testimony, Elisabeth Burgos speaks of achieving a kind of revelation by transcribing and editing the experiences of this other woman from Spanish America whose mother tongue is Quiché and whose Spanish is decidedly interlingual: "Ella [Rigoberta] me ha permitido descubrir ese otro yo-misma. Gracias a ella mi yo americano ha dejado de ser una 'extrañeza inquietante' " [She {Rigoberta} allowed me to discover another self. Thanks to her, my American self is no longer something 'uncanny'].[45] If by this is meant that now Burgos is aware of the continent's others, one can understand her sense of gratitude. But what would strike one as unusual would be the anthropologist's belief that conversations with Menchú, regardless of intensity and detail, could have diffused the sense of strangeness that must still surround the other culture, especially in the light of Menchú's overt option for a measure of secrecy: "Nosotros los indígenas hemos ocultado nuestra identidad, hemos guardado muchos secretos . . . Por eso no puedo explicar el nahual pero hay ciertas cosas que puedo decir a grandes rasgos. Yo no puedo decir cuál es mi nahual porque es uno de nuestros secretos" (40) [We Indians have always hidden our identity and kept our secrets to ourselves. . . . So I can only tell you very general things about the *nahual*. I can't tell you what my *nahual* is because that is one of our secrets] (20). And even if Menchú were willing fully to explain the concept of *nahual,* would cultural and linguistic outsiders find themselves at home there?

The idea that through the medium of writing one can give other cultures a voice is a well-entrenched gesture in Spanish American literature. But even as they attempt to speak for the other, authors often expose the impossibility of doing so. The speaker in Neruda's "Alturas de Macchu Picchu," the second section of *Canto general* (1950), says, "Yo vengo a hablar por vuestra boca muerta" [I've come to speak through your dead mouths], and concludes, "Hablad por mis palabras y mi sangre" [Speak through my words and my blood].[46] Indeed, aspects of indigenous life may be suggested in Neruda's lofty verses, but one is made aware, upon turning the poem's last page, that there are things a Spanish-language reader will not understand; the next section of *Canto general,* entitled "Los conquistadores," starts with an epigraph in Quechua that the poet chooses not to translate into his own tongue, the continent's lingua franca: "Ccollanan Pachacutec! Ricuy / anceacunac yahuarniy richacaucuta" (47).[47] Even if this is macaronic Quechua, Neruda privileges the existence of those other languages that share with Spanish the cultural spaces of Spanish America. What do those words mean? Why do they remain only in the other tongue? Despite one's best intentions and desires, an untranslatable "space between" becomes visible whose strangeness Neruda and other writers teach us to acknowledge and preserve.[48] In the chapters that follow, as I move to affiliate heterolingual authors and texts with the current discussion of Spanish American literature, I shall underscore not only what can be translated, but also that which cannot be retrieved from the other tongue. Banned from the house of Spanish, this unhomeliness may yet find a home in a reconfigured house of Spanish American literature.

3

Merlin's Craft: An Author's Ocean Blues

IN THE COURSE OF HER LIFE, THE COMTESSE MERLIN SAILED ACROSS THE
Atlantic Ocean on three occasions. The first crossing took place in
1802, when she left Cuba for Europe at the age of twelve; the second, several decades later in 1840, on her only return trip to her
native country; the third, a few weeks later, back to France, where
she would die in 1852.[1] At the outset of her second crossing, as she
sails from Bristol to New York en route to Havana, Merlin wit-
nesses an odd interlingual exchange between two fellow passengers, an Englishman and a Spaniard, who attempt to communicate
with each other in French. The author, ever the scribe with pen in
hand, faithfully records this uncanny dialogue in *La Havane*, the
narrative of that journey home:

> —Vos était remarquablement stioupid," dit milord à l'Espagnol, voyant
> que ce dernier ne bougeait pas. À quoi celui-ci répondit:
> —Y vue sa merced es un mal criado.
> —Cette homme,—reprit l'Anglais,—avé une très-irréverencious man-
> ner.—"Et s'addressant à l'Espagnol:
> —Jé défendé vos de paalé davantadge!—taisez-vos tutte suite, tutte!
> —Hérético dou diable!—Caramba! . . . que si jè me lève!"

> ["You are remarkably stupid," said milord to the Spaniard, seeing the
> latter did not move. To which he replied, "And your honor has no man-
> ners."
> "This man," the Englishman went on, "has a very irreverentious
> manner." He added, addressing the Spaniard, "I forbid you to say any-
> thing else. Shut up right now, right now!"
> "You heretic from hell! Good gracious! . . . I'm not about to get up!"][2]

Placed at the end of the first "letter" of *La Havane*, when readers
have just embarked on the author's textual homebound journey,
this heavily accented dialogue may be read as an emblem of Mer-

lin's strange position in literary history and criticism. The location
is a craft, a vessel sailing between continents, an international as
well as an interstitial space. The language of the two passengers,
curiously, is also halfway, neither English nor Spanish, and certainly not an impeccable form of French. Linguistically unhoused
in this foreign tongue, the Englishman and the Spaniard clearly
mispronounce the first-person singular pronoun, the word one uses
to refer to oneself, the two phonemes that most effectively should
mark one's position as a speaking (or writing) subject in the French
language. Against their defective "jé" and "jè", Merlin emits a perfect "je", whose unaccented condition is both typographic and
phonemic, but also symbolic: she is a master of that tongue: "La
caisse sur laquelle *je* m'appuyais était le seul meuble vacant qui
gardât encore l'équilibre; *je* l'offris à Fanny, qui l'accepta et s'y
établit tant bien que mal" (1:24; my emphasis) [The chest on
which I leaned was the only empty piece of furniture that still kept
its balance; I offered it to Fanny, who accepted it and settled there
for better or worse].[3] The author's precious *je*, however, is illusory,
for she, like the two men, is not a native speaker of French either,
and her vernacular Spanish is not the tongue employed in her literary endeavors.

Linguistically, then, Merlin shares with her unwitting informants
more than she reveals here. She, too, is an interlingual figure; her
text, moreover, clearly exemplifies the notion of the interliterary,
or writing across the traditional bounds of national literatures. The
purity of her French does not last, for it will soon be exposed to her
native Spanish, giving way to a certain *Sprachmischung* and to a
kind of writing that overlaps not only two languages, but also the
systems of two literatures. Like Esteban Echeverría's and Domingo
Faustino Sarmiento's foundational texts, Merlin's book amalgam-
ates diverse genres, fluctuating from foreign travel narrative to nativist *cuadro de costumbres,* even to a kind of memoirs. But this
wavering is more complex than that of the two Argentine writers.
Merlin emerges as a European author in search of a Cuban character, a New World expression; but one may also view her as a
Cuban writer poignantly trapped in the sounds and forms of
French literature. Her craft, then, is *entre dos aguas,* between two
waters, as the Spanish metaphorical expression reads, and that
critics and literary historians should have focused on the author's
extraterritorial condition is really no surprise. Some, though, have
underscored the other tongue to justify her virtual exclusion from

the established discussion. As we saw in the introduction, Gastón Baquero reads Merlin as an exemplum that not every Cuban who writes is a Cuban writer. Other critics justly foreground the author's role in the formation of Cuban nationalism, but pay less attention to her heterolingualism and the unhomely meanings contained only in the French originals.[4] What I seek to underscore is how Merlin's transit, or in-betweenness, or dual habitation, allows and signifies her emergence as a Cuban and Spanish American author even without recourse to Spanish translations. By speaking of Merlin's craft in this chapter's title, I seek to locate the author's literary value in her precarious navigation between languages and literatures, a condition best observed in the French original. That she is not well housed in any traditional literary-historical construct makes her an uncanny writer. Readers of Merlin sometimes disregard those aspects of her writing that do not fit into certain theories of nation and literary culture: her claims for Cuban authorship, for instance, in some cases; or the strangeness of her French textuality, in others. If I variously underscore the Cuban connections of her French prose, or the French viewpoints in her visions of Cuba, it is because I value the unhomely status of nation that Merlin's authorial undulations allow us to imagine: one's country is not only a familiar place, but also, without fear of its unraveling, a site of strangeness.

In France, where she lived for over four decades, María de las Mercedes Santa Cruz y Montalvo, also known as the Comtesse Merlin, the Condesa Merlín, or the Condesa de Merlín, among other names, was a prominent figure in the literary and musical life of Paris.[5] At her salon, located on the rue de Bondy (now rue René-Boulanger), she often welcomed important guests from her native country, men such as José Antonio Saco y José de la Luz y Caballero, literary figures now solidly placed at the center of the cultural history of nineteenth-century Cuba. One can well imagine that French with an accent, and other tongues too, were frequently spoken around her. That *La Havane* and her other writings should devote considerable attention to the interlingual and to other languages is probably a natural reaction on the part of an author for whom monolingualism and linguistic purity were rarities.

Reputedly a very talented singer, Merlin was also a friend of Maria Malibran, née García, the celebrated mezzo soprano whose biography makes up a section of Merlin's *Les Loisirs d'une femme du monde* (1838). In a certain way, opera, contrasted with literature, constitutes an insightful terrain from which to view Merlin as a cultural and literary figure. Composers and singers normally profit from their knowledge of more than one language, even in those cases where mastery of any is imperfect. We know, for instance, that Malibran "wrote to her husband in French, with many mistakes, and with many words in Spanish, Italian and English," and that Vincenzo Bellini, who lived in Paris at the same time as Merlin, was also an interlingual figure: "His written Italian . . . was uncertain; like many people whose grasp of language is weak, he readily picked up foreign turns of phrases—Gallicisms—while failing to master the language they came from."[6] Rossini's *Guillaume Tell* (1829) and Donizetti's *La Fille du régiment* (1839), written in that same period when the composers lived in Paris, employ French-language libretti. Despite nationalism, opera composers may move from one language to another with relative ease and still have a connection with their national audiences because, arguably, music comes before words.[7] Besides Rossini and Donizetti, one can cite the examples of Spontini, Cherubini, Gluck, and Mozart, even nationalist Verdi, as well as exiles such as Stravinsky and Kurt Weill, as opera composers who set foreign-language libretti to music. But if the idiom of opera can transcend the libretto's tongue, that of literature is grounded in words in specific languages. Musical audiences can appreciate works sung in languages they do not understand, but the same does not obtain in literature. As a performer, Merlin was able, for the most part, to charm a Cuban audience at her concerts in Havana;[8] as an author, however, she chose a tongue that, as we shall see, disconcerted many a Cuban reader.

Beyond Merlin's musical talents, there is also a certain operatic quality about her written words. Composing her texts in what is at times an extravagantly lyrical Romantic prosody, doing so in a foreign language that most of her compatriots cannot understand, Merlin may strike some as a haughty diva enamoured of her own sounds, but devoid of much sense. The countess's throat and tongue are perplexing: what is she doing uttering those passionate things about Cuba in French? If exacerbated emotion in other Spanish American authors—exalted Sarmiento and lachrymose Jorge Isaacs are two that readily come to mind—may be read, correctly, as part and parcel of a foundational discourse, in Merlin's cry for Cuba it may resound as alienation: her own and that of the reader. In Figarola-Caneda's biography, there is a drawing of Merlin dressed for a performance of Bellini's *Norma* (1831). As if imitating the Druid priestess who falls in love with a Roman soldier, Merlin's story may be read as an act of betrayal against her people; saved from the pyre, she is still banished from the house of literature and given an eccentric role in the more general history of culture: a woman from Havana who became a European aristocrat, but never a full-fledged Cuban writer.[9] Yet, in her works about Cuba, if not in her mundane novels set in Paris, one can identify an effort on the part of Merlin to assert herself as a Cuban writer. Authorship has repeatedly been denied to her, both through anecdotal evidence and through critical and literary-historical evaluations in which language is adduced as the only exhibit that counts.[10] But, as we shall see, *La Havane* and other texts by Merlin interrogate several axioms surrounding both the figure of the author and that of the reader, as well as the idea of nation, in Spanish American literary culture. The unintelligibility of Merlin, so operatic, so foreign, becomes the key to new soundings of the nation and its literature in which linguistic alterity will play a valuable role.[11]

Traditionally, the discourse of Spanish American literature has watched closely the biographical aspects framing any given text.[12] Literary histories, specifically, are built upon and organized around authors whose national or continental filiation, especially birth, but also longtime residence, are taken as markings of identity. Merlin may be dismissed by some as an outlandish, if not altogether alien, character in search of Cuban authorship, but, besides her heterolingualism, there is little in her biography that sets her apart from other writers from the continent. Indeed, her life journey follows many of the same patterns discernible in many other Spanish American authors, such as migration. This is especially true in the case of Cuba. From the early nineteenth century, there is no period in Cuban history when exile, either voluntary or imposed, has not been a dominant episode in the lives of writers. In colonial times, José María Heredia is banished by the island's Spanish rulers, while Gertrudis Gómez de Avellaneda lives most of her life in Spain; Cirilo Villaverde writes in the United States, and Martí himself returns to Cuba only to die a short time later. Also a heterolingual like Merlin is Félix Varela, whose works on philosophy and religion were written in Spanish, Latin, and English.[13] The situation is no different even after the Republic of Cuba is established in

1902. Lydia Cabrera studies in Paris and dies in Miami; Virgilio Piñera works in Buenos Aires; Alejo Carpentier spends years in Venezuela and France; Nicolás Guillén and Heberto Padilla hold diplomatic posts in Moscow, and the latter is exiled to the United States, like Antonio Benítez Rojo and Reinaldo Arenas; Calvert Casey dies in Rome; Severo Sarduy and Zoé Valdés go to Paris, while Mayra Montero is raised in Puerto Rico; and Guillermo Cabrera Infante, a longtime resident of London, becomes a British subject, if not an English author, as his eventual heterolingualism might suggest.

Moreover, the encounter with exile informs many of these authors' writings, and, indeed, much of the canon of Cuban and Spanish American literatures. One of the classic texts of the Romantic school, Heredia's "Niágara" (1824) marks the initial phase of a major undercurrent in Cuban literature to this day: the expression of sorrow about one's physical absence from the island. Veritable realms of memory, some of Heredia's verses are engraved in the minds of many Cuban readers: "¿Por qué no miro / Alrededor de tu caverna inmensa / Las palmas ¡ay! las palmas deliciosas, / Que en las llanuras de mi ardiente patria / Nacen del sol a la sonrisa" [Why are not here, / About the jaws of this abbys, the palms— / Ah, the delicious palms—that on the plains / Of my own native Cuba spring and spread / Their thickly foliaged summits to the sun].[14] The speaker's rhetorical questions may be said to function as archetypes that much Cuban literature since then reformulates in different genres and modes, from Avellaneda's sonnet, "Al partir" (1836) to Cabrera Infante's evocation of Havana cigars in *Holy Smoke* (1985). If in the European tradition the "where?" in the classic *ubi sunt* is often invested with temporal intimations, as one can see in Jorge Manrique or Marcel Proust, the same question in Cuban literature expresses, first and foremost and quite literally, a spatial yearning, a remembrance of things present elsewhere, invisible to speaker or narrator because of physical separation. Cabrera Infante's best-known works, *Tres tristes tigres* (1967) and *La Habana para un infante difunto* (1979), certainly deal with the past, but their melancholy thrust focuses on space, a city that the author is not about to regain. Marcel remembers Illiers-Combray from the proximity of Paris, but Havana, in Cabrera Infante's fiction, is a forbidden city; the past may be another country for all writers, but it becomes an even more remote location when actual geography intervenes. In the larger context of Spanish American heterolingualism, the title of W. H. Hudson's autobiography, *Far Away and Long Ago: A Childhood in Argentina* (1918), encapsules these notions: the past occurred literally in a distant land.

As an author, Merlin engages in the paradigmatic Cuban practice of turning absence from the homeland into the primary subject of literature. *Mes premières douze années* (1831) and *Histoire de la sœur Inès* (1832), her first works, are mostly autobiographical in nature, addressing the author's childhood in distant Cuba;[15] nostalgia for her lost birthplace is also a major theme in *Souvenirs et mémoires* (1836) and *La Havane* (1844). As in the works of Heredia and other Cuban authors, Merlin's evocation of Cuba also revolves around spatial displacement, often expressed through the symbolism of climate. Her depiction of Europe's winter, even after decades of residence in those latitudes, still occurs mostly through a tropical prism. The first experience of snow in Castile, recounted vividly in *Souvenirs et mémoires,* signals the absence of elements associated with Cuba's perennial spring: "Plus de feuilles, plus de fruits; le gazon même avait disparu. Des troncs et des branches noirs, épars ça et là, comme les débris d'un naufrage, offraient une image complète de destruction, et la nature me parut ensevelie sous un vaste linceul" [Leaves and fruits were gone; even the grass had vanished. Black trunks and branches, scattered here and there like debris from a shipwreck, afforded a complete image of destruction, and nature seemed to me buried beneath a vast shroud].[16] In this landscape after the snowfall, the child retrieves the memories of her native country as a land of plenty: "ces forêts vierges plantées d'arbres de toute couleur . . . le chant d'une multitude d'oiseaux; la douceur de l'air, la beauté du ciel, les rayons brillants du soleil" (86) [those virgin forests where trees of all colors grew . . . the singing of a multitude of birds; the air's softness; the radiant sunshine]. These may be well-worn topoi, but they signify a filiation with Cuban literature that heterolingualism does not conceal. If European space is seen from the start as the negation of cherished objects, most poignantly Cuba itself, the Old World will remain, at least partially, an alien presence in her eyes. From Cuba she may even remember the Loire Valley with nostalgia, but winter, for one thing, will still retain a certain measure of foreignness: "Néanmoins mes premières ideées sur l'hiver ayant été puisées dans les romans, j'en suis toujours frappée d'une manière neuve et piquante" (86) [but since my first ideas of winter came from novels, it still strikes me every time in a new and biting way]. Even after decades, snow is still perceived as the alien stuff of books.

Yet, during her sojourn in Havana, Merlin also underscores the strangeness of what she still thinks of as home. The city's cathedral, an edifice celebrated by later writers as an endearing expression of the New World Baroque, is, for her, frightfully reminiscent of the island's lush tropical nature, with "des fruits entrelacés par des lianes et des guirlandes de fleurs, puis des imitations de feuilles de papayer larges et lustrées . . . se tortillant avec souplesse autour de colonnes sans base, couronnées de panaches exubérants, en corolles d'ananas" (*La Havane*, 2:200) [fruits intertwined by creepers and flower garlands, and imitation papaya leaves, large and shiny . . . twisting with suppleness around bottomless columns and crowned with exuberant plumes like a pineapple's corolla]. That such exoticist passages are in French, and that they are addressed mostly to European men and women—recipients of her "letters," or chapters—problematizes Merlin's claim to Cuban authorship.

Merlin's exile, then, boasts a double edge. If the focus on absence links her with other Cuban writers, it also contains a kind of foreign vision that heterolingualism only exacerbates. The two competing images of Cuba as a domestic paradise and as a strange location of culture seem to invoke, *avant la lettre,* what Gustavo Pérez Firmat, speaking about Cuban-Americans who left Cuba at a young age for the United States, terms "life on the hyphen." Identifying a bicultural situation in which it is difficult to decide which culture is dominant and which is subordinate, Pérez Firmat views the typographical hyphen through another metaphor, that of a children's seesaw in which each side moves alternately up and down (*Life on the Hyphen,* 6).[17] The interlingual and interliterary qualities of Merlin's *La Havane* bespeak a hyphenation of this kind. As is the case with Pérez Firmat's Cuban America, this in-betweenness, in its search for equilibrium, is benign because it is not usually the source of disabling anxiety: if one at times feels unhoused in each of the two cultures, one also may feel quite at home in both. Merlin may miss France while she is in Cuba, and Cuba when she is abroad, but *La Havane* itself is a hybrid where literary practices linked with each culture and nation, even if at times they show themselves abruptly as fearful cracks in the wall, manage textually to share the same space. Yet biographers as well as critics and literary historians have, more often than not, chosen to view only the European side of her Cuban-French condition. Writing in the *Dia-*

rio de la Habana upon the publication of Merlin's travel narrative, Félix Tanco is plainly dismissive: "La señora de Merlin, por decirlo de una vez, ha visto a la isla de Cuba con ojos parisienses y no ha querido comprender que la Habana no es París" [It must be said once and for all: Madam Merlin has seen the island of Cuba with Parisian eyes, and has refused to understand that Havana is not Paris].[18] Although Tanco's quarrel is ostensibly with Merlin's book, his ocular metaphor—unlike that of Anderson Imbert regarding Hudson—wills to turn the author herself into an outsider; then again, in a period of emergent patriotism like the mid-nineteenth century, it is not surprising that Tanco should be blind to the possibility of writers being endowed with a dual, at times contradictory, field of vision.

Consequently, those who decide to affirm Merlin's Cuban side often underscore defensively the author's ties with Cuba and disregard the equally important French dimension of her writings. This is the case of Francisco Calcagno's positive note on Merlin in his *Diccionario biográfico cubano* (1878):

> Porque las bellas producciones de su inteligencia brotarán [sic] á orillas del nebuloso Sena, donde ha pasado toda su vida literaria; porque en lengua extrangera emitiera sus pensamientos y modularán [sic] sus hijos sus primeras palabras, no dejó de ser cubana, y una de nuestras principales glorias literarias, máxime cuando sus escritos són para Cuba, y cuando á semejanza de la Avellaneda y Heredia, sólo tomaba la pluma para derramar, en los recuerdos de la pátria todas las fusiones del más puro patriotismo.

> [Just because the exquisite creations of her intelligence were born on the nebulous banks of the Seine, just because she expressed her thoughts, and her children spoke their first words, in a foreign language, she did not stop being a Cuban, or one of our greatest literary glories, especially when her writings are for Cuba, and when, like Avellaneda and Heredia, she took the pen only to exude, in her memories of the fatherland, the purest patriotism.][19]

The issue of national loyalties is obviously a foremost concern. Calcagno's biographical note is emblematic of how even Merlin's most favorable reviewers must contend with the specter of the author's foreignness. Here, her personal circumstances and literary output are constructed, even manipulated, in order to make her a palatable figure to those questioning her authorship as a Cuban.

Despite its best intentions, Calcagno's review partially falsifies the nature of Merlin's writing; if she did express patriotic feelings in *La Havane* and elsewhere, she also "took the pen" to compose novels such as *Les Lionnes de Paris* (1845), where Cuba does not play any significant role—unless one decides to read, as one might, the protagonist's initial, but short-lived, interest in abolitionism as an element that gains new meanings within the systems of Cuban literature and their discussion of slavery.

The issue of patriotism raised by Calcagno is relevant because, in Cuban literary culture, an author's ideological commitments have often been a primary concern in canon formation. Martí, situated at the center of all things Cuban, is regarded both as a pinnacle of the nation's writing and as the father of Cuban independence: an icon who encompasses the political symbolism of Washington and Lincoln as well as the literary heights of Emerson and Whitman. Unlike that of Merlin, Martí's biography serves the nationalist needs of much criticism and literary history. Having died a hero's death, Martí soon becomes the yardstick against which every Cuban writer must measure himself—or herself. Indeed, as Méndez Rodenas has demonstrated, the fact that Merlin was a woman could only hamper her insertion into the male-dominated corpus of Cuban literature; that she "fits better" in feminist reconstructions of the nation's literary canon is shown in the recent inclusion of Merlin as the very first author in *Estatuas de sal* (1996), an anthology of Cuban women writers.[20] But if these gestures constitute a new vision of Cuban literary culture in which Merlin translated into Spanish is seen to play a major role, one must still consider the author's heterolingualism and its possible effects on theories of the nation and of Cuban writing. No matter whether Merlin is repressed or only her French is, the unhomely foreignness of her texts must be allowed to return, even if it haunts the more open, but still well-guarded, house of Cuban literature.[21]

La Havane is arguably one of the few masterpieces of nineteenth-century Cuban writing; its vast spaces offer an intricate response to the problem of authorship, language, and national literature. In the work's preface, addressed to the Capitán General Leopoldo O'Donnell, the island's colonial ruler, Merlin clearly depicts herself, albeit in French, as a patriotic Cuban author: "Permettez, général, que je place sous votre égide protectrice cette œuvre conçue par le sentiment patriotique d'une femme; le désir ardent de voir mon pays heureux me l'a seul inspirée" (1:v) [Allow

me, general, to place under your protection this work conceived by
a woman's patriotic feelings; only a fervent desire for my country's
happiness has inspired it]. The book itself has a heartfelt dedication to her fellow Cubans, who are thus signaled in French to read
this book: "À mes compatriotes" (1:vii) [To my compatriots]. That
Cuba matters to Merlin is obvious from the contrast between her
opening words and, for instance, those of Richard Henry Dana's
To Cuba and Back (1859), a more conventional travelogue: "To the
Gentlemen of the Saturday Club, this narrative of a short absence
from home and from their society, is dedicated."[22] Yet the work's
general dedication is gainsaid by the foreign status of its narratees.
La Havane consists of thirty-six letters addressed mostly to Mer-
lin's daughter, Madame Gentien de Dissay, born and living in
France,[23] and to a series of European (mostly French) personali-
ties: René de Chateaubriand, whose own travels had taken him to
North America and the Middle East; Prince Frederick of Prussia;
George Sand, recipient of the letter on women; and Baron Roth-
schild, to whom the letter on trade is addressed.

After its preface and dedication, La Havane soon inserts itself
thematically as well as formally in the tradition of European travel
narratives, a genre easily perceived as foreign to Cuban writing.
With great detail, Merlin recounts her journey from Europe to the
United States, where she visits several places between New York
and Washington; she then sails on to Cuba, where she lodges with
her family and is celebrated by Havana's social and cultural circles.[24] The first quarter of La Havane focuses on Merlin's transatlantic journey and her sojourn in the United States. The episodes
narrated here are heterogeneous: adventures on the high seas; an
analysis of American democracy; a meeting with President Van
Buren; a strange encounter with George Washington's niece at a
mental hospital. Unlike the rest of the text, devoted to Cuba, these
North American letters clearly follow the conventions of travel writing, and the author's general manner does not differ essentially
from European books about the United States, such as Alexis de
Tocqueville's De la démocratie en Amérique (1835–40) or Charles
Dickens's American Notes (1842). Merlin's detachment from the
world she portrays marks her clearly as a foreigner; upon landing
in New York, she explicitly introduces herself as "étrangère à tous
ces interêts, indifférente à tout ce qui m'entoure" (1:65) [a stranger
{foreigner} to all these interests, indifferent to all that surrounds
me], and proclaims her neutral approach to this new country: "Il

faut voir cette nation pour se faire une idée de ses mœurs" (1:118) [one must see this nation to form an idea of its mores]. Thus, her descriptions of North American cities abound in newly acquired, firsthand information, without any reference to her own personal past.

But in these initial chapters, even as Merlin stresses her role as an aristocratic traveler from Europe, a change begins to take place that brings out the author's hybrid filiation. Objects from Cuba start to appear in these northern spaces, and they are accompanied by an unexpected textual lyricism: "Tout en écrivant ces lignes, je m'abreuve d'eau de coco à la glace et d'ananas arrivés hier soir de la Havane;—ce qui ne manque pas de faire battre mon cœur, comme l'étreinte d'un ami après une absence de longues années" (1:184) [As I write these lines, I am drinking coconut milk with ice and pineapple, which came from Havana last night; this makes my heart beat fast, as a friend's embrace after many years of absence]. The metaphor is an early signal that Merlin's spatial progression is also a journey back in time. Earlier in the text, passion had intensified upon her receiving some Cuban flowers, "une corbeille des plus belles fleurs: tout au milieu se trouve une plante de la Havane, une fleur de mon pays!—En aspirant son parfum, mes sens ont été bouleversés, et j'ai senti une grosse larme qui roulait dans son calice" (1:68) [a basket of the most beautiful flowers, in the center of which was a plant from Havana, a flower from my country! As I inhaled its perfume, I was overwhelmed by emotion, and I felt a large tear rolling down to its calyx].

As the curtain falls on this episode, placed dramatically at the end of Letter III, one is tempted to view the lachrymose self-portrayal on glancing at objects from Cuba simply as the predictable reaction of someone imbued in the extravagant forms of much European Romantic art. But Merlin's operatic diction, even if it is French in language and form, signals here an incipient textual permutation whose ultimate result is the deep interliterary waverings of her writing. The first major change concerns the text's genre. As it approaches Havana, La Havane breaks with certain patterns of travel narratives and embraces another type of writing, one where exoticist visions are replaced with the intimacy of memoirs or autobiographies. A lofty page, Merlin's first vision of Havana after decades of absence, marks a shift in the authorial possession of Cuba. She writes to her daughter:

Mais, mon enfant, voici déjà la ville qui se mêle à ses faubourgs.—La
voilà, c'est bien elle, avec ses balcons, ses tentes, ses terrasses; puis
ses jolies maisons bourgeoises de plain-pied, aux grands portes-cochè-
res, aux immenses fenêtres grillées. Portes et fenêtres sont ouvertes;
tout est à jour, l'œil pénètre jusqu'aux intimités de la vie domestique,
depuis la cour arrosée et couverte de fleurs jusqu'au lit de la *niña*, dont
les rideaux de linon sont garnis de nœuds roses. Ensuite viennent les
maisons aristocratiques à un étage, entourées de galeries que signalent
de loin de longues rangées de persiennes vertes.—J'aperçois déjà le
balcon de mon père qui s'allonge en face du château de la Punta; puis,
à côté, un balcon plus petit. (1:286; emphasis in original)

[But, my child, I can already see the city reaching to its suburbs. There
she is, it's really she, with her balconies, awnings, and terraces, then its
pretty, one-story townhouses, with their large porte-cocheres and huge
grilled windows. Doors and windows are open; everything is exposed,
and the eye reaches the intimacy of domestic life, from the courtyard,
watered and covered with flowers, to the *niña*'s bed, whose linen
drapes are decorated with pink flowers. Then come the aristocratic
houses, the second stories of which are surrounded by galleries recognized from a distance by their long rows of green shutters. I see already
my father's long balcony, facing La Punta castle; then, next door, a
smaller balcony.]

"L'œil pénètre jusqu'aux intimités de la vie domestique," she
admits, and this uncanny gaze encompasses spaces that for other
writers arriving from abroad should be invisible. As in her previous
descriptions of North American cities, Merlin's text dwells on landmarks and architecture, but there is one crucial difference in the
depiction of Havana; this city is still inhabited by figures from the
author's early years. This is not a traveler's fresh glance at a foreign
city, but a mnemonic retrieval of home: "C'est bien elle." She can
see the balconies of her father's house, including what turns out to
be her own bedroom's smaller balcony; these are spaces where she
has stood before. She can also view a young girl's bed, whose details are magically captured from the ship's deck. Indeed, doors
and windows are wide open, following the customs of tropical regions, but one feels this is not only a literal condition. Even if everything were boarded up, the distance separating the author from
these intimate spaces—balconies, courtyards, bedrooms—would
be of no consequence, for Merlin's telescopic eye, looking for a vision of her childhood in Havana, would invent them, as she perhaps does.

Indeed, Merlin's rapprochement to the island is also an invention of the authorial self, an autobiographical figure. This journey to Cuba, unlike those of Dana and other nineteenth-century travelers, is both spatial and temporal. Suddenly, by voyaging into the past, travel writing transforms itself into memoirs. As she looks into the rooms of her old home, Merlin sees, or imagines, her former self: a Cuban *niña*. The italicized Spanish word in this passage is one of the first instances of an interlingual transaction in the text. By switching, albeit momentarily, into Spanish, the author marks herself and her writing as having a Cuban wellspring, both existentially and aesthetically. In view of this domestic space from the past that is now once again part of the present, Merlin recounts the origins of her literary vocation. It is at this house, on her own "balcon plus petit," that she locates her earliest experience of Cuba's physical splendor: "C'était de là que tout enfant, je contemplais le ciel étoilé et resplendissant des tropiques, et que mon âme, au bruit sourd et régulier des lames qui se brisaient en écume sur la grève, exhalait ses premiers parfums, s'élançait vers de saintes révélations!" (1:286–87) [It was from there that, still a small child, I gazed at the splendid starry night of the tropics, and my soul, to the muffled and even sound of the waves breaking into foam on the beach, exhaled its first perfumes and soared toward holy revelations!]. Even as she regains her lost birthplace, the country remains the past: the flower's perfume that she inhaled in New York is corresponded here not by a present smell, but by the perfumes of her childhood in Havana: the source of her art.

One can trace the same relations in other works by Merlin. Also from this same balcony, in *Souvenirs et mémoires*, she sees the fleet on which she will sail to Europe for the first time. It, too, is an indelible image: "Souvent, je me plaisais à admirer, de mon balcon, cette armée navale qui se déployait devant moi, et qui, au premier signal, devait m'emmener si loin. Je la vois encore, occupant le centre de la rade, entourée d'une multitude de bâtiments de toutes les nations" (65) [From my balcony, I would often take pleasure in admiring that fleet deployed in front of me, which, at the first signal, would take me so far away. I can still see it, occupying the center of the harbor, surrounded by a vast number of ships of all nations]. That "holy revelations" should take place at the same spot from which she beholds the harbor and its foreign sails suggests an intimate bond between art and exile. If *Souvenirs et mémoires* openly states its generic filiation, *La Havane* proceeds obliquely; the items perceived on the journey trigger Merlin's memory and the book's undulations. Thus, as she beholds the belfry of Santa Clara, the convent where she had been a boarder as a child, Merlin thinks she sees the image of Sor Inés (1:287), the nun whose story she had told in *Histoire de la sœur Inès*. Self-reflectively, the text approaches Havana as a real place to which one can travel, but, moreover, as the vague space where memory and literary art are conjoined: "Et illusions et réalités se mêlent dans ma tête troublée et font battre mon cœur à le briser" (1:287–88) [Both illusions and realities are mixed in my troubled mind and cause my heart to beat to the breaking point]. Once again, in the tradition of much Cuban literature of exile, the island's spectral shadow is what matters most.

If *La Havane* never fully abandons the model of European travel writing, its adoption of other modes of representation implies a search for a literary form that can encompass Merlin's habitation of two worlds and languages. Besides delving into the autobiographical, the long travel narrative engages in a dialogue with two other kinds of writing: the *crónicas de Indias*, as exemplified, specifically, by Christopher Columbus's *Diario*;[25] and the sketches and fiction of *costumbrismo*. The incorporation of these models is doubly pivotal, for even as they allow *La Havane* to embrace the interlingual and the interliterary and thus enter the systems of Cuban literature, they facilitate the text's negative reception among Cuban readers. Two main issues arise as one reads these intermittent oscillations of genre. The first concerns Merlin's self-depiction as a new Columbus and the island's literary discoverer. The second is a question of possible plagiarism: her so-called translation of a *costumbrista* text into French with no credit given to its author. Ironically, this heterolingual text's rapprochement to practices that link it with Cuban and Spanish American literatures also places the author in an ambivalent position.[26]

Passionately, Merlin embraces Columbus's textual and historical legacy, portraying her own figure as the natural heir to his exploits and writings, thereby claiming as her own the literary discovery of Cuba. She emerges as a devoted reader of the *crónicas de Indias*, and these first writings of the Spanish explorers of the New World constitute her sources for Cuban history: "Aussi est-ce avec une joie d'enfant que j'ai consulté nos anciennes chroniques, leur demandant tous les détails possibles sur les faits et les noms historiques qui touchent de près ou de loin à mon île maternelle"

(2:4) [Thus, with a child's joy, I consulted our ancient chronicles, demanding from them all possible details related to the events and historical names having anything to do with my maternal island]. In the twentienth century, Spanish American novelists have also inspired themselves in these texts, but such "rewritings" as Carlos Fuentes's *Terra nostra* (1975), Alejo Carpentier's *El arpa y la sombra* (1979), and Juan José Saer's *El entenado* (1983) question and modify the chronicles' European viewpoints. Merlin, however, closely mimics the gestures of these imperial writings without any sense of irony or detachment. As she approaches the coast of Cuba, on a vessel named *Christophe-Colomb*, she purports to discover a landscape that, in her musings, should still be inhabited by the long-extinct indigenous peoples of the island:

> À quelque distance, et plus prêt de la côte, je découvre le village de *Puerto Escondido*; à ces chaumières de forme conique, couvertes jusqu'à terre de branches de palmiers; aux buissons touffus de bananiers qui, de leurs larges feuilles, protégent les maisons contre les ardeurs du soleil; à ces pirogues amarrées sur le rivage, et à la quiétude silencieuse de l'heure de midi, vous diriez que ces plages sont encore habitées par des Indiens. (1:276; emphasis in original)

> [Farther away, and closer to the coast, I discover the village of Puerto Escondido. With these cone-shaped cottages, covered with palm branches down to the ground, and the thickly planted banana trees whose large leaves protect the houses from the blazing sun, and the canoes moored on the beach, and the silence of noon, you would say that these shores are still inhabited by Indians.]

Once on shore, her stay "renouvelle les charmes de l'age d'or" (1:310) [renews the charms of the golden age]; like a new conquistador, she receives fruits and gold, and remarks on the natives' meek generosity: "Les fruits, les fleurs pleuvent sur moi; car c'est une coutume créole de se faire présent en famille d'une once d'or comme d'un ananas ou d'un *mamey*; et celà avec une naïveté, une tendre bonhomie d'expression vraiment admirables" (1:311) [I'm showered with fruits and flowers, since in Creole families one is used to giving an ounce of gold as naturally as one would a pineapple or a *mamey*, and this is done with such naïveté and tenderly expressed good-naturedness that it is quite admirable].

Elsewhere, Merlin's familiarity with other colonial texts, such as the writings of Fray Bartolomé de las Casas and Bernal Díaz del

Castillo, becomes apparent, but the literary stance that she underscores and mimics is that of Columbus himself. The first intertextual claim on the *Diario* occurs in the very first pages of her
narrative, where, echoing her admired admiral, she describes Cuba
as "le plus beau pays du monde" (1:v) [the most beautiful country
in the world]. To some extent, Cuba emerges in *La Havane* as a
splendid physical space devoid of history, which is in essence how
Columbus describes it. If Columbus's vision foregrounds almost
exclusively the land's sheer beauty, many passages in Merlin also
focus on a nature that is "charmante et virginale" (1:268) [charm-
ing and virginal]. The tropics may be an inferior model for a cathedral's facade, but they are a fine setting for imagining the golden
age of humankind:

> Avec quel religieux recueillement je contemple cette végétation si
> jeune, dont la sève répand partout sa magnificence!... et les contours
> onduleux de ces côtes!... et ces mouvements de terrain dont les lignes
> arrondies semblent avoir servi de modèle aux plus beaux paysages
> rêvés par nos poëtes! Plus loin, sur des collines légèrement inclinées,
> d'immenses forêts vierges étalent sous le soleil leurs éternelles beautés,
> qui, toujours vertes, toujours fleuries, règnent sur la terre et domptent
> les ouragans. (1: 268–9).

> [I religiously gaze on this nature which is so young and whose sap
> spreads its magnificence everywhere!... and its winding coasts!...
> and these undulations of the land whose lines seem to have served as
> models for the most beautiful landscapes dreamed by our poets! Far-
> ther away, covering the hills, vast virgin forests display under the sun
> their eternal beauties, which, always green and in bloom, reign over the
> land and tame the hurricanes.]

Once again, the space of Cuba and the practice of writing are
bound together. But, in this context, it is not altogether clear whom
does Merlin mean by "nos poëtes" [our poets]. Is she alluding to
French or Cuban writers? The answer is not self-evident because,
in Merlin's text, the meaning of "nos" or "notre" [our] shifts con-
stantly to refer to one or the other country. Embracing duality, she
speaks about "nos plus riches hôtels de Paris" (1:174) [our richest
houses in Paris], "notre monde européen" (2:49) [our European
world] and "nos élégants de salon" (2:54) [the smart people at our
salons], but also about "nos *guajiros*" (2:51; emphasis in original)
[our peasants] and "notre colonie" (2:241) [our colony].

Palm trees, a recurrent motif in Cuban literature, but also in foreign writing about the island, may hold a key to Merlin's meanings. Uncanny forms of vegetation for some northerners, palm trees strike Richard Henry Dana as emblems of the island's exoticism and his own unhousedness there: "These strange palm trees everywhere! I cannot yet feel at home among them" (103). Cubans abroad, however, inscribe the palm tree as a symbol of nation and home. Cintio Vitier, one of Cuba's foremost poets and critics, identifies in Heredia's allusion to palm trees in "Niágara" "la imagen paradisíaca de la isla lejana, inocente y desdichada" [the paradisal image of the distant, innocent, and hapless island].[27] Vitier's observation, taken from his influential study, *Lo cubano en la poesía* (1958), officializes the link between nature and nation in writing by Cubans; in Vitier's ontological search for "lo cubano" [Cubanness], as his title would have it, Heredia can be easily proclaimed "nuestro primer poeta cabal" (73) [our first complete poet]. And in a classical poem by Martí (the first text in *Versos sencillos* [1891]), famously set to music in the song "Guantanamera," the speaker defines himself as "un hombre sincero / De donde crece la palma" [a sincere man / From where the palm tree grows],[28] further grounding Cuba's identity in this particular tree. (In an even more official context, the royal palm, though an import originally from India, appears on the coat of arms of the Republic of Cuba.)

In *La Havane*, however, the depiction of nature exemplifies Merlin's ambiguous stance vis-à-vis these official images of the island. If nature is the predictable site of nostalgia, it is also linked to the dubious glories of imperial conquest. The palm tree, specifically, triggers recollections of a foreign epic that contradicts the nationalist sentiments of much Cuban literature as well as literary history and criticism:

Lorsque j'aperçois ces palmiers séculaires, qui courbent leur orgueilleux feuillage jusqu'au bord de la mer, je crois voir les ombres de ces grands guerriers, de ces hommes de résolution et de volonté, compagnons de Colomb et de Vélasquez; je les vois, fiers de leurs plus belles découvertes, s'incliner dans leur reconaissance devant l'Océan, pour le remercier d'un si magnifique présent. (1:269)

[When I see the age-old palm trees with their proud leaves bending to the water's edge, I seem to perceive the shadows of those great warriors, determined and willful men, companions of Columbus and Velázquez; I see them, proud of their most beautiful discoveries, bowing before the Ocean to thank it for such a magnificent present.]

Like the Spanish conquistadors, Merlin regards Cuba's beauty and bounty as nature's gift to the newly arrived Europeans. The nature she beholds is the same Columbus and Velázquez knew in the fifteenth and sixteenth centuries; these palms, after all, are "séculaires" [age-old]. If at times her depiction of Cuba coincides with Heredia's patriotic constructs, a certain reconfiguration may be discerned in which the native soil seems to serve other interests. Palm trees are not strange for Merlin, as they are for Dana, but their associations nevertheless point to a European angle of vision that much nationalist criticism seeks to eradicate from the official corpus of Cuban literature.

In other sections of *La Havane*, Merlin further obscures the established connections between nature and nation. For instance, in Letter XXI, addressed to the Marquis de Custine, she deprives Cuba and its residents of any links with history or civilization, transforming Havana into a world where nature alone, virtually devoid of cultural imprints, prevails:

> Nos édifices n'ont pas d'histoire ni de tradition: le Havanais est tout au présent et à l'avenir. Son imagination n'est frappée, son âme n'est émue, que par la vue de la nature qui l'environne; ses châteaux sont les nuages gigantesques traversés par le soleil couchant; ses arcs de triomphe, la voûte du ciel; au lieu d'obélisques, il a ses palmiers; pour girouettes seigneuriales, le plumage éclatant du *guacamayo*; et en place d'un tableau de Murillo ou de Raphaël, il a les yeux noirs d'une jeune fille, éclairés par un rayon de la lune à travers la grille de sa fenêtre. (2:210–12; emphasis in original).

> [Our buildings lack history and tradition: the man of Havana is all in the present or the future. Only the sight of nature that surrounds him can strike his imagination or move his soul; his castles are the giant clouds pierced by the setting sun; his arches of triumph, the vault of heaven; instead of obelisks, he has his palm trees; for lordly weather vanes, the bright plumage of the *guacamayo*; and instead of a painting by Murillo or Raphael, he has a young girl's dark eyes, which the moon illuminates through her window grille.]

If in other letters, as Méndez Rodenas demonstrates, Merlin is able to offer a preview of Cuban nationalism, there are numerous instances where the historiographical stance recognizable within the established discussion is overtaken by poetical detachment of an exoticist kind. The change in the possessive adjectives in this passage is revealing. The opening "nos" [our] quickly transforms itself into "son" [his], as if Merlin's writing were less an act of self-discovery than a struggle for representing outlying entities, a remote outpost of civilization in which those elements that one can find along the Champs-Elysées—the Arc de Triomphe, the Egyptian obelisk at place de la Concorde, the Old Masters at the palatial Musée du Louvre—are translated into emblems of an untamed nature.

In *La Conquête de l'Amérique*, Tzvetan Todorov remarks on Columbus's practice of writing about humans as part of the landscape; people are routinely mentioned "quelque part entre les oiseaux et les arbres" [somewhere between birds and trees].[29] Merlin, too, associates her fellow Cubans with nature, resorting frequently to animal and botanical images to describe them. White children are "comme des cygnes" (1:290) [like swans] and a black man swimming in a river is said to surface "soufflant comme une baleine" (2:84) ["blowing like a whale"], while the people of Havana "mangent peu à la fois, comme les oiseaux" (1:304–5) ["eat a little at a time, like birds"]. Even her own cousins, seen for the first time as they row to the *Christophe-Colomb* to greet her, are metamorphosed into exotic birds: "quelque chose de souple et de délicat dans toute leur personne leur donne une grâce parfaite, et comme ils s'avancent à la fois hors de la chaloupe, folâtres, joyeux et empressés, on les prendrait pour une nichée de nos plus beaux oiseaux" (1:294) [something lithe and delicate about their persons endows them with a perfect grace, and as they move forward all at once from the boat, playful, merry, and attentive, one would take them for a brood of our most beautiful birds]. The city itself, with its colorful houses and gardens, is described as a "bouquet de fleurs sauvages au milieu d'un parterre" (1:284) [bunch of wild flowers in the middle of a flower bed]; in this context, it is logical that the Baroque cathedral would rise almost as a jungle-like excrescence. By transforming humans and cultural artifacts into mere projections of the island's flora and fauna, Merlin estranges herself from her native context and sounds less like a Cuban writer than a traveler from abroad; it is no surprise, then, that Cuban readers and critics have often regarded her as the rara avis.

Significantly, the central episode of *La Havane*, literally as well as metaphorically, is Merlin's pilgrimage to Columbus's alleged tomb at the cathedral in Havana. Repelled by its architecture but moved after seeing the tombs of her own ancestors, she stops at the stone covering the admiral's remains, calling him "un illustre héros" (2:206) [an illustrious hero] and "une belle création de Dieu" (2:207) [a beautiful creation of God], even equating him with a mythical creature, "car Hercule en fit moins et fut admis dans l'Olympe" (2:206) [for Hercules did less and was admitted to Olympus].[30] Yet, in her imagination, Columbus the explorer seems less impressive than Columbus the storyteller. She invokes him at the court of Ferdinand and Isabella, to whom "il raconte avec une modeste simplicité ce qu'il a vu, sans s'arrêter à ce qu'il a fait" (2:207) [with modest simplicity, he recounts what he has seen, not what he has done]. The oral storyteller is then replaced by the writer, and she is seduced by the image of a man dutifully writing in his logbook even as his ship traverses a dangerous storm: "Que faisait Colomb pendant que la mort se présentait à lui sous une forme si effrayante? Il écrivait le récit circonstancié de son voyage" (2:208) [What was Columbus doing as death appeared to him in such frightening form? He was writing a detailed account of his journey].

Indeed, what Merlin composes also with a sense of duty is the *récit circonstancié* of her own journey to Cuba, with Columbus's text often acting as a clear model. For her, writing about her native land is a mission, and its goal, as defined in the prologue of *La Havane,* is none other than to reveal Cuba to Cubans and Europeans alike:

> C'est un devoir aussi de rendre justice à mille de talents que l'Europe ne soupçonne pas, de révéler de charmantes vertus qui s'ignorent elles-mêmes, et un devoir sacré encore d'indiquer à mon pays les améliorations qui l'élèveront parmi les peuples civilisés au même rang que Dieu lui avait assigné par les merveilles du sol et l'ineffable beauté de son climat. (1:3)

> [It is also a duty to render justice to a thousand talents whose existence Europe does not suspect, to reveal some charming virtues that are ignored even by those who possess them, and it is a sacred duty as well to show my country the way to improvements that will make it rise among the civilized nations to that position which God assigned to it for the marvels of its soil and the ineffable beauty of its climate.]

Merlin's self-imposed mission is, then, twofold. On the one hand, she defines herself as a bridge between Europe and Cuba, because her book will uncover the natural wealth of her native land to the Old World. On the other hand, by showing the island's potential

prosperity, she also defines herself as a bridge between its unfortunate present and its expectations of future glory. I use "bridge"
twice because the horizontal figure for which it stands recalls the
horizontal lines of hyphens and seesaws, but also because those
structures, as they traverse the distance from one point to another,
are for much of their length situated nowhere. What place claims
Merlin as its own? She herself uses two verbs, "dévoiler" [unveil]
and "révéler," [reveal], repeatedly, and, in most cases, she is the
subject performing these actions, as if she alone could be the
source of knowledge about Cuba. But as she discovers the island
for Cubans and Europeans, she also reveals herself in the process,
and some of what becomes visible is problematic for both Merlin's
authorship and the nation's slowly forming vision of itself.

Clearly, Merlin's stated beliefs often violate the notions of social
and political progress that underlie much of Cuban literary history
and criticism. If her depiction of nature already contains what may
be interpreted as foreign signs, in other instances orthodox views
are expressed in no uncertain terms. On several major issues that
concern Cuba, she rejects the nationalist roads taken by such canonical authors as Heredia and Cirilo Villaverde. On the subject of
political independence, for example, her loyalty to Spain is clearly
stated, seemingly contradicting her self-portrait as a Cuban:
"Quant à nous, je le repète, nous sommes profondément, exclu-
sivement Espagnols. . . . L'intérêt de l'Espagne est le nôtre; notre
prosperité servirait la prosperité espagnole" (2:285) [As for us, I repeat, we are profoundly and exclusively Spanish. . . . Spain's interests are our interests; our prosperity would contribute to the
prosperity of Spain]. On slavery, she opposes abolition and, non-
chalantly, paints the origins of the slave trade in a positive light:
"Lorsqu'une tribu faisait des prisonniers sur une tribu ennemie, si
elle était anthropophage, elle mangeait ses captifs; si elle ne l'était
pas, elle les immolait à ses dieux. La naissance de la traite déter-
mina un changement dans cette horrible coutume : les captifs fur-
ent vendus" (2:89–90) [When a tribe took prisoners from an enemy
tribe, they, if they were anthropophagous, would eat the captives;
if they were not, they would immolate them to their gods. The inception of the slave trade caused a change in this terrible custom:
the captives were sold]. [31]There is a certain measure of tenderness
in her portrayal of some slaves, specifically her wet nurse, whose
poignant definition of liberty, apparently based on observation,
Merlin cites in Spanish: "eso quiere decir: no trabajar y pasearse"

(1:161) [that means: not to work, but to promenade]. But she normally associates nonwhites with ugliness and evil: "un nègre grand, laid, affreux à voir" (1:43) [a tall, ugly black man, hideous to see]; "un mulâtre de figure sinistre" (1:66) [a sinister-looking mulatto]. Tanco, the early harsh critic of *La Havane,* had written a narrative piece condemning slavery, and Merlin's ideological faux pas could not have contributed to a kind evaluation of the literary merits of her work.[32] Modern views of the text often focus on it as a representative of European colonialism. An edition of *Viaje a la Habana* published in Cuba in 1974, for instance, condemns the writer with very faint praise by proclaiming on its back cover that "la obra constituye un documento interesante para el lector cubano, por los temas, los panoramas y la visión colonizante que encierran sus páginas" [the work constitutes an interesting document for Cuban readers, because of the themes, surveys, and colonizing viewpoint its pages contain].[33]

What the work presents is a fearful vision of the nation itself, one that the publishers of this edition of *Viaje a la Habana* seek to exile from the country's substance by labeling it as "colonizante": the discursive influence not of a Cuban author, but of a foreign agent. The institutions of Cuban literature often privilege authors and texts that seem to show a clear line of progress toward a more ethical nation; the tradition of antislavery narratives, for instance, is situated at the heart of the established discussion. Yet Merlin's reactionary views are also rooted in Cuban culture, and simply to brand them as foreign leads to a whitewashed construction of Cuban literature. Merlin is a ghostly figure not only because of her unhomely tongue, but because of the double fractures she reveals in the house's walls: a Cuban who writes may not resemble what Cuban writers are imagined to be linguistically and ideologically. Moreover, she also seems to be another country's writer as well: Merlin's literary-historical difficulties are, to an extent, grounded on her authorial self-fashioning.

It is an aesthetic merit, if not a nationalist virtue, that Merlin herself should do little to repress the specter of her own unhomeliness. Refusing to choose between the two places it communicates, the text of *La Havane* repeatedly takes two seemingly diverging roads in which Merlin shows herself as both French and Cuban: an apparent impasse for the self-proclaimed Cuban author, but a wonderful forest of forking paths for the reader willing to go along. Writing from tropical Havana to her French son-in-law, she mo-

mentarily forgets Cuba and recalls the soft autumnal landscape of
the Loire Valley as the true site of civilization:

> Vous souvenez-vous, mon cher Gentien, de ces belles soirées d'au-
> tomne passées si doucement au château de Dissay, lorsque le soleil,
> d'un rouge enflammé mais sans chaleur, projetait ses rayons sur la
> pointe de vos peupliers, et que, ses derniers lueurs pâlissant par degré,
> allaient s'égarer entre les découpures et les bas-reliefs de vos tourelles?
> . . . Mon souvenir me ramène aussi vers ces prairies artificielles que
> j'aimais tant à contempler . . . C'est, mon ami, que vous êtes dans un
> pays civilisé, plus façonné que vrai. (2:381–83)

> [Do you remember, my dear Gentien, those beautiful autumn evenings
> so sweetly spent at the chateau of Dissay, when the sun, burning red
> but not hot, shone on the top of your poplars, and when its last glim-
> mers, gradually vanishing, wandered along the indentations and bas-
> reliefs of your turrets . . . My memory also takes me back to those arti-
> ficial meadows that I so loved to behold . . . What happens, my friend,
> is that you live in a civilized country, more molded than real.]

Thematically, this passage matters because it is a fleeting glimpse
into Merlin's other life, the aristocratic spaces of Europe that in *La
Havane*, because of its focus on Cuba, remain mostly hidden. But
in an oblique fashion, the final two sentences also reveal the difficult task of writing about Cuba and becoming a Cuban author. If
readers of Spanish American literature may see in her praise of
French civilization a contact with Sarmiento's formula, the words
"artificielles" and "façonné" are more revealing. What France, unlike Cuba (or Argentina) seems to possess is not only order and
method, but a tradition of art and a semblance of craft: a general
sense of perfected cultural forms. By contrast, Cuba emerges as all
too real, not only because the island's physical space is wilder than
that of the Loire Valley, but because there are no literary models at
Merlin's disposal to encapsule the overwhelming actuality of Cuba
and the duality of her own condition. The protocols of travel writing are not enough: its formal aspects may serve their purpose
when writing about the United States, but in Cuba—in Merlin's
Cuba—they prove to be insufficient. Trying to locate a new form, it
is not surprising that she should resort to the figure of the reputed
discoverer, but that, in the event, is no lasting solution either. The
question, ultimately, is less how can one be Cuban and French at
the same time, but rather how can one be a Cuban author when

Cuban literature does not yet have a form of its own, let alone one available to an author in French. The issue of her hyphenated personal identity is one that Merlin, after all, resolves to an extent, as the naturally shifting pronouns seem to reveal; metaphorically, she clarifies her liaisons by naming Cuba "mon île maternelle" (2:4) [my maternal island] and France "ma mère adoptive" (1:2) [my adoptive mother]. But to be a Cuban author, and not just a Cuban who writes, is a different matter. Beyond proclaiming herself a discoverer, Merlin's most important revelation will be in the various trails of the text itself.

Searching paradoxically for a Cuban form in French, *La Havane* experiments with various genres, especially those that are perceived to be intrinsically linked with the incipient national literature. A model is found in the popular school of *costumbrismo*, which aims at the detailed representation of local cultural patterns and forms of speech. The origins of this modality are European, but in Spanish America the *cuadros de costumbres* acquire a different function as vehicles in the creation of national literatures. In an age characterized by what José Antonio Portuondo calls "afán de criolledad" [zeal for creoleness] and "empeño diferenciador" [determination to be different], *costumbrismo* emerges as a perfect medium to underscore those elements that are perceived as distinctively national.[34] As Salvador Bueno indicates, its peak in Cuba occurred between 1830 and 1840, coinciding with Merlin's arrival in Havana; in fact, his description of the school's thematics might be adapted into a blurb for the back cover of *La Havane*:

> Percibimos entre líneas la existencia de aquellos criollos acomodados en las amplias casonas de antaño, sus paseos en quitrines y volantas por las calzadas y alamedas, asistimos a sus festejos, sus ingenuas reuniones de familia, recorremos las calles soleadas de las viejas ciudades, los campos donde los guajiros laboran en vegas y caseríos. Y chocamos con el espectáculo indignante de una sociedad apoyada en el trabajo esclavo, en los sufrimientos y humillaciones de miles de hombres.

> [We perceive between the lines the existence of those affluent Creoles in their rambling houses of yesteryear, their promenades on *quitrines* and *volantas* along roads and boulevards; we attend their celebrations, their naïve family reunions; we travel along the sunny streets of old cities and in the countryside where the peasants toil in *vegas* and *caseríos*. And we run into the shocking spectacle of a society resting on slave labor and the sufferings and humiliation of thousands of men.][35]

All of these subjects appear in *La Havane,* but one writer's *cuadro de costumbres* in Spanish may easily become someone else's exoticist travel narrative in French. Can Merlin write about this society with a native's eye and tongue? The authors whose works Bueno gathers in *Costumbristas cubanos del siglo XIX* write from a position in which Cuba is never a foreign land, never a space regarded from afar, but a place they claim to know intimately. They also write in the country's official language, and, indeed, one of their objectives is the representation of popular speech, as in Francisco de Paula Gelabert's "El puesto de frutas," collected in his *Cuadros de costumbres cubanas* (1875): "—*¿Tú lo ve,* muchacha, *tú lo ve...? Anda, jarrea pa* tu casa, que luego te van *a meté guano* si te tardas *en la pueto de fruta*" (455; emphasis in original) [You see him, girl, you see him...? Go, get going to your house, because they're going to hit you good if you're late from the fruit stand]. In *costumbrismo,* as in other Spanish American forms, the narrator's "correct" literary diction contrasts with the nonstandard Spanish of many of his characters, but everyone—authors, characters, and readers—are ultimately at home in one and the same tongue.

Nevertheless, it is the characters who make "mistakes," and these, on occasion, are due to the interference of other tongues. The interlingual is generally seen in a comic vein by narrators whose language is a "pure" form of Spanish. Gelabert's text, for instance, parodies what seems to be an African-influenced dialect, as the lack of gender agreement in "la pueto de fruta" indicates. Beyond class considerations, a favorite target of other *cuadros* is the affected Spanish spoken by those in contact with other European languages, specifically English and French. In José María de Cárdenas y Rodríguez's "¡Educado afuera!" (1845), for instance, the protagonist's speech is ridiculed for its abundance of Anglicisms and Gallicisms:

—Son *falsas bellezas*—dijo—, aquí no hay gusto, en Europa, ésas son bellezas *campañardes,* campesinas, como dicen ustedes. Aquí no hay un tipo delicado . . . ¡Facciones toscas *que todo* eso! Una *complexión* morena... ¡oh, *que esto es* terrible! Lo mismo que las frutas... En este país no se dan buenas frutas... oh, en Europa... Las *blackberries,* que llaman los ingleses... moras en español... Aquí no hay *nada comparable.* (emphasis in original)

["They are false beauties," he said, "people here have no taste; in Europe, they're country beauties, peasants, as you say. There are no delicate types here... Rough features as all that! A dark complexion... oh, that this is terrible! Same as the fruits... No good fruits can be grown in this country... oh, in Europe... The blackberries, as the English call them... 'moras' in Spanish... There is nothing comparable here."][36]

Since she writes in French, one could more easily imagine Merlin as the object depicted by the *costumbristas* than as the author of her own sketches of manners. But, quite unexpectedly within the fabric of her French text, Merlin introduces an approximation of the type of writing that those Cuban authors were practicing, in Spanish, at the time. In fact, the imitation in *La Havane* of that trend is arguably the main reason for the work's fame, or infamy, among literary critics and historians. Letter XXIX, addressed to a mysterious Madame ***, is a lively piece of narrative *costumbrismo*, which also happens to be a close translation of "Una pascua en San Marcos" (1838), a novella by Ramón de Palma. Despite Merlin's best intentions (as a letter to her collaborator, Philarète Chasles, seems to suggest), Palma is not given any credit in the text, and the literary circles of Havana condemned what they perceived as the French noblewoman's craftiness.

Most histories of Cuban literature, if they mention Merlin's name at all, underscore the issue of plagiarism.[37] Méndez Rodenas proposes a reevaluation of Merlin's act in which the use of texts by Palma and other Cuban writers might be akin to "Carpentier's self-conscious use of the chronicles of European voyagers to America and of the Spanish American *novela de la tierra* . . . in *Los pasos perdidos*."[38] Yet, Carpentier's adoption of those texts is never a mirror-like repetition; letter XXIX, on the other hand, would fall within what Gérard Genette categorizes as plagiarism in *Palimpsestes*. But if one examines Merlin's European context, the issue turns out to be more complex than a simple act of dishonesty. As Christopher L. Miller points out, plagiarism was a widespread practice among French Romantic travel writers; in fact, even Gérard de Nerval, in his *Voyage en Orient* (1850), "copied passages" from Silvestre de Sacy's *Chrestomathie arabe* (1826) and from texts by Edward William Lane.[39] What is different, and most significant, in *La Havane* is that Merlin's appropriation comes not from other foreign travel narratives, but from the most nativist examples of Cuban writing. Méndez Rodenas rightly postulates that reworking Palma's novella would seem to be Merlin's only chance to execute what Cuban writers at the time were doing. But by engaging the practices of *cos-*

tumbrismo in Letter XXIX (and elsewhere), Merlin is also allowing to diffuse—if only in a few places in the text and often clumsily—her own heterolingualism: following the example of Cuban writers, she attempts to represent the quirks of local Spanish with utmost precision.

That Merlin in Letter XXIX does not translate into French the dialogues of slaves, but leaves them in the original dialect of Spanish, is for Max Henríquez Ureña a "detalle curioso" [curious detail].[40] Merlin herself explains her reasons: "Ce dialogue m'a paru si naïf et plein de charmes dans le langage créole, que je n'ai pas voulu en priver ceux de mes lecteurs qui connaissent la langue espagnole" (3:46) [I found this dialogue so naïve and full of charm in the creole language that I did not want to deprive my Spanish-speaking readers of it]. Here and elsewhere, the presence of not very brief passages in regional forms of Spanish may be described, indeed, as both curious and charming. But there is also a farther-reaching critical and literary-historical significance. By welcoming the interlingual and the interliterary into its fabric, *La Havane* arguably becomes an element in the systems of Cuban literature, for many of its meanings would be unintelligible if read outside of them—just as some elements in Cabrera Infante's *Holy Smoke*, which I discuss in chapter 5, will depend on Merlin's exiled figure for a fuller understanding. Besides trying to do what other Cuban authors do, Merlin, the intermittent revenant, also summons a reader who can regard without nationalistic trepidations these odd literary and linguistic detours.

The strangeness of a French text that quotes phrases in a dialect of Spanish influenced by African substrata cannot be overestimated. In one short passage, Merlin encapsules the history of transatlantic crossings of various peoples and cultures. On a visit to the Vuelta Abajo region, Merlin and her friends run into a black man whose speech obviously strikes her as different, and she tries faithfully to reproduce, within the French text, the man's peculiar phonetics and syntax. In *Souvenirs et mémoires,* she had rendered the speech of slaves in nonstandard French: "Moi ne vouloir plus rien; moi être trop heureuse pour rester seule!" (69) ["Me not want nothing more; me be happy enough to remain alone"]. In Letter III of *La Havane,* while she is in New York, a French-speaking man of mixed race frightens her; she can describe his diction—"sa parole brève et rare" (1:66) ["his curt, strange speech"]—but does not quote him. But when *La Havane* is finally at home, Merlin mimics the original Spanish:

> —A qui appartiens-tu, *muchacho?* lui demanda Pepe.
> —Moi? à *don Rafé Braboso..., si, sino.*
> —Et où vas-tu?
> —*Yo? yo va a un San-Savao, à compra uno poco tasao... uno poco arao... uno poco sa... uno poco... poco... no me acuero. Aqui ta paperito que habla lingua.* (3:340; emphasis in original)

["Who do you belong to, *muchacho?*" Pepe asked him.
"Me? To *Mr. Rafael Barboso..., yes, sir.*"
"And where are you headed?
"Me? I'm going to San Salvador, to buy a little tasajo... a little rice... a little salt... a little... little... I can't remember. Here's little paper that speaks tongue.]

One may argue that the incorporation of this local dialect into *La Havane* is one more instance of unabashed exoticism on the author's part, akin to the use of foreign tongues in much travel literature. Indeed, works that deal with other cultures are often marked by the imprint of other languages, and foreign words sometimes appear almost as fetishized possessions. In Merlin's case, however, the foreign language is not merely a token of someone else's alterity, but a pretext for not concealing her own linguistic duality. Although she translates this dialogue into French for the sake of her European audience, it is, as she admits, the Spanish-speaking reader who truly finds any significance in the approximative transcription of local speech. The dialogues in regional forms of Spanish imply both a detachment from French literature, whose readers will in all probability find Merlin's skilled ears meaningless, and a rapprochement to the practices of writing of the incipient Cuban literary tradition. Ultimately, however, interlingual passages such as these are tokens of a more profound condition in the author's literary makeup. Merlin, who at the end of Letter I, as she sails to the New World, overhears and records two men speaking accented French, now in Letter XXXV, as *La Havane* comes to an end, documents yet another tongue spoken with weird inflections. Linguistically unhoused, the text seems always to detect those speakers who, like Merlin herself, are not easily sheltered within any one language.

In Letter XXII—which Cabrera Infante later adapts—Merlin records a dialogue between two young women from Havana's upper class, her own original social milieu. One can surmise her intimate knowledge of the language in the careful notation of this sociolect, one that she would probably find unremarkable, had she not been taken to Spain and France at an early age and exposed to other dialects and languages, because this is how she herself would speak. The dialogue appears in a bilingual transcription, the author's French version followed by the Spanish original. Merlin's act of translation is not altogether exact, but what matters is the virtual repetition, the doubling and almost mutual mirroring of languages: if one is a monolingual reader of French, the familiar gives way to what is a strange language; or if one's language is Spanish, the foreign tongue freely admits a domestic form:

—As-tu vu, Pepilla, comme elle l'a regardé? Avec quelle fureur elle a brisé son éventail lorsqu'on le condamna à m'embrasser? disait une jeune fille à son amie en s'appuyant sur son épaule.
—Lo viste, Pepyia, como lo miró? —Ya, lo vi, ya. —Y con que furia rompió el abanico, cuando le condenaron á darme un beso?... —Y el! que colorado se pusò! (2:223, emphasis in original)

["Did you see, Pepilla, how she looked at him? With what fury she broke her fan when they sentenced him to kiss me?" a girl said to her friend as she leaned on her shoulder.
"Did you see, Pepiya, how she looked at him?" "Yes, I saw him." "And with what fury he broke the fan when they sentenced him to kiss me?..." "And him! How he did blush!"]

The subtle transformations of La Havane are most meaningful to readers who, like Merlin, are bilingual and can understand the text's two versions, both of which, arguably, are the original: the French was written first, but the Spanish was heard first. These interlingual passages, when translated into Spanish, lose perforce the interplay between the familiar and the strange through which the text's unhomeliness becomes visible.[41] In the original, Merlin resorts to italics not unlike those employed by costumbrista authors to mark their characters' peculiar speech. But, here, the italics that surface as she inscribes her own native tongue seem especially poignant, for they, along with the awkward spelling and the French accents graves, so odd on Spanish words, constitute a sign of the author's own extraterritorial predicament. As a narrator, she lacks one language that she can truly call her own, for the French, a foreign tongue, is often just a cover for some submerged Spanish, which, in turn, reveals itself marked as foreign and framed by another language. Merlin's literary craft, then, like the first interlingual dialogue in Letter I, is strange: a mélange of languages whose unhousedness is exposed even as it is sheltered by Merlin's original form of authorship. The focus of *La Havane* on the interlingual is ultimately an oblique form of authorial and textual self-reflection: Merlin's stance vis-à-vis two tongues and the spaces between them becomes an acknowledgement of her own linguistic and literary strangeness.

Although it is concealed in most formulas of nationhood, strangeness may well have its adepts, readers who can understand, or might even see themselves mirrored, in Merlin's uncanny displacements and unhomely revelations. If her writing is often rejected by the institutions of Cuban literature, there are readers—then and now, now and then—who resemble her. A copy of the first volume of *La Havane* housed at Widener Library bears the following words, carefully inscribed by a nineteenth-century hand:

> Mademoiselle Amérique Urbano
> Souvenir de mon bien-aimé papa

I do not know anything about this reader from far away and long ago, but one can easily imagine her and her cherished father as members of a Spanish American household in France, "una familia lejana," as Carlos Fuentes would have it. The reader's name is significant, for "Amérique," a French term, implies a nostalgia for the New World—now conceivably the old continent, in Urbano's eyes—and a linguistic transformation emblematic of exile. Indeed, in the second volume, after a few lines of verse, one can read the same inscription followed by a phrase in a different hand: "Que Dieu guide [ce?] pauvre exilé" [May God guide {this?} poor exile]. These readers, whoever or wherever they were, seem to have found in this book an author who spoke to them. It is perhaps no coincidence that the first complete translation of *La Havane* appeared outside of Cuba, seemingly for readers who do not live in the country where they were born. This translation's title is *La Habana* (1984), plain and simple, instead of the other version's title, *Viaje a la Habana*, which brands Merlin as a traveler from abroad and not as a Cuban author.

Still, the issue of heterolingualism raises other questions. One may wonder what languages the Urbanos spoke and read. Could they understand the interlingual and interliterary oscillations of *La Havane,* or was their reading impeded by Merlin's incursions into Spanish and Cuban literary forms? What about the average Cuban reader who does not know French? Will a translation do? Can one render Merlin's interlingual figurations in conventional Spanish? How readers perform an author's heterolingual text remains an unresolved issue, one that may also find an answer in Freud's discussion of the unhomely.

4

Hudson's and Bombal's Lost Horizon: Expectations of the Unhomely Reader

TOWARD THE END OF W. H. HUDSON'S *THE PURPLE LAND* (1885), Richard Lamb, the novel's English-born protagonist and narrator, reveals to a native of the Banda Oriental,[1] or Uruguay, the fair if violent South American republic where the author lays the scene, that he has a literary project he must fulfill:

> "Do you know, Demetria," I said, "when the long winter evenings come, and I have plenty of leisure, I intend writing a story of my wanderings in the Banda Oriental, and I will call my book *The Purple Land*; for what more suitable name can one find for a country so stained with the blood of her children? You will never read it, of course, for I shall write it in English and only for the pleasure it will give to my own children—if I ever have any—at some distant date, when their little moral and intellectual stomachs are prepared for other food than milk."[2]

That this instance of self-reflection in Hudson's first novel should concern the intertwined issues of language and reading signals explicitly what is perhaps the most intricate quandary faced by Spanish American heterolingual authors: the unavoidable fact that the foreign tongue seems to exclude those who might be among an author's most receptive readers. The passage dramatizes Hudson's linguistic and literary conflict in several ways. Lamb's words make it clear that those whom this story is about will not be able to become its readers, so Demetria and the other South Americans will have to remain as passive subjects in Lamb's storytelling. If they cannot read the text, one also wonders about real-world readers from Uruguay, or those of Argentina, the place where Hudson was born and to which he never returned after emigrating to England in his thirties. At this point in the story, Lamb is still married to Paquíta, an Argentine woman, and one can well imagine that their

124

Anglo-Argentine children—if they ever have any children—could become one day the book's ideal readers: interstitial figures with a plausible knowledge of Hudson's English language and the South American scene. But the story is told as a flashback, so we already know Paquíta will die; by the end of the novel, Lamb remains a childless man. Who, then, in the text, will read Lamb's winter's tale? Is there only one implied reader? If the novel seems addressed to an English and English-speaking figure, one still perceives certain shadows that invoke another kind of reader.

It is not an uncommon practice in Spanish American fiction for narrators to tell stories of characters who will not be able to read what is written about them. In those works, however, a character's inability to read does not usually stand as a metaphor, as it does in Hudson's text, for a broken link in the chain of author and national readership. If for reasons of language Hudson cannot look to the traditional Spanish American reader of the continent's fiction, the implied English reader of his text is not an ideal recipient either. From the viewpoint of English literature—which is, after all, the cultural context within which Hudson wrote and published—*The Purple Land* may simply be viewed as the story of an Englishman's adventures among foreign people, a notion supported by the imperial resonances of the first edition's title: *The Purple Land That England Lost*.[3] But, on closer examination, other signs emerge that the average English reader will likely not be able to interpret. The text, as I will show in this chapter, calls for a third figure, one whose horizon can perform the full range of Hudson's interstitial authorship. Hudson is not the Spanish American *hombre de letras* who discusses the nation's problems for his literate fellow countrymen in the language they all share, nor is he the metropolitan author discoursing about exotic beings from whom they, author and readers, stand at a safe emotional distance.[4] A writer with a singular cultural identity, Hudson invokes a reader who resembles him. This figure one might playfully term the River Plate Reader: a hybrid whose bicultural condition—linguistic, literary—is especially in tune with the virtually invisible nuances of Hudson's practice of writing. I choose the toponymic "River Plate" advisedly: strangely, the Spanish "Río de la Plata" does not become "Silver River" or "River of Silver" in English, as one might expect, but an uncanny "River Plate," an eccentric coupling of English and Spanish in which the vestiges of the latter are not concealed. Ideally, the River Plate reader—who, of course, does not need to be an Anglo-Argentine in real life—will be quite at home in Hudson's unhomely textuality: an outpost halfway between, yet also within, two continents, two languages, and two literary traditions.

More generally, outside of Hudson's context, I will refer to this secretly implied figure of many heterolingual texts as the unhomely reader. It knows the language of the work that it reads, but it suspects and eventually confirms the subtle sway of another tongue and other literary systems beneath the surface: elements that ought to be interpreted for the best performance of the text. The unhomely reader, like the signs it reads, may be textually invoked in a vague fashion, as in the case of Lamb's unborn children, or it may be briefly suggested, as in *La Havane*. If Merlin's various narratees—Chateaubriand, George Sand, even her daughter—do not really share the author's extraterritorial condition, there are instances where Merlin records a dialogue in Spanish, as in the texts of *costumbrismo*, for the benefit of those who do know that tongue. There is ample evidence that many of Merlin's real-world readers did notice the imprint of Cuban literature in her work, especially, of course, the passages interpreted as plagiarism. But the unhomely reader notices, or feels, other things: the strong foreign accents of the Englishman and the Spaniard who speak French on the voyage out; the strange transcriptions of Spanish dialogues using French diacritics; the uncanny transformation of the travel narrative into a literary journey back in time. If one is in tune with Merlin's essential unhomeliness, even the plagiarism acquires a different signification: it is not an act of piracy, but an opening through which another literary world filters into the text. The unhomely reader, then, does not care only for the plainly visible surfaces of the text; it probes dormant elements in its nooks and crannies, sitting down cozily with the book in a strange room of its own.

Sometimes a heterolingual text will not give obvious signs of the unhomely reader. But silence and invisibility cannot fully hide this reader's latent status and eventual *aparición*, or appearance. This kind of apparition occurs in María Luisa Bombal's *House of Mist* (1947), the author's own English "version" of *La última niebla* (1935), an innovative text in the Chilean and Spanish American narrative avant-garde. Composed in the United States, *House of Mist* is normally read as a translation of the Spanish-language "original," but I would argue that it is, in effect, a new work: one that tells more or less the same story, but abandons, because of its implied and real-world readership, the daring thematics and structure of *La última niebla*. But if Bombal is textually aware of the text's U.S. American reader, one may also detect in *House of Mist* a long series of elements that become significant only in the context of the Spanish American literary tradition that Bombal seems to have put aside, even concealed. English, the other tongue, emerges then not only as the tool in which the story of Helga, the main character and narrator, is told, but as the strange space in which Bombal's own history of exile and self-translation is apparently hidden but ultimately revealed. The homely appearance of *House of Mist* seeks, at a first glance, to cover up the kind of literary and linguistic quandary that Lamb openly states at the end of his own text. But, if one excavates this placid surface, a measure of secrecy is soon revealed that opens tacitly into the realm of the unhomely.

The complete works of Hudson were published in London in the 1920s: twenty-four volumes bound in green, boasting the author's golden profile on each cover. On the back of each tome, among drawings of trees, birds, and deer, one can read this inscription:

W. H. Hudson
Born on the South American Pampas
Natus Circa 1846—Obiit London 1922

In these phrases, the erasure of Argentina's name is significant. Hudson's origin is set vaguely in time, and in a place that does not seem to have a specific identity: a country that somehow fails to exist in the annals of history. His ultimate destination, however, is precise: modern London, the cultural and political heart of the British Empire. Indeed, Hudson's story may be told to suggest a colonial's progress from an imperial periphery into the heart of civilization. That the Argentine Republic, the so-called Fifth Dominion, was never officially an English colony matters little in this paratextual context: the pampas are represented as mere space, and Hudson, who wrote both *British Birds* (1895) and *Birds of La Plata* (1920), loved the kingdom of nature more than he cared about the politics of men. Leaving his native land before the 1880s, the period when "structures imitative of French châteaux and English country mansions began to sprout upon the pampas,"[5] Hudson is now commemorated at Hyde Park: a green space where urban encroachment is kept at bay, but a metropolitan space nevertheless. "A very great writer; and—to my thinking—the most valuable our Age has possessed," claimed John Galsworthy.[6] With its insistence on "value" and "possesion" and its proud capitalization of "Age," Galsworthy's dictum turns Hudson into something of a commodity: a breath of country air in the metropolis's lungs. But this shady nook in the park may also be seen as an enclave of the foreign. In Hudson's archaic prose, comforting to some, there blow at times strange crosswinds that threaten to erase the well-surveyed limits between the bodies of Argentine and British literatures. The writings of Hudson are like a drafty house with signs for a reader who will not only like the gusts, but who will actually open windows and doors to welcome them in.

Despite his present critical marginality, Hudson's status as an English author has never been really doubted: although his parents were American, not British, Hudson's literary nationality is not a matter of dispute within the discussion of English literature.[7] If anything, it is only the Argentine connection that remains mostly concealed, as the inscription cited above reveals. In Argentina and the rest of Spanish America, however, two contradictory readings of Hudson coexist. Lamb's ominous foreshadowing aside, the reception of Hudson in the region has been relatively favorable—at least in comparison to Merlin's fate. For one, *The Purple Land* has been translated into Spanish several times and published by official agencies, such as Uruguay's Ministerio de Instrucción Pública y Previsión Social and Caracas's prestigious Biblioteca Ayacucho, whose editions are normally reserved for the classics of Spanish American literature. In Argentina, specifically, Hudson is for some a beloved author. Borges, whose partial English ancestry and early bilingualism make him something of an Anglo-Argentine, praises *The Purple Land* as "fundamentalmente criolla" [essentially Creole, native to South America][8] and, although he denies him a place in his *Historia de la literatura hispanoamericana,* as we saw in chapter 2, Anderson Imbert still perceives an Argentine quality in Hudson's English prose. Ezequiel Martínez Estrada, one of Spanish America's foremost essayists of the twentieth century, devotes an entire book to Hudson's biography and writings; that *El mundo maravilloso de Guillermo Enrique Hudson* (1951) should rechristen Hudson with a Spanish name that the author himself never used may be read as a benevolent act of naturalization: Hudson's Argentine origins are restored by means of translation.[9] In the larger discussion of Spanish American fiction, Luis Leal reads Hudson's

Green Mansions (1904) as the continent's first "novela de la selva" [jungle novel], thus situating the author as the first link in an illustrious narrative tradition that will eventually include such classic works as José Eustasio Rivera's *La vorágine* (1924) and Alejo Carpentier's *Los pasos perdidos* (1953).[10]

Yet, even those who have written admiringly about Hudson's links with Argentina frequently still label him as a foreigner. Alicia Jurado, the author's painstakingly detailed biographer, calls Hudson's birthplace his "patria física" [physical fatherland] and England his "patria cultural" [cultural fatherland], while Jean Franco, who writes the introductory essay to the Ayacucho edition, calls him in her *Spanish American Literature since Independence* "the English writer whose youth was spent in Argentina."[11] Even Borges, after underscoring the nativist elements of *The Purple Land*, concludes on an ambiguous note: "Percibir o no los matices criollos es quizá baladí, pero el hecho es que de todos los extranjeros (sin excluir, por cierto, a los españoles) nadie los percibe sino el inglés. Miller, Robertson, Burton, Cunninghame Graham, Hudson" (350) [To perceive or not to perceive the Creole nuances may be quite unimportant, but the fact is that of all the foreigners (not, of course, excluding the Spaniard) no one perceives them like the Englishman—Miller, Robertson, Burton, Cunningham Graham, Hudson] (145).[12] Borges's inclusion of the author among those English-born writers who lived or traveled in Argentina mirrors Martínez Estrada's mistaken inclusion of Hudson in the same category.[13] The "viajeros ingleses," as Martínez Estrada calls them, may very well capture in writing the quintessence of the pampas; but, it must be noted, they still occupy the foreign category of travelers. Borges's and Martínez Estrada's great praise of Hudson, then, is also a kind of faint damnation. An Argentine writer of sorts, an English traveler of sorts, the heterolingual Hudson fails to achieve the full status of Spanish American author.

These dual interpretations of Hudson's figure and texts invoke, once again, the extreme practices of literary taxonomies. As one reads those who write about Hudson, one often notices the need to classify him as either an Englishman, or an Argentine, or, at best, an Anglo-Argentine. The focus is solely on the writer, while the nature of those categories into which he is willed to fit remain unexamined. I seek to read *The Purple Land* not for what it may tell us about the author's nationality, but for what it may suggest also about the concepts of nation and national, or even continental, literature. Hudson's writing is indeed rooted in British literature, but it invokes certain practices associated with the literary traditions of the River Plate region, such as *literatura gauchesca* and, to a lesser extent, *costumbrismo*.[14] These modes of representation, however, do not travel into, or within, Hudson's foreign tongue unchanged, but rather undergo and trigger a series of permutations: they appear altered, and so is the text onto whose alien textuality they are grafted, and so are the concepts of Argentina and Spanish America, as well as those of Argentine and Spanish American literatures. Those who read *The Purple Land* in English, and who are familiar with the currents of Spanish American literature in the nineteenth century, may notice the author's uncanny rapprochement to nativist forms even as he writes in the other tongue: Hudson is best read within the systems of British and Argentine literature so that his text can make the most sense. Here, as in Anderson Imbert's *Historia,* the biographical matters. If Hudson had not been born in Argentina, one may be inclined to view the author's involvement with *literatura gauchesca* as the act of a foreign traveler in search of the picturesque, signifying little. But, as I examine below, Lamb heeds and records the verbal art of the gauchos with utmost attention, a gesture that one can interpret as a meditation on his own practice of writing outside the main language of Argentina. His malaise regarding his own storytelling, coupled with his admiration for that of the gauchos, may be read as Hudson's lament about his own interstitial difficulties, but also, moreover, as a suggestion of the possible unhomeliness of nations as well as that of the national and continental literary traditions.

That Hudson was not altogether pleased with the ways in which his first work was received is made evident in the preface to the second edition (1904) of *The Purple Land*: "A few notices of the work appeared in the papers, one or two of the most serious literary journals reviewing it (not favourably) under the heading of 'Travels and Geography' " (v). If the specter of the travel genre follows Hudson in his first literary venture, it is because the text, on one level, can indeed be read as the account of an Englishman's journey to Uruguay. The fictional plot, episodic in nature, follows Richard Lamb's voyage around the country from his arrival in Montevideo through his departure back to Buenos Aires. The narrative often indulges in lengthy, precise descriptions of the country's landscape and geography: "Continuing my journey through the Durazno district, I forded the pretty River Yí and entered the Tacuarembó department, which is immensely long, extending right away to the Brazilian frontier" (39). As Lamb traverses the Banda Orientál— the República Oriental del Uruguay is so named because of its position on the eastern shore of the Uruguay River—he often foregrounds his own act of observing the natives, called Orientáls, as well as other outlandish forms of life: "Here I broke my journey at an estancia where I had an excellent opportunity of studying the manners and customs of the Orientáls, and where I also underwent experiences of a mixed character and greatly increased my knowledge of the insect world" (30). The narrator's phrase ironically recalls a title such as Edward William Lane's *An Account of the Manners and Customs of the Modern Egyptians* (1836), one of the classic works of English Orientalism. If the citizens of Uruguay are rightly called Orientáls as a translation of the Spanish *orientales*, the label, in the Victorian age, inevitably evokes the intertwining discourses of empire and exoticism. As Lamb's gaze takes in the paroquet, ostriches, and pet armadillo that live inside a native's house (31), it also focuses on the manners and physical traits of the humans: "Anselmo was a fine specimen of the Orientál gaucho, dark and with good features, his hair and moustache intensely black" (75).

What matters here, though, is not simply the people and things that Lamb sees, but the style in which he describes them. If his language bespeaks a distance from the gauchos, its own emphatic features—"excellent opportunity," "fine specimen," "intensely black"—also denote a vision equally detached from a certain discourse of exoticism. Moreover, Lamb's words may denote Hudson's dissatisfaction with the modes of representation available to him in writing about his old world. In this regard, the "English" word "Orientál," with its peculiar diacritic (*oriental* has no accent mark in Spanish) may be telling the story of Hudson's literary journey: as he writes in another tongue about his *orientales* from South America, these men and women who, in a neo-Columbian turn of events, run the risk of resembling those other "Orientals" in Asia. Inscribing them with an accent not only grants them a separate status, it also gives birth to an odd interlingual creature that underscores the author's own sense of unhomeliness in the literary culture of England and Europe.

In its intermixture of humans and nature, Lamb's vision does often recall that of Columbus in his *Diario,* or that of Merlin in *La Havane.* Foreshadowing Rima, the bird-woman of *Green Mansions,*

Lamb depicts one of the first gauchos he meets outside of Montevideo as "this curious old Orientál bird" (23); later, he reverses the terms and describes birds as "the feathered people" (119). These cross-species affections—in which Lamb's own name will also be significant—may be explained in the context of Hudson's own ornithological writings: he is, after all, the author of a book lovingly entitled *Birds and Men* (1901). But these figurations, I propose, are also emblematic of the author's "experiences of a mixed character" (30), which is how Lamb ambiguously describes his first encounters with the gauchos. In this English novel, the Orientál gauchos metamorphose from closely watched creatures into highly eloquent voices whose creation of texts—stories, songs, and poems— both undermines and reanimates the text's English prose. The bird-like gauchos, as we shall see, speak, sing, and recite, and Lamb—as listener, narrator, storyteller, and, ultimately, translator—delivers an unforeseen portrait of the gauchos as verbal artists. What's more, in Lamb's comments on and record of the gauchos' oral styles, one can read an oblique reflection on the predicament of the author's interstitial writing. In a foreign tongue and literary context, Hudson mimics the gestures of those Argentine and Uruguayan authors—writers such as Estanislao del Campo and José Hernández, to name just two—who use the customs and manners of the gauchos, as well as their diction, as the thematic and linguistic foundation of their own texts, which now stand at the center of the national and continental canons. Delicately, *The Purple Land* and other writings by Hudson rise as strange birds in the region's literary landscape. Yet, by writing back from the heart of empire and hovering insistently, if vaguely, over the River Plate region, Hudson fashions an uncanny habitation of his own and incorporates it into the bodies of Argentine and Spanish American literatures. That the process whereby this occurs may seem clumsy and ambivalent at times is a signal of Hudson's tentative exploration of various literary systems, none of which accounts fully for what this text does.

As in many heterolingual texts, *The Purple Land* regards the world it portrays with a measure of melancholy. In this sense, it does not differ either from Ricardo Güiraldes's *Don Segundo Sombra* (1926), a lyrical evocation of the vanishing lifestyle of the gauchos and one of Argentina's canonical works. Güiraldes views the gauchos from a distance that is essentially temporal; that of Hudson, however, as he constructs South America, is also spatial and, most obviously, linguistic. As it often happens with the travel narratives among which it is traditionally classified, *The Purple Land* is crisscrossed with foreign words. Its English reader is abundantly exposed to such words as "señor," "rancho," and "maté." Many other Spanish words, printed in italics, are defined for the sake of this reader, who, like a traveler abroad in possession of a phrasebook, may end up mastering with time an alien lexicon: "*tropilla,* or troop of horses" (16); "*chiripá,* a shawl-like garment fastened at the waist with a sash, and reaching down half-way between the knees and ankles" (22); "the sudden south-west wind called *pampero*" (71). In Güiraldes's novel, as in other Spanish American regionalist texts, there is also a linguistic division between the narrator's literary register and the nativist diction of most characters (including the narrator's younger self), but these differences do not achieve the status of interlingualism. The apparent barrier is surmountable, because the author is able to represent in detail the interplay of both styles of Spanish, not simply a few words from gaucho speech framed by his own. In *Don Segundo Sombra* and other works, the reader, even if he or she must resort to footnotes or a glossary to learn the meaning of some words and expressions, is still able to appreciate fully the flavor and connotations of dialectal differences. That one learns how others in the nation (or continent) speak may also be viewed as a step in the process of mutual knowledge and even community; if divisions among social strata are textually underscored, a growing sense of intimacy ultimately obtains. Even in *La Havane,* interlingualism, with its careful depiction of local phonetics and syntax, may be recognized at once as a form of Cuban *costumbrismo.* In Hudson, however, the other tongue emerges first mostly as an element within an exoticist discourse. That he needs to explain the most basic lexical items reveals, in the eyes of the Argentine reader, the foreignness of his textuality and the sheer distance from which he writes about his native continent; that he does not engage in Merlin's audacious interlingualism may also be regarded as an absence of true engagement with local forms and practices.

Yet, if Spanish words are ambivalent signs in this text, Hudson's consideration of *literatura gauchesca* as a model for writing represents a more complex involvement with the River Plate. The gauchos in *The Purple Land* are not so much men of action as they are linguistic and literary beings, and Lamb's dealings with them are marked by his realization of their unusual prowess in telling a

story, singing a song, or reciting a poem. The gauchos are, as Nicolas Shumway puts it, "the true symbol of an emerging nation,"[15]
and their oral literary traditions are easily regarded as the source
of much national art. Hernández's *Martín Fierro* is Argentina's national poem partly because it convincingly imitates the diction of
the gauchos, even if, as Borges and others claim, the outcome is
gauchesque, not gaucho, poetry.[16] The act of singing with which
the first canto of *Martín Fierro* opens is an invocation of the Greek
and Latin epic, but also a conscious device to rewrite the tradition
with a distinctly Argentine accent: "Aquí me pongo a cantar / al
compás de mi vigüela" (53) [Here I come to sing to the beat of my
guitar] (3). Hudson's text, however, as it considers the art of the
gauchos or some of the practices of the gauchesque genre, in English, must ultimately acknowledge its linguistic inadequacy. As
narrator and fictional author of *The Purple Land,* Lamb is unable to
compose a work in the gauchesque tradition. Then again, Lamb's
shortcomings, one may argue, are precisely the oblique manner in
which the text both inscribes itself into Argentine literature and
marks that tradition with a distinctly heterolingual, specifically English, accent.

Lamb's encounter with the old gaucho Lucero occurs early in the
novel. In a *pulpería,* a classic space of Argentine writing defined for
the sake of the English reader as "store and public-house all in
one" (21), Lamb looks at Lucero and notices his obvious physical
difference. But if the gaucho has "a dark dry skin" (21), almost like
an ideal parchment on which to write, he also possesses very good
eyes that inspect Lamb, and the gaucho soon usurps the metropolitan stance of surveying and speaking: "after bestowing a searching
glance on me out of his dark hawk-like eyes, he resumed his talk"
(22). Having seen Lucero see him, Lamb, very much the foreigner,
makes a conscious effort to become one with the gaucho audience:
"After calling for rum and water, to be in the fashion, I sat down on
a bench, and, lighting a cigarette, prepared to listen" (22). As he
attends to this speech, Lamb once again surveys the Oriental's
body, underscoring his barbaric aspect: "his left foot was bare,
while the right one was cased in a colt's-skin stocking, called *bota-
de-potro,* and on this distinguished foot was buckled a huge iron
spur, with spikes two inches long" (22). But then again, and most
significantly, Lamb is seduced by the gaucho's verbal artistry: "so
vivid and minute were his descriptions—sparkling with passion,
satire, humour, pathos—and so dramatic his actions, while won-

derful story followed story, that I was fairly astonished, and pronounced this old *pulpería* orator a born genius" (22). While the gaucho exhibits his poetry, Lamb becomes a docile listener, very much the antithesis of the fierce conquistador.

If the narrator's authorial evaluation of Lucero's skills, albeit positive, seems an instance of European paternalism, the gaucho himself soon submits Lamb to a narrative test of his own couched in a respectful question: "My friend, I perceive you are a traveller from Montevideo: may I ask what news there is from that city?" (23). The narrator, just pronounced an alien figure in this place, confesses to the reader his own verbal insecurity in the face of "this curious old Oriéntal bird, with such ragged plumage, but whose native woodnotes wild had such a charm in them" (23). Trying to avoid "mere commonplace phrases" (23) in his carefully crafted reply, Lamb manages to produce only a "grotesque speech" (23). But the mutual testing continues, however, and Lamb asks Lucero what news about the countryside he should report upon his return to Montevideo. Once again, the gaucho's speech, enriched with metaphors and vividly performed, thrills Lamb. Finally, Lucero tells his interlocutor what he suspected—and what the reader suspected he suspected—all along: "But, señor, though you speak as we do, there is yet in the pepper and salt on your tongue a certain foreign flavour" (25). To which Lamb, no longer a mere urban outsider, must admit, "You are right, . . . I am a foreigner" (25). That Lamb should expect a possible victory in a foreign tongue may stand as a sign of the text's aspirations, which, though unfulfilled, remain a valuable site for reading Hudson's unhomeliness.

Even if both men speak in prose, there is in this dialogue a trace of the competitive elements of poetic art that Johan Huizinga analyzes in *Homo Ludens* (1938).[17] Obliquely, they debate the relative merits of English prose and River Plate poetry, and Lucero playfully rises over Lamb as the best "poet-seer" (120), to borrow a phrase from Huizinga. Two things matter in this game: who observes and, more importantly, who can best speak about what he observes. That in these matches Lamb should turn out to be the inferior raconteur ultimately complicates the hierarchies of empire and colony. If the novel's first edition is entitled *The Purple Land That England Lost*, these initial chapters may well be called "The Purple Land in which England Lost," or, perhaps, "The Purple Land in which English Literature Did Not Win." Lucero's superior narrative skills become apparent once again when he recounts to his wife the news from Montevideo, which he has previously inquired from Lamb. The foreigner, hearing how much better the gaucho's telling of the same story is, acknowledges his own defeat in front of Lucero's wife. Lamb's metaphorical evaluation of Lucero's tale curiously reverses the habitual order of imperial transactions: "Señora . . . you must not give me credit for all you have heard from your husband, I only gave him brute wool, and he has woven it for your delight into beautiful cloth" (27). Here, the English narrator furnishes the Oriental with raw materials, which the gaucho then weaves into a marvelously crafted text. This finished product, significantly, does not appear in Lamb's narrative, but is only reported upon: its actual words are a notable absence in the fabric of *The Purple Land*. Spoken in the style and language of the gauchos, Lucero's verbal creation cannot be reproduced in his listener's tongue or Hudson's text: there exists a better tale told in Spanish that cannot be rendered in English.[18]

Lamb's inefficacy as a gauchesque poet, or even as the gauchos' translator, becomes manifest again as the episode comes to an end, when, after listening to a ballad sung by a young gaucho, he expresses his sense of frustration at not being able to reproduce it faithfully in the reader's language: "Here are the words translated almost literally, therefore without rhymes, and I only regret that I cannot furnish my musical readers with the quaint, plaintive air they were sung to" (28). The tune is absent because literature, obviously, does not usually occupy itself with musical notation.[19] But if the words themselves are far removed from the usual lexicon and meters of gaucho poetry, it is because Lamb, with the English reader in mind, is copying it in the wrong language. The protocols of *literatura gauchesca* in the River Plate region differ from the gaucho's oral poetry, of course, yet urban gauchesque poets can still imitate the style of the gauchos: they, like Güiraldes's narrator and characters, share the common space of Spanish. Lamb must deal in English, and, despite his best efforts, what he translates "almost literally" into that tongue does not sound like anything that one would immediately recognize or read as gaucho or gauchesque poetry:

> O let me go—O let me go,
> Where high are born amidst the hills
> The streams that gladden all the south,
> And o'er the grassy desert wide,
> Where slakes his thirst the antlered deer,
> Hurry towards the great green ocean. (28)

In the prologue to his *Rimas,* as we saw in chapter 1, Esteban Echeverría regarded the desert as the ground on which to build the national literature. A similar space seems to be invoked here, but Hudson's bucolic "grassy desert wide" lacks the connotations of barbarism that it has in much Argentine writing of the nineteenth century. Then again, these stanzas "translated" from the Spanish do contain some strands that might remind one of themes in Argentine literature: "My heart within the city pent / Pines for the desert's liberty: / The streets are red with blood, and fear / Makes pale the mournful women's faces" (29). In these lines, one finds vestiges of Argentina's civil strife as depicted in texts by Echeverría and Sarmiento; the escape to the desert recalls as well the end of the first part of *Martín Fierro.* If this desert seems slightly familiar, yet strange, it is because one can hear through the foreign tongue and structure distant echoes of Argentine works written in Spanish. Echeverría's "La cautiva," for instance, ends with a description of the protagonist's final resting ground in the desert, also called the *llanura,* or plain, under an *ombú* where birds find shelter; an image not unlike this one surfaces at the end of Hudson's verses: "I do not love the burial-ground, / But I shall sleep upon the plain, / Where long green grass shall round me wave— / Over me graze wild herds of cattle" (29). If the formulaic treatment of civilization and barbarism, entrenched in other authors, is not at work in Hudson, one can still perceive the vague imprint of some kind of Argentine intertext. The residue is plausible enough to have caused Eduardo Hillman, a translator of *The Purple Land,* to believe in the probable existence of a Spanish-language original for the young gaucho's poem, as he suggests in a footnote to his version: "He traducido estos versos casi palabra por palabra; pero aunque dice el autor haberlos vertido casi literalmente del castellano al inglés, no he logrado obtener nada que se asemeje a lo que debió ser la rima original" (38 n. 1) [I have translated these lines almost word for word; but, although the author says that he rendered them almost literally from Spanish into English, I have not been able to obtain anything resembling what must have been the original rhyme].[20]

Curiously, if this footnote concedes that Hudson's version of the poem was done almost literally, Hillman's rendering of the passage in which Lamb admits so reads simply "literalmente" (38), camouflaging the original text's modicum of insecurity. That Hillman's Spanish version of Lamb's English is hardly "almost word for

word," as he claims in his footnote, further complicates the authorial chain of custody, as it were. In its transmission from "original"
gaucho text in Spanish, through Lamb's "translation" into English,
and back into Spanish in Hillman's text, the poem that the Argentine reader of *La tierra purpúrea* encounters has a definite ring of
nonpoetic foreignness. In an unexpected turn of events,
Lamb's—or Hudson's—unhomeliness is faithfully mirrored in Hillman's awkward lines:

> Quiero irme donde alto entre los cerros,
> Brotan los arroyos que alegran todo el sur.
> Corren al grande y verde océano,
> Por el herboso y vasto llano,
> Donde su sed apaga el gamo. (38)

> [I want to go where high amidst the hills,
> The streams are born that gladden all the south.
> They run towards the great green ocean,
> Through the grassy and vast plain,
> Where slakes his thirst the deer.]

Yet, that Hudson's and Hillman's versions of a poem recited by a
young gaucho stand as copies without an original may be read as
a comment on the Romantic artifice whereby national literatures
and folkloric traditions are bound together. These "almost literal"
versions underscore the sense of willful construction implicit in
both *literatura gauchesca* and the critical discussions that elevate it
as quintessentially Argentine: the literary tools of authors who
write books can never reproduce the practices of oral poetry, nor
can critics demonstrate the veracity of their own constructs on ontological grounds. In this context of essential loss and limited approximation, Hudson's version of gaucho poetry in English can be
read, conceivably, as an extreme illustration of the same artifice in
which other Argentine and Uruguayan authors often engage. Thus,
as Hudson's heterolingual textuality overtly exposes the failure of
its mimicking, Lamb's failed translating may be read not only as an
act of fictional self-reflection, but as a meditation on gauchesque
poetry and, more generally, on the possible nonexistence of national (or continental) literary traditions. Hudson, for reasons of
language, could never be a gauchesque poet; at the most, he might
be taken as a gauchesque poet manqué. That Hillman should
search for Hudson's original text signals not only the translator's

faith in literary archaeology, but a general sense that Hudson, like the gauchesque poets, wants to situate the source of his art in popular forms. But no text is found. This absence, however, is a meaningful abode, for it posits the ghostly—a figure variously visible and invisible, a figure that may not even exist—as the touchstone of the nation.

If something seems to be lost in the various acts of translation surrounding *The Purple Land,* something too is gained which may be less tangible, but whose actuality can be sensed through the process of reading. Later in his perambulations around the Banda Oriental, Lamb "translates" another ballad sung by a gaucho, and this time what emerges in the English text is a poem under which one detects the shadow of a *décima,* one of the favored stanzas of oral poetry in Spanish. Besides the requisite ten lines, Lamb's text exhibits, imperfectly, something of the stanza's meter and rhythm, but only if one chooses to read it, in an interlingual and interliterary gesture, with a Spanish poetic accent:

> Yesterday my senses opened,
> At a rap-a-tap from Reason,
> Inspiring in me an intention,
> Which I never had before,
> Seeing that through all my days
> My life has been just what is.
> Therefore when I rose I said,
> To-day shall be as yesterday,
> Since Reason tells me I have been
> From day to day the same-self thing. (45)

In fact, the uncanny resemblances between this short poem and the Spanish verse may have prompted both Hillman and Idea Vilariño (another translator of the novel) to render Lamb's "translation" as a *décima*—Vilariño's classically perfect, Hillman's wanting.[21] The English original may not be a fine example of gauchesque poetry, but something perhaps more precious in the archaelogy of heterolingualism: an unhomely text, ten lines of poetry under which certain readers can strangely perceive another language and literary tradition. As a translator, Lamb may be a traitor, but the essential betrayal displaces both Argentine and British literature by creating a space between one and the other, a room for both their houses. Hillman's homely verses may yet be the best

literary figuration through which the monolingual Argentine reader
can look into this secret space of the nation.

Because of Lamb's appreciation of the verbal art of the gauchos,
one can understand why, as he first considers the project of writing
a book upon his return to England, he rejects certain forms that he
relates to European literature, but is yet unable to define what new
kind of writing he will practice:

> How unutterably worn out, stilted, and artificial seems all the so-called
> pastoral poetry ever written when one sits down to supper and joins in
> the graceful *Cielo* or *Pericon* in one of those remote semi-barbarous
> South American estancias! I swear I will turn poet myself, and go back
> some day to astonish old *blasé* Europe with something so—so— (32;
> emphases in original).

At this point in the narrative, Lamb is distracted by the sound of an
insect's wings, so the exact configuration of his literary project will
be postponed. One can intuit, though, the seductions of exoticism,
and one may suppose that Lamb will write a text addressed to the
English reader; after all, the novel published in 1885 is entitled *The
Purple Land That England Lost*. If, in the second edition, Hudson
omits the second part of the title because " 'tis of our gains, not our
losses, we keep count" (v), one may also think of other reasons.
This is not a novel about imperial desires, but about one Englishman seduced with the idea of losing England for good, even when
his other home, Argentina, is already lost.[22] The plot of *The Purple
Land* may easily be read as the story of a possible hyphenation:
the narrative of an Englishman named Richard Lamb who may become a South American: an Anglo-South American.[23] That Uruguay, and not Argentina, is the setting for Lamb's adventures may
be seen as negligible, given the geographical and cultural proximity
of the two nations, and the fact that from the Old World, all Latin
American countries, happy or unhappy, are frequently made to resemble each other. In the context of the novel, however, the Banda
Oriental emerges as a second opportunity for the protagonist to remain on this continent. Twice does he lose Argentina, and twice
does he find refuge on the other side of the River Plate.

Lamb's adventures in *The Purple Land* are for the most part, in
essence, amatory, and not always do they concern Paquíta, his Argentine wife. The novel opens with the couple's arrival in Montevideo from Buenos Aires, whence they escape because of their illegal

elopement and clandestine marriage. Lamb defines the magnitude of his actions in terms of his foreignness: "And I had taken her—stolen her—from her natural protectors, from the home where she had been worshipped—I of an alien race and another religion, without means, and because I had stolen her, an offender against the law" (4). As he rambles around the Banda Oriental while Paquíta remains in Montevideo, Lamb, something of a non-Latin Don Juan, meets and even courts other women, but, since he is a married man, any projects of creating a household with any of them are thwarted from the beginning. The story of Lamb and Paquíta, in any event, ends sadly: they return to Argentina; Lamb is imprisoned; she dies of sadness. Curiously, these last events are narrated in the first two paragraphs of the text, in which we also learn that Lamb returns to Uruguay for a second time. It is not altogether clear, but it may be there, in that third country of his in which he arrives twice, where he will compose *The Purple Land*, the book that will give pleasure to his children, if, as he tells Demetria, he ever has any.

Given the text's focus on love and nation, especially in regard to Lamb's status as a foreigner, one may read *The Purple Land* as a strange kind of Latin American "national romance," those nineteenth-century novels that, as Doris Sommer suggests, seek to reconcile through fictional love the heterogeneous elements within nations: a conjunction of Polis and Eros, or of Benedict Anderson and Michel Foucault, as Sommer would have it.[24] That this is a tale of two nations, Uruguay and Argentina, and that Lamb's sentimental journey in either one do not result in offspring, makes one wonder to what extent he becomes fully integrated into the life of either. In the course of his travels, he meets a man from Edinburgh who has found the life he wants in his new country, with a wife named Candelaria, six children, and even a new name, "Don Juan" (255). This "un-Scotched Scotchman" (257) stands in contrast to the colony of "English gentlemen" that Lamb encounters in an earlier episode and profoundly dislikes. They are arrogant and predictable even in the way they speak, repeating the phrase "don't you know" as a self-parodical leitmotif (53–55). The episode of Lucero precedes that of the Englishmen by only a few chapters, which makes the contrast between the gaucho's speech and that of the Englishmen particularly obvious: "Here we stand, a colony of English gentlemen: here we are, don't you know, far from our homes and country and all that sort of thing" (65).

Here, too, stands Lamb, who returns to the Banda Oriéntal with neither family nor home. One is left to wonder who eventually he will grow to resemble: the childless Englishmen who remain decidedly English; or John, who is now Don Juan? The end of Lamb's tale of possible hyphenation is not told—the novel, in fact, ends quite abruptly—and the only key that the reader may consult in order to fill that gap is the text of *The Purple Land* itself, a hybrid work in which the language and writing of the River Plate are more than just a ghostly shadow. That he does not become one of the colony of Englishmen is clear, because he does not write at all like they speak; but one cannot presume, either, that, following John/Don Juan, he will be un-Englished and become just Ricardo, as he is now and then called by the Orientáls. One can more easily imagine him on one shore of the River Plate, thinking of the other, from which he has transported himself; or writing in one language, thinking of another, into whose literary systems he cannot translate himself. His Anglo-Argentine or Anglo-Oriéntal children remain an absence in this story, but a reader emerges who may fill Lamb's seemingly void act of writing with meanings.

It is not strange that María Luisa Bombal, having changed language and literary context, should begin *House of Mist* (1947) with a few words to her new reader. Writing now for a vague U.S. American figure whose horizon of expectations—she may suspect—are not those of her old Spanish-language audience in South America, the author clarifies for that reader's sake some of what may be perceived as her text's quirks:

> I wish to inform the reader that even though this is a mystery, it is a mystery without murder.
> He will not find here any corpse, any detective; he will not even find a murder trial, for the simple reason that there will be no murderer.
> There will be no murderer and no murder, yet there will be... crime. And there will be fear.[25]

These words are an instance of fictional self-reflection, but, on another level, they are also a curious act of masking and unmasking—a cover-up and a confession—that only Bombal's old reader in South America would be likely to "get." What the new reader is not told here is that this regardful author has a past, both literary and otherwise. There could be a measure of fear. In Spanish, she has written two Modernist works of fiction in which the reader is offered no guidance of this kind.[26] Those texts were published to great critical acclaim in Buenos Aires and Santiago de Chile, in whose streets, incidentally, Bombal once shot several bullets at an old lover; there was no murder and no corpse then, but there were detectives and a trial. Once acquitted, Bombal left her native continent and headed north, like Hudson, remaining in the United States for almost three decades. Years later, other readers, perhaps, might fear other things. Should one be afraid that María Luisa Bombal, one of the greatest names in Chilean and Spanish American writing, might have become for a long period of time a foreign author in another country? Is there any significant role for the Spanish-language reader in this linguistic and literary permutation? Is there, perhaps, yet another reader implied even in these opening lines, a figure that Bombal wants to retain for the duration of the text?

In *House of Mist,* the mystery is not only the issue of genre that the author addresses directly in these opening lines, but something else that concerns reading as much as it may the law: the truth, the whole truth. Even as the reader is told something that should reassure him or her, the author comes tantalizingly close to revealing something else that may be shocking, something that should best remain concealed. That only a reader with a knowledge of Bombal's South American past can read between these lines and suspect another story—one told with irony—is the first sign that *House of Mist* may shelter two radically different tales in its seemingly candid fabric. One, the most apparent, is the romantic and rather exotic story, as the prologue states, of "the strange house of mist that a young woman, very much like all other women, built for herself at the southern end of South America" (3). The second story is also a mystery of sorts: not the story of Bombal's true crime, but one that also pertains to South America. Secretly, ironically, this is a complex story of linguistic and literary unhousedness; it is told in English, and those readers who do not repress Bombal's past in another tongue and literary tradition, with its own set of cultural and aesthetic norms, will perform it best.

Frequently misread as little more than a translation into English of *La última niebla* (1935), Bombal's first novella,[27] the text of *House of Mist* is best understood as a new work, the author's longest. The changes from one text to the other are profound. The author herself explains the radical transformation in terms of genre and viewpoint: while the first text focuses poetically on the main character's inner life, the second is concerned with external events, more like a traditional novel.[28] This, indeed, may be taken as a fine description of the thrust of each text. Much of the plot, if one may call it that, in *La última niebla* takes place in the nameless protagonist's mind, to which the reader has access with relative transparency;[29] in *House of Mist,* though, what seems to matter most is the byzantine episodes surrounding Helga, who resembles her counterpart in the first text mostly in that they are both first-person narrators. What seems less convincing is the analogy that Bombal traces between her own literary evolution and that of James Joyce. If the text of *House of Mist* does "develop the subject" of *La última niebla,* as Joyce's *Ulysses* "develops" *Portrait of the Artist as a Young Man,* it is also quite possible to read Bombal's English-language novel almost as an unwriting—through proliferation—of the novella she had composed in Spanish. The changes from one work to another include not only the most obvious ones of language and genre, but also far-reaching alterations of plot, atmosphere, and characterization. Upon the publication of *La última niebla* in Buenos Aires, Amado Alonso, one of the continent's foremost critics at the time, praised Bombal for her first work's subdued art and tight construction, traits that its English counterpart does not reproduce.[30] Where *La última niebla* is brief and obscure, *House of Mist* amplifies and clarifies to the point of betrayal. As Ágata Gligo explains, Bombal's old audience must have felt disconcerted upon reading what she had written in New York: "Donde se espera un mundo de sombras y emociones, surgen diálogos concretos y explicaciones lógicas para todo lo que ocurre" [Where one expects a world of shadows and emotions, there emerge concrete dialogues and logical explanations for everything that happens].[31]

Indeed, so different is the new text from *La última niebla* that the latter has been translated independently into English as *The Final Mist.*[32] Interestingly, Bombal herself worked on a Spanish version of *House of Mist,* which was provisionally titled "Embrujo" (Spell), but she never completed the translation. One can only speculate about the unfinished status of "Embrujo," but it might have to do with the unhomely nature of heterolingual texts. To render the other tongue in its "original" linguistic and literary systems is a difficult task, because it runs the risk of altering the meaningful absences on which heterolingualism rests. The strange yet familiar sounds of Hudson's *décima* in English are lost once they are rendered in Spanish—unless they can be mirrored, as we saw in Eduardo Hillman's version, by sounds equally strange and familiar. A straightforward translation of *House of Mist* into Bombal's first language can easily capture the obvious patterns of the plot, but the text's other story of unhomeliness—one that concerns the nation— may depend, paradoxically, on the foreign tongue. What Bombal does in English, I will argue here, may easily be lost in Spanish.

In Gligo's report, the reference to "dialogues" and "logic" fits well into Bombal's own reading of *House of Mist* as more akin to a traditional novel than the previous text, but it still does not account for the specific nature of those new elements, which turn out to be, upon examination, not just novelistic, as the author suggests, but fantastically *novelescos*. The new text's dialogues, for instance, are often magniloquent: " 'It's not true. You're the one who's always been a tyrant—and still are.' 'Certainly, and I will prove it by taking my wife back with me right now to the hacienda' " (64). Logic, too, at times seems overly stretched. The touchstone of *La última niebla* is the protagonist's lasting uncertainty about a night of passionate love spent with a stranger: she, like the reader, never learns whether this central event in the story actually occurred, or was only a dream. In *House of Mist,* a similar mystery is conveniently solved through a bizarre series of events that ultimately restores Helga's sense of virtue as it violates all sense of verisimilitude. Following certain conventions of melodrama, the English-language work abounds in coups de théâtre and extreme sentiments, but sexuality itself, openly treated in *La última niebla,* is absent in *House of Mist.* If one compares the narration of each protagonist's nocturnal encounter with the man who is not her husband, one sees textual resemblances among the two works: "una pequeña plaza" (18) becomes "a small square" (72); "una calle estrecha y en pendiente" (19) is rendered as "straight up the narrow street" (72); and "verja" and "cadena enmohecida" (19) are still recognizable in "old iron gate" (72). But the actual physical union between the man and the woman, daringly recounted in Spanish, is suppressed in English. Curiously, what is vague in *La última niebla* is made explicit in *House of Mist,* and vice versa. Time, represented as a misty substance in the first text, becomes precise in the second one. As if to challenge the famous dictum that modern authors can no longer write such a conventional phrase as "the marquise left at five o'clock," Bombal, the Modernist, seems to revel in precisely such statements: "The Countess can see no one at this hour" (58); "The Countess is going to the opera tonight" (75).

Yet these changes, which one may be tempted to dismiss as mere concessions to a new audience seeking fiction's most obvious thrills, are double-edged signs addressed also to another reader. The Countess de Nevers, for instance, is not just a picturesque figure, but a meaningful element in Bombal's subtle analysis of the interplay between native and foreign in South America. It is true that if one believed in the linear evolution of literature, one might speak about a regression here, from avant-garde forms to the predictable conventions of old-fashioned romance, and in this Bombal would not be alone. From Cervantes's embrace of conventions in *Los trabajos de Persiles y Sigismunda* after having written *Don Quijote*, to Woolf's traditionalism in *The Years* after *To the Lighthouse* and *The Waves*, literary history offers many examples of an author's seeming volte-face. In Bombal's case, there is evidence that financial reasons prompted the composition of *House of Mist*. Wanting to sell the rights of *La última niebla* to a motion picture company, Bombal and her husband approached several studios; Paramount Pictures expressed some interest, but also much skepticism, for reasons that Bombal summarized thus, "Muy bonito, pero demasiado corto y no vamos a filmar un poema en prosa. Aclare el asunto: ¿Soñó o no la protagonista? Póngale final" [Very nice, but too short; besides, we are not going to film a prose poem. Make it clear: did the protagonist dream or not? Give it an ending].[33] Bombal is ready to oblige: she writes a longer work, a novel that can be made into a movie, with a protagonist who did dream; there is also an ending—and a happy one at that. That working within these rather narrow parameters she produced a work that still addresses less marketable concerns is a sign of Bombal's continued practice of verbal ambiguity; it is an indication also that more than one reader is implied in this text.

It is a truth almost universally acknowledged that authors from Spanish America often interest foreign literary markets because of the perceived exoticism of their writings. Given Bombal's provenance, one can well imagine that this issue may have played an explicit or subliminal role in her transactions with Hollywood, or in those with Farrar, Straus in New York, which eventually published the novel. Whatever the actual conversations may have been, if one compares *House of Mist* to *La última niebla*, one soon notices the English-language text's insistence on the story's alien setting. This is a departure from her other works as well, which take place in countries that are, or may well be, Chile or Argentina, but where geographic specificity, let alone local color, is minimal, if existent at all. Indeed, in the Spanish American literary context of the times, Bombal's fictions of the 1930s—composed shortly after such classic novels as Gallegos's *Doña Bárbara* and Rivera's *La vorágine*— stand out for their nonregionalist preoccupations. In *La última niebla,* for instance, the mist-covered house is first described as a "casa de campo" (9) [country house], a more or less neutral term that could be applied to houses anywhere in the Hispanic world, while the rest of the text is written in a decidedly nonregional Spanish. That this country house should be marked as a clearly Spanish American hacienda throughout *House of Mist* fits well into the work's explicit setting, even if in the continent's southernmost countries, other terms—*estancia* and *fundo*—are more commonly used. If hacienda is sometimes used in *La última niebla* (and also *La amortajada,* Bombal's other long text in Spanish), the effect is altogether different: the fact that the term may be used throughout Spanish America, and not only in one country, gives the text a non-regional connotation that the English lacks—in a sense, it displaces the story beyond the specificity of the Southern Cone. Moreover, in *House of Mist,* the misty "southern end of South America" (3) mentioned in the prologue may not be the customary Latin American landscape of the tropics, but it still fulfills, generally, the reader's expectations of alien horizons. Beyond setting, the melodramatic plot of *House of Mist* may also be a response to preconceived notions about Spanish American literary culture. Obviously, love stories told on a high key are hardly the exclusive province of Spanish America; in fact, one of the strongest intertexts of *House of Mist* seems to be Daphne du Maurier's *Rebecca* (1938) or Hitchcock's version thereof (1940). But if Spanish American authors, like their European and American counterparts, have always freely explored multiple aspects of the human experience, the tendency to link "Latins" with those stories where love and passion play an emphatic role may have influenced Bombal in this new narrative stance.

Yet, the concrete geography and melodramatic airs of *House of Mist* will serve not only the novel's exoticist level, but also its tale of unhomeliness, one that Bombal's previous fiction in Spanish already suggests, but that this new work expands as it tells the story of its own heterolingualism. Whatever the causes may have been for these changes, there is extraliterary evidence of Bombal's disenchantment with the U.S. American literary scene, and it concerns specifically the issue of the reader. In 1967, she writes to a friend complaining about the futility of "empeñarse con libros que esta gente no entiende. Han de ser escritos especialmente para ellos y fue en ese sentido que *La última niebla* se transformó en *House of Mist*" (quoted by Gligo, 145) [keeping at it with books that these people do not understand. They must be written especially for them and that's how *La última niebla* was transformed into *House of Mist*].[34] Yet there is proof that Bombal's verbal art, not only her finances, profited, albeit perhaps unwittingly, from playing by the rules of this other reader's game.

Having developed from its seed in *La última niebla* into a strange voluminous creature, *House of Mist* is much more than a mindless divertimento. In its intricate twists and turns, one can read not only the romantic tale of Helga, the nameless woman who now has a name, but also a fictional meditation on the drama of heterolingualism and exile. Although not an autobiographical novel in any sense, *House of Mist* tells an oblique story of migration and foreignness that appears intertwined with the process of writing outside of one's language and literary culture. The key to this second tale resides, quite specifically, in several details absent from or having minimal importance in *La última niebla,* but that *House of Mist* either introduces or amplifies. These include, first, the protagonist's foreign name, Helga; her illegitimate birth to a Danish woman; her devotion to fairy tales; her passion for Daniel, her childhood friend and later husband, an unsophisticated landowner; Daniel's twin sister, the Countess of Nevers; Teresa, Daniel's first wife, whose place Helga appears to be usurping; and her possible affair with Landa, a man who turns out to be a foreigner. Finally, there is also one Spanish word, *tranquera* [fence gate], which is the text's only italicized one-word instance of interlingualism. That all of these elements are also part and parcel of the outlandish melodrama of *House of Mist* underscores the double face of Spanish American heterolingualism: even as it seems to turn its back on home, it maneuvers the foreign signs to house itself meaningfully in the literary culture of origin. As she wears the mask of local color, Bombal unmasks from time to time to let the reader glimpse her formerly patently audacious face, and to examine the mask itself, an artifact whose polysemy may not be obvious at first.

The protagonist's name, Helga, matters because of its double outlandishness: it is a strange name in the United States, but also in South America—except perhaps in southern Chile, a land German immigrants settled since the nineteenth century. Being the first sign of the character's relative foreignness in her native country, it is also the primary clue that *House of Mist* is not only a story of South American exoticism, but also one of unhomeliness. Let us recall once again the prologue, where Bombal defines her novel explicitly as the story of "the strange house of mist that a young woman, very much like all other women, built for herself at the southern end of South America" (3). Appealing to the reader's interest in the exotic and, more generally, in the human condition, this sentence contains in a nutshell a summary of Bombal's literary output in Spanish—tales about women, "very much like all other women," where the regional is secondary—as well as a preview of the exotic geography that *House of Mist* underscores. If Helga's story is universal through its focus on love and marriage, it is also a tale about an unusual woman not completely at home in a place—and in a text—where such appelations as Señora Rivas and doña Teresa are most common. Once the text reveals that her mother was a Danish woman with whom Helga's married father, a native of the country, had sustained a long, secret romance, Helga's orphanhood becomes an element not only in this quasi-Victorian yarn of literal unhousedness—the plot follows Helga from house to house—but a meaningful clue, suspected all along, in a more elusive tale that links illegitimacy with virtual foreignness. Like the second Mrs. de Winter in *Rebecca*—or like Cinderella, also a major intertext in the novel—Helga does not have a true home, but she stands to gain one through marriage. That in this melodrama she turns out to be a half-foreigner as well—the illegitimate daughter of an immigrant woman shunned by a conservative society—invokes another reading of *House of Mist*, one in which husband and house stand as metaphors for Helga's full citizenship, visible signposts of home in Helga's quest for a place in her half-country. When Daniel and Helga first meet as children, in the garden of his uncle's vast estate, he stresses her strangeness: "Helga! So your name is Helga! What a funny name!" (12). He cannot suspect yet, of course, that she will acquire a less unusual name by marrying him: Helga will become Señora Viana. That Daniel shares a surname with Javier de Viana, the Uruguayan author of such titles as *Campo* (1896) and *Gaucha* (1899), can only serve to foreground, at least for a reader familiar with Spanish American literature, this character's roots in a land that is not quite Helga's yet.

In *House of Mist,* the narrative conventions of fairy tales emerge as ambivalent markings of the text's dual movements. On the one hand, they underscore Bombal's apparent naïveté in this phase of her writing career, while, on the other, they are the threads secretly leading into the nucleus of this examination of foreignness. A half-foreigner in the New World, Helga views her life and narrates her story very much in the manner of fairy tales, traces of which are found throughout the text. Like the main characters in Hans Christian Andersen's "The Ugly Duckling" and "The Little Mermaid," Helga is an outsider. Her first words to Daniel when they first meet as children are an allusion to a fairy tale, which can only accentuate her own outlandishness—even as it suggests the author's apparent simpleness. In the boy's South American garden, she is looking for the mythical Prince Toad, and she says as much: "I was looking for the Prince" (8). If Bombal's signs may sound at times as guileless as her protagonist, their interplay in the text has an eye on a variety of readers, ultimately revealing a complex canvas of significations.

Like Cinderella, Helga is not invited to a "fancy dress party" (11), and must live with relatives who not only mistreat her, but have a fearsome aspect as well: "Aunt Adelaida, so very long and thin, with her big colorless eyes staring into space, with her profile like a bird of prey, was indeed the striking image of one of the witches in my books" (20). Then again, as Adelaida's characterization continues, it also responds to specific types in Spanish American literature: "Aunt Adelaida spent her mornings in church and her afternoons in bed, suffering from the same heart ailment which had been fatal to my father" (20). The text's transposition of the imaginary landscape of fairy tales to the concrete spaces of much of the continent's literature is a small example of what the whole text actually fulfills: a foreign tool—another tongue, another mode of representation—may yet tell the nation's domestic story, especially if one views the nation, as this text proposes, as a site where the strange and the familiar coexist.

In Bombal's naïve yet reflexive fiction, the imprint of the fairy tale problematizes the concepts of foreign and native. The fairy-tale books to which Helga refers when she speaks about Aunt Adelaida are a legacy—the only one, really—from her Danish mother; since she is a poor orphan whose relatives will not pay for her schooling, these are the books in which she learns how to read and write.[35] To locate the origin of Helga's practice of reading and writing in these foreign texts explains the dreamlike quality of her narrative even as it underscores the strangeness in her that others are quick to perceive. Daniel, the native son, is surprised not only at Helga's name, but at her unusual imagination and diction, the fact that everything she perceives is represented by means of fairy tales, including himself, whom she describes as "exactly like the enchanted Bear in my fairy tales" (8). Yet, in the context of Bombal's heterolingualism, Daniel's reaction to Helga's style foregrounds the book's doubly extraterritorial condition: *House of Mist* depicts an outlandish South America, but it also tells the tale of one character who is herself an exotic being in that continent. The antipodes, then, have their own antipodes: if the United States can look at the south with strange eyes, so can South America at the north. But this fairy-tale intertextuality, even as it functions as an emblem of strangeness, also emerges as a sign of commonality and, even more importantly, of the difficulty of distinguishing between the foreign and the native, north and south, Europe and the New World. Seen from both North and South America, the fairy-tale archive, with its princes and castles, may bespeak a foreign European past, yet these stories, known to children throughout the Americas, also constitute a fertile terrain for viewing the existence of transculturally shared connotations. In this international network of literary relations, Helga speaks a language that is strange, yet familiar, in the country. She is, after all, only *half* a foreigner, one whose language may be strange, but, in the final analysis, understandable across several cultures and continents. If Daniel is astonished at hearing her words, it is due to Helga's peculiar diction, but also to his narrow or provincial imagining of the national community.

Helga's story, like that of Richard Lamb in Hudson's novel, is also one of hyphenation, expressed through the intertwining concepts of house and tongue. But if Lamb is unable truly to adopt the language of the gauchos, or to avoid his literal and figurative unhousedness on this continent, Helga manages not only to legitimate her fairy-tale vision and diction, but to use these as instruments in finding and speaking about a true home. In the figurations around her Danish-South American hyphen, fairy tales may appear to tilt her one way, yet they also serve, as we shall see, as the gate into her eventual insertion in the nation's heart, by which I mean both an emotional and a physical location. *House of Mist* emerges as another foundational fiction of sorts, but one that, unlike *The Purple Land,* has a fruitful ending; it concerns Helga's love story as well as that of her mother.

In this romantic tale, the character of Daniel functions as Helga's cultural opposite: the man she loves will guarantee her full naturalization. Readers who tend to see *House of Mist* mostly as a narrative amplification of *La última niebla* may fail to see how Daniel's development in the English text allows the emergence of a tale of Eros and Polis absent in the first work. Not much is known about Daniel there, except that his labors in the country seem to interest him more than his wife does. In *House of Mist,* however, Daniel becomes a fully rounded character, closer to that of Ricardo in *La amortajada* than to his namesake in *La última niebla.* At first, he is depicted as a rather conventional romantic figure whose physical traits may be linked with the author's adoption of a screenplay-like shorthand. In Helga's words, Daniel is "this tall, taciturn, handsome young man" (8); predictably, that one can substitute "dark" for "taciturn" becomes evident just a few lines below, when she speaks of his "curly, brown hair" (8). His mist-covered house, where he lived with his first wife Teresa and into which Helga will move when she marries him, is also a conventional feature; its prototype may well be a mansion like Manderley in *Rebecca.*

In Helga's eyes, however, Daniel is first and foremost a man of the country, in both senses of the word: his rural habitation will stand as a site around which to consider a traditional view of a nation's essence. She may speak about him as if he were a fairy-tale character, but the image that surfaces most potently, in Helga's odd mélange of words and worlds, is that of a Spanish American feudal lord, a figure whom she reveres: "The presence of the Bear was all I needed . . . the absent smile that lit his face at times when I was helping him out of his poncho or waiting on him at table, as if he had been one of those dazzling knights spoken of in my fairy tales" (48). The act of removing items of Daniel's rural, or "national," attire is one that she performs and recounts once again, when he asks her, in order to humiliate her, to take off his spurs: " 'With pleasure!' I exclaimed. And kneeling down swiftly on the stone floor, I began to undo the straps of those beautiful spurs with silver buckles that tinkled so prettily as he walked" (81). This toying with sadomasochism has a precedent in *La amortajada,* where Ricardo persecutes Ana María and other girls, but here it also tells a story of cultural fetichism: Helga will do almost anything, it seems, to worship the tangible signs of Daniel's rootedness in the country. He, on the other hand, does not love her; he still thinks of Teresa, his first wife, whose death seems to have been foretold not in fairy tales, but in some traditional ballads, which the text of *House of Mist* reproduces as its only instance of prolonged interlingualism (46–47; 105–6). Ultimately, as we shall see, the friendship between Helga and Serena, the singer of these folktales, will be instrumental in making Daniel transfer his love from Teresa to his new wife.

That Daniel stands as a strong figuration of rural South America becomes evident also in his turbulent relations with Maria, his twin sister, also known as Mariana or the Countess of Nevers. Sent to Europe as a child, Mariana returns to South America with a new name, a title, a foreign husband, and a rather extravagant lifestyle. In the story, Mariana appears at first as a dangerous token of deracination, but ultimately she emerges to provide a significant twist to the conceptualization of the nation, one that will admit into its fabric the idea of strangeness and foreignness. The conflict between brother and sister concerns the lands that they have inherited from their uncle, who built the house in which Daniel and Helga live. More generally, their discord is a reformulation of the entrenched debate about civilization and barbarism in Spanish American literature. Each sibling represents one of these poles in an extreme fashion. Daniel Viana is a kind of rural caudillo with little education, abusive of his wife, unwilling to care for the collection of manuscripts, paintings, and tapestries inherited from his uncle; Mariana de Nevers, with her European upbringing, lives in the capital, is married to a French aristocrat and takes a foreign lover, and is not overly concerned, despite her limited resources, about her profligacy. In a way, the hyperbolic figures of Daniel and Mariana are the unlikely offspring of Sarmiento's polemical debate, but they serve the novel's two intertwining stories well, as characters in Helga's sentimental education and elements in her tale of foreignness and nationhood.

That the clash between Daniel and Mariana should be read as a meditation on the nation—its spaces, its cultural limits—is first suggested by the appearance of the word *tranqueras,* or fence gates, in the text; it is the only Spanish word in the novel printed in italics, in fact, the only example of interlingualism in *House of Mist* where a word's meaning is not likely to be known by the average American reader. Unlike in *The Purple Land,* where regional terms are abundant, there are very few words in Spanish in Bombal's text besides such commonly known terms as "Señora" and "hacienda," which are never printed here in italics. The first appearance of *tranqueras* occurs when Mariana's journey to her hunting lodge is impeded by Daniel's refusal to open the road that leads to it through his property. Mariana protests, "Are you going to lend me the keys of your *tranqueras,* or force me to make a detour on roads that would break down my carriages and my nerves?" (52) The second appearance of the term, used twice, is in an argument between Daniel and some peasants from Mariana's lodge, who are trying to get to a lake where they suspect the boy Andrés may have drowned: " 'That's not the reason to break down the locks of my *tranqueras* and to come over to shoot at my ducks!' 'Oh no, don Daniel, sometimes we may jump over your *tranqueras,* but nobody has ever thought of going after your ducks' " (100). The *tranqueras* are markings of how *House of Mist,* rather unpredictably, without forsaking its U.S. American reader, takes up a classic theme of Spanish American literature. The conflict between civilization and barbarism triggers a discussion of the nation's patrimony, one whose eventual resolution will benefit Helga's lot. A compromise is ultimately achieved whereby the foreign and the native are united and housed within the nation's culture.

Who shall possess the land and houses of South America? Oddly, an accord is reached through Helga's convoluted melodrama, in which several characters are involved. Helga loves Daniel, but cannot turn down, simply to please him, Mariana's invitation to a magnificent ball at her house. As a poor orphan, she was not able to go to any parties, but now, thanks to Mariana, she has the chance. Daniel decides to attend as well, so that he can finalize a contract with Mariana's husband regarding the purchase of their hunting lodge. Once again, a fairy-tale imagination takes over the story, and Mariana emerges as a fairy godmother of sorts: she may be devoid of a magic wand, but is wearing "a black velvet dress spangled with thousands of little golden stars that scintillated at every movement of her body" (65). Melodrama ensues. Daniel, upset that Mariana's husband is away in Europe, decides to remain upstairs in their room and not go to the ball, while Helga, knowing that her husband is still in love with Teresa, lets herself be seduced by Landa, a man she has met briefly before when, walking in the woods of Mariana's hunting lodge, she had been chased by his greyhounds. In that predicament, Helga's dispossession had once again become obvious: "He was a tall young man, slender and dark. He looked at me silently for a few moments. I must have seemed queer lying there, pale, disheveled, covered with mud, with the dogs jumping all over me" (55). Rescued then by Landa, Helga had begun to fall in love with him, and she now decides to spend the night at his house.

Who shall possess Helga's heart? What heart will Helga possess? Sometime later, when Daniel finally forgets Teresa and learns to love his wife, Helga will regret that night of passion, but this, fortunately, will turn out to have been only a dream. Daniel helps her reconstruct the events: she had really fallen asleep on a sofa and heard Mariana go out with Landa; a fan that she thought she had forgotten at Landa's house is retrieved from between the sofa's cushions as evidence of Helga's innocence. But then, a terrible realization hits the protagonist: how can she remember a little clock on the mantelpiece of Landa's house? In one final coup de théâtre, Helga discovers that she is in effect remembering her mother's old house, where she had not been for years; to complete her happiness, the house, Daniel tells her, now belongs to her, a bequest in her Aunt Adelaida's will.

One may wonder what these twists and turns may have to say about the nation. The key resides in the various amatory possibilities suggested in the plot as well as in the invocation of folk ballads—the wellspring of much national art—as a counterpart to Helga's fairy tales. Both Daniel and Helga are coupled romantically—if not sexually—with two characters each: Daniel with Teresa and Helga; Helga with Daniel and Landa. Both Daniel and Teresa are natives of the country, while Landa is a foreigner; Helga herself possesses an ambivalent status. If Landa supplants Daniel in her imagination, it will be Daniel's fault, insofar he still loves Teresa, whose rootedness in and hold over this land are suggested by the traditional ballads people believe tell her story. Helga, on the other hand, is perceived by Daniel as the purveyor of the strange textuality of fairy tales. The turning point in *House of Mist* comes when Helga's friend, Serena, is finally able to convince Daniel that Teresa had never loved him.

Significantly, the first clue that Serena provides Daniel of Teresa's indifference is in the third stanza of the ballads, which, if it tells the truth, reveals that Teresa must have committed suicide:

Aguas abajo
La hallaron muerta
Ahogada y fria [sic]
Quiso morir!

Down the river
They found her dead,
Drowned and cold
She wished to die! (106)

It is Helga's true friendship with Serena, the singer of these ballads, that provokes Daniel's change of heart. Serena's words make it clear: "She wished to die! Do you hear, Daniel? She wished to die!" (106). The final piece of evidence is in Teresa's wedding ring, lost in the lake where she drowned; found by the boy Andrés before he himself drowned—when Mariana's workers tried to convince Daniel to open his *tranqueras*—it bears the inscription, "David" (107), the first name of Landa, with whom it is now revealed Teresa was in love. In an interlingual gesture of sorts, the name "Serena" recalls *sirena,* the Spanish word for "mermaid," thus uniting the folkloric traditions of South America with the fairy-tale world of Andersen, one which, after all, also boasts a folk origin; an alliance between these two imaginary realms brings about the story's happy ending.[36] With Daniel's love for Helga also comes a new friendship with Mariana: they decide to exchange her lands for his art collection. As for Helga's sense of unhousedness, that, too, comes to an end, when she has not only her house of mist, but also her mother's house in the city.

    The text does not say much about this house, where Helga's mother and father lived a love story of their own. We only have a brief glimpse into "that classical inner patio upon which all the rooms in our colonial houses converge" (153). In this archetypal space of Spanish America, also at the core of Borges's poetry, the unhomely reader who understands Bombal in her intricate trails and trials across languages and literatures has nothing to fear. The foreign now resides at the heart of the nation. But then again, this may all simply be a fairy tale—a happy ending that literary history does not yet register. After all, somewhere outside the reach of Helga's hearth, there lives, perhaps unhappily ever after, David Landa, a foreigner.

5

Babel; or, Explosion in the Library: Our Authors as Literary Historians

A GHOSTLY FIGURE IN MUCH OF THE ESTABLISHED DISCUSSION OF CUBAN and Spanish American literatures, the Comtesse Merlin appears unexpectedly in Guillermo Cabrera Infante's *Holy Smoke* (1985), a long, inventive history of tobacco written in English from the author's London exile. As it reveals Merlin to the reader, Cabrera Infante's text briefly adopts some of the conventions of traditional literary histories: listings of names, noms de plume, dates and titles; inclusion of biographical data deemed meaningful; and even cross-references to other writers with whom an affinity is perceived with the author under consideration:

> After her trip to Havana in 1840 the Comtesse de Merlin (1789–1852) published in Paris a book called, inevitably, *Voyage à la Havane*. The Countess, born in Cuba with an aristocratic name (Maria de las Mercedes Santa Cruz y Montalvo) became in France a French noblewoman by marriage and a Parisian from head to toe by make-like. She was thus able to look at Cuba with fond but foreign eyes, exactly like José Maria de Heredia, the French poet, would do fifty years later.[1]

Evidently, *Holy Smoke* is not in any way a scholarly work (it is not a conventional history of tobacco, either), but one may take Cabrera Infante's bit of literary archaeology as an element in one author's ambivalent, if ultimately receptive, meditation on the vagaries of Spanish American heterolingualism. That he is writing in English is, of course, no insignificant detail. An author with an illustrious career in Spanish that includes the language's highest honor, the Premio Cervantes, Cabrera Infante adopts another language as a literary vehicle, and this act is one more angle from which to examine the linguistic parameters of Spanish America's national and continental literatures. If these traditions rest on the bedrock principle of monolingualism, one may well argue that a heterolingual text such as *Holy Smoke* should be excluded from the literary corpus, even if composed by a major figure of the Spanish American boom.[2] But if one believes that an author's œuvre cannot be fragmented so that it may be comfortably subsumed into one given discourse, then Cabrera Infante's permutation ought to be read as a change in linguistic signs, but also, plausibly, as a new figuration of many of the literary codes that he had employed before: two languages connected in the figure of one author. In this regard, critics would be justified in reading across languages, an act whose consequences ought to affect the monolingual axioms of literary institutions.

If Cabrera Infante's heterolingual writings—*Holy Smoke,* but also short fiction such as "Nest, Door, Neighbours" (1973) and "The Phantom of the Essoldo" (1984)—should be viewed in relation to his previous works and, therefore, as elements dependent on the systems of Spanish American literature, one may also inquire into the effect that an official acknowledgment of these texts might have in the reading of heterolingual authors who never wrote in Spanish, like Merlin and Hudson. Reading *La Havane* and *Holy Smoke* side by side, as I do here, will produce a strange effect. It is as if two mirrors were placed face to face, and each work became an image of the other, one on which each could also behold its own reflection: *Holy Smoke* becomes more meaningful when seen through, or against, the content of *La Havane,* while Merlin's authorship is housed more significantly in Cuban literature when inspected through Cabrera Infante's English lenses. The spectacle of this game of mirrors may be an astounding sight, as one sees how Cabrera Infante translates and adapts a passage from Merlin's French text, probably by means of a Spanish translation, into his own English-language writing: Merlin's book is taken off its shelf, dusted and read, cut and pasted, rewritten in English—a second foreign tongue—and then placed in another shelf where readers, one may argue, are more likely to see it. Cabrera Infante's act, then, may well be a major step in the official acknowledgment of heterolingualism. As for Cabrera Infante's own text, by finding other works it resembles, it openly exposes its unhomely nature as well as certain meanings that otherwise would not be clear. Through Cabrera Infante's attention to Merlin's book, it will become evident not only that *Holy Smoke* is a book about remembering Havana, but, more specifically, about imagining one's own continuous absence from Havana; in this, the choice of another tongue plays a symbolic role, but, moreover, it introduces a whole new series of meanings that Spanish would probably not allow. Cabrera Infante himself defines *Puro humo* (2000), the Spanish translation of *Holy Smoke*, as "más que nada una crónica erudita de la relación entre el puro y el cine" [First and foremost an erudite chronicle of the relationship between cigars and cinema].[3] The author's claim is more difficult to substantiate in the English original, where the virtual sameness of the signifiers "Havana" and "Havanas" dominates the text in an openly self-conscious fashion.

Literature that reflects on the acts of writing and reading is of course a very old practice in the Hispanic tradition, and it is one that emerges with renewed strength in Spanish America's narrative fiction of the past several decades. Borges's stories, as is well known, often comment on their own textuality and, more generally, on the status of fiction itself, while authors linked with the narrative boom of the 1960s have extensively probed the literary traditions—national as well as continental—to which they belong. Some of these meditations have been essays, such as Carlos Fuentes's *La nueva novela hispanoamericana* (1969) and José Donoso's *Historia personal del "boom"* (1972),[4] but others have taken place in the realm of fiction, as in Fuentes's vision of the novel of the Mexican Revolution in *La muerte de Artemio Cruz* (1962) or Cabrera Infante's parodies of the Cuban literary canon in the various tellings of Trotsky's death in *Tres tristes tigres* (1967). Beyond the aesthetic pinnacles of these and other authors—Julio Cortázar, Gabriel García Márquez, Severo Sarduy, Mario Vargas Llosa—the boom is a watershed in the thinking and writing about Spanish American literature because of the culmination—if one believes, as many do, in literary-historical "progress"—it seems to represent. If there is no critical consensus on what, or whom, should be sheltered under the boom's resplendent umbrella, there seems to be at least an agreement on the clear sense of solidity that the international reception of these writers imparted on Spanish (or Latin) American literature. Some authors, particularly Cabrera Infante, have questioned the validity of such concepts as "Latin American literature" and even "Latin America," but few, if any, would quarrel with the premise that the landscape of writing by authors from Spanish America, whatever its literary contours may be in the end, seems decidedly more fertile and engaging, from the viewpoint of

aesthetics, than when Anderson Imbert published the first edition
of his *Historia de la literatura hispanoamericana* in 1954.

It is this sense of literary self-confidence, justifiable or not, that
may facilitate the incorporation of heterolingualism as a possibility
of Spanish American literature. That a retrieval of long-forgotten
or ignored texts should occur in literature itself, rather than in the
discussion about literature, comes as no surprise given the critical
mindset of these authors.[5] If Merlin acquires a new presence
through Cabrera Infante's fiercely centrifugal gesture of writing in
another tongue, other heterolingual writers—the French authors
born in various parts of the continent, poets like Heredia, Lautréamont, Laforgue, and Supervielle—may reenter the imaginings of
Spanish American literature through *Una familia lejana* (1980), a
novel in which Fuentes dissects the cultural ties that bind France
and the Spanish-speaking nations of the New World. As we shall
see, Fuentes's tale is a self-reflective act, in that his fictional consideration of heterolingualism concerns not only other authors, but
his own Spanish-language practice of writing as well. At the end of
the novel, the reader learns that its narrator is named Carlos Fuentes, a man whose story is both familiar and strange if read against
the real-world Fuentes's literary record, especially in regard to the
possible choice of writing in another tongue. Ultimately, however,
Una familia lejana interrogates not only the monolingual parameters of Spanish American authorship, but, beyond that, the validity
of all historiographical undertakings, including literary history. In
the end, the fabric of *Una familia lejana*—the pleasure of its storytelling, but also its contradictions and eventual opaqueness—
invokes a reconfiguration of Spanish American culture at whose
core lies, paradoxically, a veritable sense of unhomeliness.

In an interview conducted in the 1980s, Guillermo Cabrera Infante
was asked a question that concerned both his status as a Cuban
author and the more general issue of representation in art: "In your
fiction written in exile you have lovingly and wittily detailed Cuban
life, its voices, places, rhythms, etc., so that your work seems a kind
of 'À la recherche du temps cubain.' Do you see yourself as the
only real chronicler of Cuban life?" Cabrera Infante's answer was
as forthright as the question itself: "Not the only one but the best,
and as Margot Kidder likes to say, I'm not kidding."[6] Beyond his
habitual facetiousness, the author's written response to the question seriously dismisses three major Cuban fiction writers—Alejo

Carpentier, José Lezama Lima, and Virgilio Piñera—when it comes to the verbal depiction of Havana.[7] This mordant stance has turned Cabrera Infante into something of an enfant terrible, indeed, one of the continent's most polemic literary figures. If his relentless criticism of Fidel Castro's regime is no longer as exceptional as it was decades ago, his rejection of the very notion of Latin America as little more than an improbable *idée reçue* is still bound to raise some eyebrows in a literary culture where authors, more often than not, speak reverentially of supranational unity. Asked specifically by another interviewer about the existence of a Latin American identity, Cabrera Infante soberly considers the linguistic alterity of indigenous populations, only to end on a biting note that is nothing short of *épatant*: "Existen millones de seres humanos en el continente . . . que no hablan español siquiera. ¿No es una burla llamarlos latinos? Mejor hacían los griegos al llamar bárbaros a los que no hablaban su idioma" [There are millions of human beings on the continent . . . who don't even speak Spanish. Isn't it a mockery to call them Latins? It was better when the Greeks called those who didn't speak their language barbarians].[8] On the boom, his comments have been equally acerbic: "Except for Borges, I don't see I have much in common with the so-called Boom, which was a political club of writers."[9] If one recalls the etymology of the word "politics"—*polites*, someone who knows his or her way around the city—one can see that Cabrera Infante is no politician: he often presents himself as a rather impolite persona non grata in the continent's *ciudad letrada*.

Beyond these extraliterary pronouncements, the author's apparent self-exile from the Spanish American literary tradition is arguably most conspicuous in *Holy Smoke* and the other works in English, texts in which the imprint of Borges is less a polemic stance involving politics than a common doubt about the possibilities of representation. On a first level, Cabrera Infante's heterolingualism may be seen as one more step in a process of detachment from Spanish America begun when he first moved to Britain. If the blurbs on the back cover of *Three Trapped Tigers,* the English translation of *Tres tristes tigres,* already define the author as the only English writer who writes in Cuban, and if Cabrera Infante himself regards his work as that of "el único escritor inglés que escribe en español" [the only English writer who writes in Spanish],[10] *Holy Smoke* takes this conceit beyond mere authorial and paratextual rhetoric: Cabrera Infante may seem to emerge, finally, as a British

author working, as British authors do, in English, a kind of Cuban
V. S. Naipaul, given their common West Indian origins and, perhaps, flair for controversies.

Indeed, Cabrera Infante's new heterolingualism does go against
the idea of Spanish America as one literary community with Spanish as the common tongue of authors and readers—a notion that
the rise of the boom and its continental readership did much to
advance. Yet, it may be housed more easily within Cuban literature. Possibly because of Cuba's long history of forced or voluntary
migrations, writing in another language might be more common
among authors biographically linked with the island than in other
national traditions. Merlin, José-Maria de Heredia, Augusto de
Armas, José Martí, and Alejo Carpentier were all heterolinguals, at
least occasionally, while, more recently, linguistic plurality has
risen as one of the main features of the literature of exile, including
Eduardo Manet's novels and plays in French as well as the varie-
gated corpus of Cuban-American writing: María Irene Fornés's
plays in English; José Kozer's Spanish-language poetry;[11] Roberto
G. Fernández's novels in both languages; and the novels in English
of Cristina Garcia and Oscar Hijuelos, with various degrees of interlingualism.

Then again, *Holy Smoke* may strike one as different from other
Cuban heterolingual texts because of its seemingly willful, almost
provocative, detachment from the Spanish-language body of
Cuban literature. Merlin, as we saw, composes her travelogue in a
foreign language, but one can see, nevertheless, an attempt to in-
sert the text into Cuba's incipient literary tradition through its
genre fluctuations. Heredia's poetry focuses on various periods of
history, as in the cycle of sonnets of "La Grèce et la Sicile" and "Le
Moyen Âge et la Renaissance," but *Les Trophées* (1893), where his
poems are collected, ends with "Les Conquérants de l'or," his longest text, dealing with the Spanish conquest of the New World.[12]
Even when they write in English, Cuban-American authors habitually display their attachment to Cuba's main language by permeat-
ing their texts with Spanish words and phrases, as we saw in
Cristina Garcia's *Dreaming in Cuba*. But because it emerges as the
English text of an author who may well choose to write in Spanish,
Holy Smoke is read more easily than other heterolingual texts as
one that flaunts its extraterritorial nature through a notorious engagement with the language and literature of Britain. Yet, that English is indeed not a frivolous choice, but a requisite element in a

literary project that ultimately, like Merlin's travel narrative, addresses the author's exilic condition, may become obvious only in the text's gaps: its surrendering, specifically, of the possibility that Havana—Cabrera Infante's *temps perdu*—may be a *place* regained by literature. In his search for a lost space, the author now may seem to concede a failure, but one in which the absence of Cuba and Cuban voices—those "voices, places, rhythms" mentioned in Wilson's interview—suggests another kind of verbal triumph.

In a way, the presence of English is nothing new in Cabrera Infante's work. In Cuba, at the beginning of his career, he was censored by the authorities for writing a short story containing "English profanities."[13] *Tres tristes tigres* abounds in words and phrases in English; moreover, translations of his works into English have often been done with his collaboration.[14] But *Holy Smoke* eschews Spanish almost completely; moreover, if Havana and Cuba are not absent from the text, their treatment is overwhelmed by multiple allusions to other locations. Yet, as one reads not only what the text openly says, but also what it seems to conceal, one can corroborate the book's essential engagement with Cuban literature, well beyond the metonymic relation between "Havana" and "Havanas" (as in "Havana cigars"), which I treat below. Indeed, one can read *Holy Smoke* as the third, and strangest, work of a literary trilogy about the city, one that began with *Tres tristes tigres* and continued with *La Habana para un infante difunto* (1979). A more intricate text than what its semiofficial status as a compilation of cigar and tobacco lore may at first suggest, *Holy Smoke* tells the story of one character—identifiable in some ways with the author, as in previous works—for whom thinking, reading and writing about Havanas is, indeed, a good way to evoke Havana, but, more importantly, a metaphor for the literary impossibility of regaining that forbidden space.

In Cabrera Infante's chronicles of Cuban life, the two long novels set in Havana in the 1950s—"my Havana books" (315), as he calls them in the Wilson interview—are monumental creations, works that in effect are viewed by many as almost synonymous with the city. The first, *Tres tristes tigres,* was begun while the author still lived there, but it was revised and published in exile, so it is commonly read as a novel about things past: Havana as a lost city, or, more specifically, as in the title of his unpublished script, "The Lost City."[15] The author's will to revisit the old spaces of home, if only through literature, is announced in the title of the second novel. *La*

Habana para un infante difunto mimics not only the sounds and syntax of Ravel's title, *Pavane pour une infante défunte* (1899, 1910) but also the paratextual gesture of dedicating the work of art to someone: the pavane is for a princess, while Havana is for an Infante that no longer lives there, who no longer is the resident of Havana that he used to be. That the author should reward himself with his creation may be seen as unusual, and it probably is; in this case, one may read it as the text's first instance of humor, but it is also a poignant reminder of Cabrera Infante's passionate liaison with his absent subject: regardless of its possible status as autobiography,[16] its author has always insisted that "Infante" must be capitalized, and that the name be preserved in the title of the novel's English translation, *Infante's Inferno* (1984) (Souza, *Guillermo Cabrera Infante,* 140). Interestingly, the evolution of "Cabrera Infante" into just "Infante" engages a kind of Anglicism: the Hispanic practice of using the last name of each parent gives way to an English nomenclature, one that seems to announce the author's linguistic metamorphosis.

Reading *Holy Smoke* as the third text in the trilogy of Cuba's capital, what one notices first is that "La Habana" is now called "Havana." This transformation, of course, may be deemed inevitable now that the author writes in English, but the signifiers "La Habana" and "Havana" will play altogether different roles in the city's literary representation. The substitution of "Havana" for "La Habana" allows, first and foremost, a clearer phonetic and visual correspondence between "Havana," the city, and "Havanas," the cigars, ostensibly the subject of the work, which, superficially at least, displace Havana. (If the two English words are virtually identical, the same does not obtain in Spanish, where "Havanas" would be rendered as either "habanos," "cigarros," or "tabacos.") In *Holy Smoke*—the third Havana book—the metonymic relation between Havana and Havanas is at the heart of Cabrera Infante's new angle of vision: Havana filters into the text as an unreachable space, seen only through a veil of smoke, darkly. Havana, no longer home, is not even much of a literary possibility anymore; in an anti-Proustian gesture of sorts, the text ultimately rejects the notion that the past—or, as it often happens in Spanish American heterolingual texts, the physical space linked to one's past—can ever be regained through writing.[17] The title of a 1988 essay collected in *Mea Cuba* (1992) alludes to this sense of irrevocable loss; proclaiming the city's, not the author's, death, *La Habana para un infante difunto* now becomes "La Habana para los fieles difunta," which means "Havana, defunct to its faithful." But what kind of fidelity is this? The essay is a review of *La Habana,* a book of photographs by Manuel Méndez Guerrero; Cabrera Infante's main criticism concerns the city's representation: the absence of people in the photographs, as if Havana were just an uninhabited collection of admirable monuments.

In *Holy Smoke,* the death of Havana is not proclaimed yet. The lifeless being is not so much the city, which, after all, still sits on the coast of Cuba, but one of its old inhabitants, the author himself, who writes between the lines not so much of his former self, but about his literary demise vis-à-vis the city, even his own death in another country.[18] The text's association of "Havana" and "Havanas" reveals that the city is still the cherished subject of Cabrera Infante's writing, but there is now a new despondency, an even darker reality to consider. If *Tres tristes tigres* and *La Habana para un infante difunto* are rapprochements to life and living in the joyful metropolis of the past, *Holy Smoke,* despite its jovial tone, emerges as an obscure reflection on the prospects of death outside of Havana. If the "dead Infante" in the second novel's title may be interpreted as a nostalgic reference to the past, one that Ravel's melancholy music suggests, the phrase gains, through its ghostly apparition at the end of *Holy Smoke,* the concretely mournful undertones of Ravel's title. On that last page, *La Habana para un infante difunto* metamorphoses into "Le Havane pour un instant parfum," a strange phrase in French that means something like "The Havana [cigar], perfume for an instant." (As in English, the correspondence between the city and the cigar is very close, only a matter of grammatical gender; that Merlin's *La Havane* sounds almost like "le havane" will be an important consideration here.) "Le Havane pour un enfant parfum" appears as the title given to Mallarmé's nameless poem whose last line is "Ta vague littérature," which Cabrera Infante uses as the title of the second part of *Holy Smoke,* a personal anthology of texts and anecdotes about cigars. I shall examine in detail the possible meanings of Mallarmé's poem, often read as an *ars poetica,* in Cabrera Infante's text, but suffice it to say for now that one misquotation of it reveals the self-reflexive nature of *Holy Smoke,* especially as it concerns its treatment of death through the double veil of figurative smoke and literal heterolingualism. If *Holy Smoke* seems to repress the fear of not returning to Havana, even through literature, the author's citation—indeed, his rewriting—of Letter XXII of Merlin's *La Havane* constitutes a momentary vision of this submerged theme. Letter XXII tells a story of smoking and death in Havana, and its uses in *Holy Smoke* afford a clue for interpreting the three trios of words—pavane, La Habana, Le Havane; infante, Infante, instant; défunte, difunto, parfum—whose transtextual journey from Ravel's piece to the second novel's real title to the Mallarmé poem's apocryphal title—from French to Spanish to French—signals an evolution in Cabrera Infante's view of his own art.

When Cabrera Infante switched from Spanish to English and rendered "La Habana" as "Havana," he invoked a name not devoid of certain connotations in his new language: "Havana" does not draw a blank. Indeed, of all Spanish American cities, Havana may well be the one whose name appears most often in the titles of works—a most visible paratextual site—by English-speaking authors, especially U.S. American. A list may include poems, such as Langston Hughes's "Havana Dreams" (1933) and Wallace Stevens's "Academic Discourse at Havana" (1936), which begins with an image of color and sound: "Canaries in the morning, orchestras / In the afternoon, ballons at night" (142).[19] In *Havana Mañana* (1941), a travel guidebook of sorts, Consuelo Hermer and Marjorie May, even as they warn tourists about the city's sartorial formality, underscore "prettiness" in women: "Fans are still used with much coquetry. Lorgnettes are everyday equipment, for no Cuban woman would dream of hiding her beautiful eyes behind spectacles. . . . In the summer you can even carry a lacy parasol." In Graham Greene's ironic *Our Man in Havana* (1958), there is not only espionage, but also "duennas" and talk of girls growing up quickly in the tropics; *North of Havana* (1997), a thriller by Randy Wayne White set partly in Cuba, contains an epigraph by Greene and one by H. M. Tomlinson: "I had never seen primitive man in his native place till then." Reviewing Martin Cruz Smith's *Havana Bay: A Novel* for Amazon.com, Dick Adler speaks of "this hot Havana, ripe with the fruity smell of sex." There are films too: *Weekend in Havana* features Carmen Miranda, while *Havana* aims to be a story of revolution. Through its title and epigraph, a recent book, Wendy Gimbel's *Havana Dreams: A Story of Cuba* (1998), brings us back to Hughes's poem, whose interlingual lines, while they cite the fabric of *Havana Mañana,* mark the city with the language most people there speak: "Perhaps the dream is only her face— / Perhaps it's a fan of silver lace— / Or maybe the dream's a Vedado rose— (*Quién sabe?* Who really knows?)."[20]

The city also reappears in other languages and cultural forms, such as French and German opera. In Kurt Weill's *Aufstieg und Fall der Stadt Mahagonny* (1929), which has a libretto by Bertolt Brecht, the character of Jenny, a prostitute, sings an aria that summons up a conventional image of sexuality, dollars, and the tropics: "Ich bin aus Havanna, / meine Mutter war eine Weiße. / Sie sagte oft zu mir: / 'Mein Kind, verkauf' dich nicht / für ein Paar Dollarnoten, so wie ich es tat. / Schau dir an, was aus mir geworden ist' " [I come from Havana; my mother was a white woman. She often said to me: 'My child, don't sell yourself for a few dollar bills, as I have done. Just take a look, what has become of me.][21] Not heeding maternal advice, Jenny sells herself for thirty dollars, and later sings to regret it. But her "Havanna-Lied," as it is sometimes called, is not the first operatic consideration of love and interest in a context that alludes, either through words or music, to Cuba's capital. In her famous "Habanera"—often spelled "Habañera," with the exotic diacritics—Bizet's Carmen, too, sings charmingly of "l'amour!," yet this is a sentiment, here in the first act of Henri Meilhac's and Ludovic Halévy's libretto (1875), not devoid of cynicism.[22] Brecht's text has no other references to Cuba, and Carmen actually lives near the ramparts of Seville, not Havana, but one still wonders whether these outlandish citations of the city may hold any significance for Cuban authors—not only Cabrera Infante, but Merlin and others too—who write not of "La Habana," but of "La Havane" and "Havana" instead. If Cabrera Infante has specifically repudiated the view that Havana in the 1950s was "un burdel para los americanos" [a brothel for the Americans][23]—one more image within the foreign discourse of the city—the truth is that "Havana" and its incarnations in other tongues hardly suggest a tabula rasa. Why, then, speak about the city in a tongue where the vision of Havana is more fixed within specific parameters than it is in Spanish?

In *Holy Smoke,* "Havana" will imply some of the associations contained in these foreign depictions or allusions, but this is not a new thing in Cabrera Infante's practice of writing. *Tres tristes tigres,* particularly the section titled "Los visitantes," had already viewed the city through the self-revealing eyes of American tourists, writing an English-inflected kind of Spanish. One may think that adopting English in *Holy Smoke* implies the intention of repossessing the sign of "Havana" in an act of "writing back" to the imperial power, now in its own language. There is some of this ideological impulse in the text, but the foreignness of "Havana" emerges most powerfully as a self-conscious reminder that the city of words is never the real place: to write about an absent city, regardless of an author's talent or desire, is never an actual journey to the city. If "La Habana" is the name used in Cabrera Infante's past life there—an aleph of voices, places, rhythms, etc.—and in those fictions trusted to regain it, "Havana" is more of a motionless artifice: its connotations are narrower, because of its not infrequent, yet rather unvaried, uses in English and other foreign languages, thus emerging as a sign of diminished expectations from the realm of literature. Twice removed from the original, "Havana" is a copy that discloses itself as such, especially to readers aware of the specific artifice of the English signifier. It is as if a disenchanted author, sensing that "La Habana" is too rich to be put in writing, had stepped into a library of foreign books and libretti, read them, tested the various signifiers for the city in different languages, and discovered, as expected, that in the end none would retrieve Havana, but that any— say, "Havana"—would serve to expose the failings of mimesis and evocation.

More than a concrete search for Havana, then, *Holy Smoke* should be read as a circuitous voyage around the sign "Havana" mostly by way of its virtual twin, "Havanas." That the author has chosen English to undertake this journey is, indirectly, an invocation of certain polemics surrounding the literary figure of Borges, often accused of ignoring Spanish America and favoring European cultural forms, especially those of England.[24] Indeed, in a Borgeslike gesture, the text of *Holy Smoke* includes multiple citations from English literature, beginning with three among its four epigraphs. To quote from another literary tradition does not mean, of course, that a text is inserting itself into a foreign corpus, but, in the context of Spanish American writing—and of Cabrera Infante's stance regarding Latin America and his self-identification with Borges—the presence not only of English, but also of British literature, may be construed as one more sign of willful detachment. There are many textual allusions to the Hispanic tradition, but authors from the British Isles by far prevail: Marlowe; Shakespeare; Sterne; Dickens; Burton; Carroll; Wells; Wilde; Joyce; Maugham; Saki; Waugh. Cabrera Infante makes it clear that there is a good reason for the abundance of English-language authors; in the introduction to "Ta

Vague Littérature," he tells the reader that because English boasts a literature on the subject richer than that of other languages, it is "undoubtedly the language of smoking" (241).

In effect, writing in English does not entail that the author, like Borges, will regard England with any degree of reverence. Cabrera Infante's attitude toward his new home far from Havana is often ambivalent: if English may be perceived as a sign of affinity between the author and his adopted land, it is also the tongue in which distances become apparent.[25] Early in the text, for instance, the supposed scientific rigor of English lexicography—and the views of foreign lands contained therein—are regarded with irony, as when the narrator considers the possible origin of the word *cigarro*:

> Most probably *cigarro* comes from *cigarra*, cicada in Spanish. Male cicadas are called *cigarros* in southern Spain. These insects are as big as cigars, with thick long wings and dark brown colouring. It is not difficult for the Andalusian animism to see a cicada in a primitive cigar. This is, by the way, the etymology accepted by the *Oxford Dictionary of English Etymology*, which of course has a better track record with words than any other etymological dictionary available. (16)

This view of etymology as a kind of sport, as the phrase "better track record" suggests, is an ironical take not only on England—a quirky land of games, even in its academic discourse—but also, more importantly, on the possibilities of representation. In this, one detects a profound connection with Borges, in whose texts, as is well known, the act of writing—including nonfictional genres, such as the encyclopaedias featured in "Tlön, Uqbar, Orbis Tertius"—implies an invention of the world rather than a reflection thereof. That Cabrera Infante's Oxford dictionary should focus on the possible links between cigars and cicadas may be seen as absurd, but the passage exemplifies in fact the narrator's wandering search for Havana in *Holy Smoke*. What matters is the statement's humor, obliqueness, and ultimate falsehood. Havana is approached here through a series of associations: an English discussion about cigars in Andalusia necessarily invokes the worlds of Mérimée's *Carmen* (1845) and Bizet's opera, in which the protagonist's "Habanera" is a foreign reelaboration of a Cuban sound that may cite Havana, but only as a distant residue of the real city. Cabrera Infante in *Holy Smoke* most often speaks about the city only vaguely, as a vestige distantly fathomed in whatever matter the text literally addresses.

Nevertheless, there are enough personal and historical allusions to Cuba to suggest that one can perhaps still capture the past, at least through humor. The book's dedication relates the theme of tobacco to the author's life: "To my father who at age 84 doesn't smoke yet." In turn, his own biography is also intimately linked with Cuba's history and the conventional story of tobacco. Cabrera Infante's birth in Gibara, perhaps the site of Columbus's first landfall in Cuba, places him in a symbolically charged milieu, for Gibara is "also that bay named by Columbus Port of Surfs: exactly the spot of soot where Rodrigo de Xeres, a man made of smoke, discovered smoking for Europe and the world" (24). Throughout the text, smoking continues to be presented as an activity at the core of the Cuban nation; even the Spanish-American War is said to have begun "when a cigar butt blew up the *Maine* in Havana: the noisiest exploding cigar ever" (153). Moreover, in Cuba before the Revolution, tobacco was everywhere: "You see, in Havana all men smoked Havanas" (187). More significantly, since the nineteenth century, tobacco is identified with the Cuban experience of exile. Cabrera Infante describes how one can buy a cigar made in Tampa with Cuban-seed leaf, and the conclusion is, "Down there [in Florida] they have more than one-hundred years of experience in making Havanas away from Havana" (70).

Humor and puns, which in Cabrera Infante's writings often camouflage loss, intermittently allow a more melancholy strain to emerge in the text. At one point, the author posits what is perhaps the central question in *Holy Smoke*, one that is preceded by an observation about beauty and the word "Havana": "And yet, 'the luxury, the elegance, the snobbishness of smoking a cigar, and therefore its aesthetics,' writes the anthropologist Bronislaw Malinowski, 'are certainly forever associated with three syllables: *Havana*.' But what of the Havana far from Havana then?" (124). The perfect correspondence in English between "Havana" and "Havanas," or just "the Havana," gives rise to a textual polysemy—an aesthetics, even—in which writing about Havanas smoothly transforms into writing about Havana. To evoke Havana, or the rest of Cuba, entails a spatial as well as temporal displacement that ends not in the city of Havana, but in the fields where Havanas are grown: "Were you able to drive on a road to the past (the past being 1955, take a year or two) in a Nash Rambler, and on leaving

Havana were the time traveller to go across the province in a westerly direction, once you crossed the boundaries of Havana province you'd go on to Pinar del Rio" (32). Pinar del Río, where the region of Vuelta Abajo is located, is reputed to grow the best tobacco in Cuba, and therefore it is, in a certain way, a spiritual pinnacle of the Cuban nation, for tobacco, unlike sugar, is regarded as a noble crop, a lofty craft akin to winemaking.[26] But traversing this privileged territory is now an impossible journey for an exile, who may then espy tokens of Havana by visiting London's cigar shops. On Baker Street, he finds an establishment exhibiting "a beautiful poster of Romeo y Julieta cigars that must have been printed in Havana *circa* 1930" (62). Reminding one of a text by Borges, here is an instance of a journey across space, time, tongues, and modes of representation: Shakespeare's play crosses the Atlantic to Cuba, is translated into a cigar brand, then a poster, which then travels "back" to London, so that many years later a Cuban author can inscribe it as the residual presence of Havana.[27]

But this sentiment is approached with extreme caution in *Holy Smoke*. Beyond the incessant wordplay that lightens the tone of the text—eating meat is called "a beef encounter" (30), or a tobacco worker becomes "our man in Havanas" (39)—Cabrera Infante views the immoderate reaches of nostalgia with suspicion. He recounts Oscar Wilde's trip to the postbellum South, where upon praising the moon of Virginia he is told: "Ah, but you should have seen it before the war, Mr Wilde" (32). The discourse of Cuban-exile nostalgia has often been hyperbolic, and its clichés have been parodied by some Cuban-American writers, as in Roberto G. Fernández's novel, *Raining Backwards* (1988), where a character states, "Everyone knows that Varadero was the most beautiful beach, not only in the world but in the whole universe!"[28] As an addendum to Wilde's conversation in Virginia, Cabrera Infante remarks, "Many exiles (and quite a few inmates on the island) are ready to swear that the sun was milder before the Revolution" (32).[29]

In this context, abandoning the Spanish language altogether may help to defamiliarize nostalgia. In *Holy Smoke,* the author presents another view of the past, a period already covered and recovered in the two novels, but now, in English, seen just briefly. Toward the end of the book's first part, the author evokes La Antigua Chiquita, a restaurant in Havana, and it is the act of smoking that triggers the workings of memory:

What Wilde said of music is also true of smoking: it always makes you remember a time that never was. Though that past sometimes really existed. But it is not called music now, it is called nostalgia. I was yesterday at La Antigua Chiquita. Yesterday was sometime in 1957 and it was evening. It was evening at La Antigua Chiquita. It happened more than a quarter century ago but it was yesterday, for unlike music memory has no time. La Antigua Chiquita was a noted restaurant in Havana. (28–29)

The fact that La Antigua Chiquita is located in Havana is not revealed until the eighth sentence, and this initial reticence in naming the geography of nostalgia ultimately accentuates the dramatic appearance of Havana. Each of the four paragraphs that follow this one start with a mention of La Antigua Chiquita, and each may be read as a fleeting glimpse into the author's youth in the lost city. He calls it "my world in the evening" (29), a phrase that arguably subsumes much of Cabrera Infante's œuvre, not only the novels about Havana, but also his writings on film, collected in *Un oficio del siglo veinte* (1963), *Arcadia todas las noches* (1978), and *Cine o sardina* (1998), and now, tangentially, also the text of *Holy Smoke*. At the restaurant, the author remembers ordering a cigar: "It said, in burnt lettering, *25 Aromas de Luxe. 1957 Crop/Hand-Made in Havana Cuba* and on top, on the sliding lid, *Marca Independiente* and the characteristic laurel wreath circling the proud name of the brand" (31).

The interlingual labels—Spanish, English, and a "de Luxe" that looks more French than it does English—is a preview of the way in which the three languages will ultimately function as a discreet tool in the text's cautious tale of nostalgia. Havana and 1957 no longer exist, and the clearest emblem of their having vanished is the cigar itself, which becomes ashes as it is smoked: "This cigar is gone, the smoke as the unsmoked. They are visitors from another era: as far away and long ago as a distant planet we once visited" (31). *Far Away and Long Ago* (1918) is, of course, the title of W. H. Hudson's autobiography, whose nostalgic subtitle is "A Childhood in Argentina." Like the Anglo-Argentine author, Cabrera Infante forsakes Spanish and Spanish America and goes to live in England and write, at least occasionally, in English. In *Mea Cuba,* the last essay is entitled "El ave del paraíso perdido," and in it Cabrera Infante traces his own history as a reader of Hudson, from his first encounter with a translation of *The Purple Land* at a secondhand bookstore in Havana, to his search, once in exile, for Hudson's books in the libraries of London. Overtly nostalgic, the essay establishes an affinity between both authors based on the common experience of living outside of their native countries. Cabrera Infante's language on Hudson at times invokes the world of discoveries, even archaeology; he claims to make "descubrimientos americanos en cada libro suyo, *trouvailles*" [American discoveries in each book of his, *trouvailles*],[30] and he views Hudson, in turn, as a kindred spirit who also goes about London finding New World things in the most unexpected places, as when he uncannily detects from the street the song of an Argentine bird inside a house in Chelsea (483–84)— just like the man who walks around London in *Holy Smoke* finds the Romeo y Julieta poster in the cigar shop. That Cabrera Infante, in his elective affinities, should quote the title of a work by another heterolingual writer is an important element in the indirect story of exile that *Holy Smoke* tells. Even as he incorporates Hudson's words, Cabrera Infante, an unhomely reader, tells an unhomely history of Spanish American literature: authors and readers who find each other meaningful beyond the linguistic boundaries of the official discussion.

If nostalgia in "El ave del paraíso perdido" intensifies through the text's last paragraph, *Holy Smoke* soon curtails the sentiment with humor. After the author's remembrance of things past at the restaurant in Havana, he states: "Say good-bye, Time Traveller, said I, . . . *Dis au revoir, Marcel. Di adiós, tú. Adiós tú*" (31). However, this farewell to Proust—which also echoes the title of Eduardo Sánchez de Fuentes's "Tú," a nostalgic *habanera*—is equivocal, for it actually recalls not the conclusion, but the opening of *Du côté de chez Swann* (1913)—the first scene in the series— when Marcel is asked to take leave of his mother and her guests: "Oui, allons, va te coucher" [Yes; run along; off to bed].[31] Just as the initial memories in Proust's text focus on Marcel's leave-taking, so do those of Cabrera Infante, but he, unlike Proust, says good-bye to his beloved subject as well as to his native tongue. Indeed, the utterance "Di adiós, tú. Adiós, tú," ending as it does with the personal pronoun, has a distinctly Cuban resonance, one that the rest of the text will seek mostly to disguise—if to no avail, since *Holy Smoke* does end despite itself by telling a story of remembering Havana, one that finishes, significantly, with a title in French.

In this tale of cigars, the author distinguishes between the duration of smoking and that of remembering the act, but he does so,

again, obliquely, by alluding to Henri Bergson's title: "A good cigar
should last forever—or a few seconds: it's all on the lips of the
holder: *matière et mémoire*" (76). Although the text seems to refer
to the impression that good smokers know how to smoke slowly for
better enjoyment, the French phrase invokes a time that extends
beyond the mere physicality of smoking; to behold this beauty,
however, it takes a special vision, one that can appreciate the
meaning of gaps, both in life and in texts. As he underscores the
unstoppable flow of time, the author recollects and, moreover,
transforms previous texts. In an intertextual entanglement of Cinderella's happy story and one of Luis de Góngora's classic texts, a
sonnet on the theme of carpe diem (1582), Cabrera Infante speaks
of the possible transfigurations of a cigar: "The smoker who meets
a Condal, for instance, can look for the glass slipper, now made of
cedarwood instead of crystal, and see how just before midnight the
cigar becomes fragrance, then smoke, then myth, then ashes, then
memory, then nothing" (126). In the unhomely shadow of the
Spanish text, through the smoke of a Havana cigar, one can see
how the city named in the cigar vanishes, *se esfuma,* it becomes a
thing of the past that cannot be recovered. Moreover, the beholder
himself, the one whose recollections may preserve the memory of
Havana, will die too. The *tercetos* with which Góngora's sonnet
ends distinguish between a *tú* who is being addressed, and an *ello,*
her physical body, and both entities, because they are in the end
interdependent, will finish by turning into nothing:

> goza cuello, cabello, labio y frente,
> antes que lo que fue en tu edad dorada
> oro, lilio, clavel, cristal luciente,
>   no sólo en plata, o viola troncada
> se vuelva, más tú y ello juntamente
> en tierra, en humo, en polvo, en sombra, en nada.

> [enjoy thy neck, hair, lips, and brow
> before that which in your golden age
> was gold, lily, carnation and bright crystal
> becomes not only silver, but a violet cut short,
> and thou and all of it together turn
> into dirt, smoke, dust, shadow, nothing.][32]

The distinction between "tú" and "ello" also obtains in the text of
Holy Smoke, where the voice that remembers Havana in the third

person is addressed directly: "Adiós, tú." If Cabrera Infante is *tú*, Havana is *ello*, but in the final analysis it does not matter, for both are one and the same. In this sense, the text is not only about the end of a cigar, or of Havana, but also about the demise of that voice, *tú*, whose writing has been entwined with the verbal act of remembering that city.

That *tú* and *ello* will both end in "nothing" is suggested, if vaguely, in the last text of *Holy Smoke*, the nameless poem by Mallarmé called here "Le Havane pour un instant parfum." We have seen how "La Habana" may easily become "le havane," the Havana cigar, just as it does in the pair Havana/Havanas. In order to understand the change of "difunto" into "parfum," one must also take into account Cabrera Infante's rewriting of the last line in Góngora's sonnet: "fragrance" is the first step in the Havana's disolution, and by this is meant not only the act of smoking a cigar, where the aroma is a primary sign of its eventual vanishing, but the practice of writing about Havana, where the city's perfume— redolent of Havanas, thus reawakened by smoking—may be both what triggers memory—the sense of smell also invokes Marcel's past—and a metaphor for the author's art through which Havana appears, at least for an instant, in the semblance of a living thing. Yet if, in remembrance of Ravel's funereal title, the name "Infante" now becomes a brief "instant" in time, suggesting the author's mortality, the text by Mallarmé will be misquoted as if to conceal the inevitable passage.

Mallarmé's poem (1895) is traditionally read as an *ars poetica*, where the cigar becomes an image to express how life should be best transposed into poetry: as a smoker sheds the cigar's ashes so that it can burn better, so the poet should exclude the real from his poetry, because, as the last two lines claim, "Le sens trop précis rature / Ta vague littérature" [Too fixed a sense erases / Your art in its faint traces]. In *Holy Smoke*, the poem, aided by its placement in the text and its false title, also functions as a key to Cabrera Infante's new heterolingual text and aesthetics. "Ta Vague Littérature," for instance, first appears textually as an interlingual phrase when Cabrera Infante employs it as the title of the second part of the book, the anthology of literary texts or anecdotes that ends, in a circular fashion, with Mallarmé's poem. If the phrase itself is French, one's reading of it ought to be interlingual—but not in one step. First, one views it as "Tabac Literature" because "tabac" pronounced with a Cuban accent may very well sound like "ta vague;"

from there, it is only one more language to "Tobacco Literature,"
which is in effect an accurate description of the book's second part.
"Ta Vague Littérature," then, unites three languages to mean
something new: a French verse becomes an English interlingual
phrase, if one can keep in mind the workings of English syntax,
French semantics, and Spanish phonetics all at once. But this is
not the only way in which Cabrera Infante rewrites Mallarmé. Beyond the poem's false title and the interlingual usage of its last line,
Mallarmé's text, in the hands of Cabrera Infante, contains a
change that may be read as one last expression of hope in the face
of imminent eclipse. The original poem[33] begins with an image that
is suggestive of death:

> Toute l'âme résumée
> Quand lente nous l'expirons
> Dans plusieurs ronds de fumée
> Abolis en autres ronds (164)

> [The entire soul evoked
> When slowly we expel it
> In many a ring of smoke
> Till other rings annul it] (77)

The phrase "expirer l'âme" means "to die," but Cabrera Infante
changes "expirons" into a life-preserving "aspirons"—not to expel,
but to breath in. The reality of ever reaching Havana, in life or in
literature, is excluded from *Holy Smoke,* but at the last minute the
deadliest image in Mallarmé's poem is replaced, or hidden, by one
evocative of life. In this last breath of *Holy Smoke,* the text refuses
to acknowledge the old truths: literature is nothing but vague repre-
sentations, one cannot go home again. Yet, this optimism—this in-
halation of Havanas—is only a matter of seconds: the perfume of
Havana lasts only one instant. Beyond Mallarmé's notion that reality may destroy literature, there is also in *Holy Smoke* the existential awareness that literature cannot abolish the hazards of real
time. As in Góngora's sonnet, all ends in nothing; even worse, it
might be too late to seize the day.

In this context of renunciation of Havana, we may once again
consider Cabrera Infante's vague literary-historical approach to
Merlin's *La Havane.* On the one hand, the author's words, which I
cited at the beginning of this chapter, are an unusual act of recognition. Merlin, the virtually forgotten writer, is retrieved by a fellow

Cuban, and a long passage of Letter XXII, translated into English, is quoted in his text: this may well be the first time most Cuban readers have actually read anything by Merlin. On the other hand, one may also argue that Cabrera Infante's words, especially those framing the passage from *La Havane,* actually gainsay the possibility of reading Merlin as a full-fledged Cuban author. Once again, as is often the case with heterolingual writers, an ocular metaphor informs literary evaluation. If, as we saw in Chapter 2, Anderson Imbert could focus on Hudson's Argentine eyes to grant him the status of an Argentine writer, Cabrera Infante emits here an opposite judgment on Merlin's literary vision, one that dismisses the heterolingual Heredia as well. The author's words bear an uncanny resemblance to those of Félix Tanco, who in the 1840s had faulted Merlin for looking at Cuba "con ojos parisienses" [with Parisian eyes].[34] The reader's blindness is excused by blaming the author's vision, and the author stands accused of lacking any true insight into the national condition.

But briefly speaking about Merlin with a scholarly mask, Cabrera Infante is about to imagine a literary history of Cuba unlike any other seen before: one into which strange authors and languages are admitted, titles of works are invented, and literature itself tells its own story of detours and dissonances better than any official history has. In Cabrera Infante's citation of Merlin, what one sees is as telling as what remains invisible. In the translation of the passage quoted in *Holy Smoke,* two sentences are omitted that may have some bearing on Cabrera Infante's own self-perception as an author. In the first, Merlin speaks of an elderly relative who wants to know what kind of report she plans to transmit to Europe about the island of Cuba; *Holy Smoke* includes Merlin's mention of this man, but deletes her description of him as a refined spirit "qui figurerait très-bien dans les salons de Paris et de Londres" (2:215); [who could play a fine role in the salons of Paris and London]. The second sentence, omitted entirely, is a comparison between Cuba's moonlit night and dawn in England and France (2:220). That these and other passages are deleted may be due to Cabrera Infante's interest in accelerating Merlin's leisurely narrative, but it is curious nevertheless that two gaps should concern the two authors' places of residences outside of Cuba. Would mentioning both European capitals and countries in such a context give rise to a perilous analogy between Merlin and Cabrera Infante, one that would count *him* out of Cuban literature? In each of the authors' tales of two cities—Havana and Paris, Havana and London—one can surmise how one writer's Parisian eyes may be used as a lens to look at, or into, those of one possible Londoner, a former resident and writer of Havana. If he once proclaimed his wish to be out of Spanish America's narrative boom, and if he rejoiced at his metamorphosis into a British writer, one can detect in Cabrera Infante's *œuvre* written in exile a clear will to assert his status as a Cuban author; the titles alone—*La Habana para un Infante difunto* and *Mea Cuba*—are acts of possession over his lost city and country, just like naming her book *La Havane* was Merlin's beachhead in the literary recovery of her absent birthplace.

Yet, notwithstanding the apparent definiteness of the label "foreign" applied to Merlin's eyes, Cabrera Infante's reading may be regarded obliquely as the location of another, more profound kind of insight. If Merlin is a Parisian "by make-like," as he claims, it may be argued, then, that she is still inherently a Cuban, and that her act of mimicking a French author is nothing but an obvious mask—like those Martí speaks of in "Nuestra América." Given her insecurity in her adopted land—the fact, to paraphrase Borges, that her French condition, not being an "act of fate," must then be an "affectation"—those qualities in her writing that most clearly bespeak a European authorship, such as exoticism, are not, as it were, the real Merlin, but another kind of screen altogether, one needed to disguise her own foreignness in France. Merlin's sudden exposure in *Holy Smoke* emerges, then, as a polysemous endeavor, a masking and an unmasking: even as he presents her to the reader in the guise of an outsider, Cabrera Infante reveals the face his words would conceal. It may be his own face, too, because, after all, one may descry in *Holy Smoke* a strange optic not unlike that of Merlin. Here is an author whose "La Habana" is now "Havana," a foreign sign beneath which a "fondness," resembling Merlin's, for the old familiar haunts in that city is plainly in sight. Indeed, the heterolingualism of *Holy Smoke*, as an emblem of the author's melancholy views, is not altogether different from that of *La Havane*.

Merlin and Cabrera Infante, then, emerge as birds of one feather; that of the two she is more of a rara avis, given her exclusive use of French as a language of writing, is of little consequence in the end, because strangeness is bound to surface as a constitutive element in the lives of nations. What Cabrera Infante achieves as he subsumes Merlin's words into the fabric of his own text is an oblique acknowledgment of heterolingualism as a meaningful practice in

Cuban literature. Despite its French textuality, the passage from Merlin's Letter XXII makes better sense when read as an instance of *costumbrismo*; its detailed focus on the quirks of local mores and patterns of speech—depicted interlingually, as seen in the Pepiya/ Pepilla dialogue I cited in chapter 3—calls for an unhomely reader who can perceive the aesthetic norms of Cuban literature as they filter strangely into the other tongue. Likewise, despite its English textuality, Cabrera Infante's invocation of Merlin's text in *Holy Smoke* is understood more clearly within the systems of Cuban literature: *costumbrismo*, but also, more importantly after *La Havane*, that mode of representation in an interlingual and interliterary variation invented by Merlin. Writing, like her, from a position of in-betweenness, Cabrera Infante finds in Merlin a precursor of sorts, and his text, by being an imitation of her imitation, recuperates *La Havane* as a possible matrix in Cuban literature. If literary critics and historians tend to speak of Merlin as a foreigner, Cabrera Infante himself speaks like a foreigner, not only in another tongue, but in a language resembling that of Merlin in which, for instance, Spanish is recorded and then translated, giving rise to the interlingual: " 'What do you mean *calzones*?' she exclaimed. 'Longjohns'?" (157).

If these uncanny affinities exist, why, then, does Cabrera Infante refer to Merlin's text as "a book called, inevitably, *Voyage à la Havane*?" (155). No such book may be found at any library. Was he simply unaware that *Viaje a la Habana* was the abridged Spanish version of *La Havane*, the only title that ever existed in French? Or else, *felix culpa*, one may attach another meaning to the author's words: a book written in a foreign tongue about a place from which one is destined to be absent forever can only be read, inevitably, as a *Voyage à la Havane*. Yet, through Cabrera Infante's reinvention of Merlin's book, we can begin to imagine a new library of Cuban literature where these strange volumes may yet occupy a prominent shelf.

In the metaphorical house of Spanish American literature, where rooms may differ according to an author's perceived rank, one can easily envision Carlos Fuentes as a figure in the atrium, guiding those who enter here around the official spaces of the house, but also leading them, from time to time, to concealed nooks and crannies where the house reveals its unhomeliness. Fuentes is no ghost—indeed, he is arguably the most consistently visible of

Spanish American authors—but his imagination often ventures into regions where familiar things may suddenly become strange, or where the strange may be deemed as an intrinsic, if often repressed, element of the continent's culture. This is the case with *Una familia lejana,* a labyrinthine fiction that takes one to rooms where Spanish American self-fashioning, in close contact with the culture of France, is seen as coming dangerously close to vanishing; yet the fact that the author is not afraid to go *there* allows, as I will discuss here, an act of salvage, one that concerns the possible revelation of Spanish America's heterolingual authors as figures in the house. In a sense, *Una familia lejana* is the tale of a haunted house: the Clos des Renards, in Enghien-les-Bains outside Paris, where a series of uncanny events seems to occur. But one may also read this text as the story of a haunted household: a Spanish American lineage whose split existence on both sides of the Atlantic engages once again the old issues of civilization and barbarism, the native and the foreign, and, more importantly, the difficulty of narrating the story of Spanish American culture, where writing in another tongue is an intrinsic, but especially troublesome, element.

The novel's convoluted plot involves several characters—a family of sorts—whose surname is Heredia, like that of the two nineteenth-century poets from Santiago de Cuba who chose different tongues as literary vehicles.[35] José María Heredia wrote patriotic verses in Spanish and became one of the leading names in Spanish American Romanticism, while José-Maria de Heredia, his cousin, left his native country at an early age for France (where his mother was born), eventually becoming a Parnassian poet and a member of the Académie française. If the first Heredia is part of the canon of Cuban and Spanish American literatures, the other Heredia is at most a curious margin within them.[36] Distant relations, the Heredias undergo a literary rapprochement through the meditation on writing, culture, and history of Fuentes's text, which leads to a retrieval of the second Heredia and other French-language poets from Spanish America. Indeed, the novel makes a case for reading heterolingual authors as meaningful presences in the continent's literature. By revealing their existence and incorporating lines from their texts into its own fabric, *Una familia lejana* tinges itself with a foreignness that gainsays the monolingual premises on which the continent's literary culture is built, while at the same time it bestows on the heterolinguals an aura of familiarity—as the novel's title already indicates—not obvious in other contexts. But Fuentes's reflection takes place as part of a narrative text in which the story—the *historia*, both "story" and "history" in Spanish—remains mysteriously opaque and essentially contradictory even when it reaches its purported dénouement. By the end of the novel, the blueprints of Spanish America's cultural history may seem less clear than before: by means of the text's focus on the mazelike fabric of heterolingualism, both Spanish America and "historia" emerge as unsettled, if still necessary concepts.

Of the two Heredias, the one whose writings matter most in *Una familia lejana* is the Francophone poet; the epigraphs of chapters 13 and 14, for instance, are lines taken from sonnets in *Les Trophées*. But the Hispanophone Heredia is also invoked, if obliquely, in the novel's discussion of Spanish American identity. Hugo Heredia, one of its main characters and, as the novel concludes, also a narrator, is an archaeologist working in the Toltec ruins of Xochicalco, in central Mexico. The novel's first episode in Spanish America takes place at this site, a backdrop that summons up one of José María Heredia's canonical poems, "En el teocalli de Cholula" (1820), in which the speaker, in a romantic gesture, sits at the foot of an Aztec pyramid and reflects on the barbaric elements, past and present, of the continent's history.[37] An exile from Cuba in Mexico, where he dies, Heredia fashions a speaker who dwells on images of human sacrifices—"sacerdotes horribles, salpicados / con sangre humana rostros y vestidos" (51) [horrible priests, their faces and clothes splattered with blood]—as a reminder to the recently independent nation, torn by internecine strife, of how despotism may lead to its own self-defeat: the pyramid at Cholula stands empty, the poem suggests, because the Aztecs themselves provoked their own downfall.[38] This vision of Spanish American violence is mirrored in the behavior of archaeologist's son, a young boy named Víctor Heredia, who mistreats those whom he considers his inferiors, such as the indigenous servant at a house in Cuernavaca. Soon, these acts of cruelty are repeated in Paris, where the novel's plot moves: Víctor whips the Spanish servants of Branly, his and his father's French host. Beyond Heredia's poem, Fuentes's text discusses Spanish American identity through the formula of civilization and barbarism, particularly as it concerns the imperial relations between Europe and the New World. But *Una familia lejana* problematizes the old conceptualizations. If some Spanish Americans, like Sarmiento, regard civilization as originating across the Atlantic and migrating to American shores, Fuentes's text presents an opposite journey: a wild child of the Americas transports his brutality into the very heart of Europe. But this may well be seen as a return trip, for it soon becomes evident that Víctor is a creature of the Spanish conquest, and his behavior a sad aspect of its aftermath; Branly's servants recognize in him a brutality they have already experienced in Spain: "así eran esos señoritos de España y de ultramar, señoritos de horca y cuchillo, vamos" [that's how young gentlemen were in Spain, and across the ocean, well! there they were young lords of gibbet and blade].[39]

If Spain and Spanish America share a common fabric in Fuentes's fictional world, as one can see in *Terra nostra,* the first chapters of *Una familia lejana* initially design Mexico and France as complete opposites: the former is a land of violence, while the latter emerges as the abode of reason.[40] The text's opening scene, where most of the narration also takes place, is the dining hall of the Automobile Club de France, overlooking the civilized expanse of the Place de la Concorde; during the French Revolution the square functioned as the site of executions—it was then called Place de la Révolution—but the novel views it now as a location of European civil order. With these refined spaces as a backdrop, Branly, a French aristocrat in his eighties, recounts to another man—whose name, it will be revealed in the penultimate chapter, is Carlos Fuentes—the tale of his journey the previous summer to Mexico, specifically Xochicalco, where he met the Heredias. Fuentes, as he frames and narrates the story that Branly tells him, contrasts the twilit softness of the Île-de-France on that November afternoon with the blinding sun of the summer morning in Xochicalco, with its volcanoes and ravines. At this point, Branly's story, set in Mexico, and Fuentes's story of Branly's storytelling, set at the Automobile Club, seem worlds apart, yet both—stories and worlds—will eventually merge to the point of becoming one and the same: everything, it turns out, is inextricably linked with everything else.

The next section of the novel treats the Heredias' visit to Paris in September and their stay at Branly's *hôtel particulier,* a mansion "construida según las reglas del barroco desapasionado de Francia" (22) [constructed according to the dispassionate principles of the French baroque] (17). The allusion to the Baroque is important; it appears as a wild factor latent in the culture of France, which Branly's contact with the Mexicans—and with a Frenchman of mixed Spanish American and French descent—is about to wake.

Indeed, Branly's orderly life is perturbed by a game that his Mexican guests play in every new city they visit: to look in the telephone directory for people who may share their names. Thus they find a mysterious man named Victor Heredia (the "French" Heredia), and young Víctor's prize for "winning" at the game is to visit his namesake. At this point, the novel's storyline is about to shed its classical directness and take a baroque turn. Branly and the boy arrive at the Clos des Renards, where the French Heredia lives, a space whose very architecture and landscaping seem at first to exemplify the triumph of reason and logic that the novel associates with the French mind: "un jardín de la inteligencia, un tablero de ajedrez donde la selva salvaje de cierta imaginación romántica era vuelta a domar por la exactitud geométrica de arbustos, céspedes, pensamientos y urnas de piedra dispuestas en perfecta simetría" (35) [a garden of intelligence, a chessboard where the wild woods of a surely romantic imagination had been checkmated by a geometric precision of shrubs, greensward, pansies, and stone urns placed in perfect symmetry] (31).

But Branly observes that something is missing from this otherwise perfect French garden: "ese elemento del orden que al duplicarlo acentúa la simetría: el espejo de agua" (31) that [element of order that as it duplicated would accentuate the symmetry: a mirror of water] (31). *El espejo de agua* (1916) is the title of a book and poem by Vicente Huidobro, the Chilean who lived in Paris and wrote in Spanish as well as French. In the heterolingual library of allusions that *Una familia lejana* collects, Huidobro's present, yet missing, text obliquely engages the issue of representation, which, in stories and history, may be regarded as an impulse toward making sense. If at first one may read Huidobro's deletion as an obscuring of heterolingualism, one may also interpret it, paradoxically, as calling attention to the practice and making its absence in literary histories more conspicuous. Texts in other tongues, because of their hybrid nature, suggest a story that undermines symmetry and order, elements that national stories, including those told by literary scholarship, often underscore. In Huidobro's aesthetics, specifically, the poet is commanded not to reflect reality, but to create it; the mirror of water, in that sense, implies the problematic relationship between texts—or, more generally, the institution of culture—and the world they seek to represent and thus domesticate.[41] *El espejo de agua* also complicates the telling of Spanish American literary history, because it also exists in a French version, a heterolingual double: *Horizon carré* (1917).[42] In this sense, Huidobro's mirror, whose refusal to focus traditionally on reality is banished from this rational space, functions as a link to the second intertext in this fragment, Borges's "La muerte y la brújula" (1942), in which symmetry suggests a semblance of order—indeed, a narrative logic—that is ultimately revealed as deceitful. Heredia's house mirrors Triste-le-Roy, the villa in Borges's tale where the detective, through the rational stories he tells himself, becomes blind to reality.[43] In the end, despite its facade, the suburban villa of Clos des Renards will reveal itself to be as mendacious as Triste-le-Roy: orderly stories and locations marked by symmetry—their spatial figurations—hide realities that are far more complex than one may be willing to accept.

The most puzzling aspect of *Una familia lejana* is the French Victor Heredia's story, which, narrated by himself to Branly and then reported to the reader by Fuentes, is one in which migration and linguistic change—from the Caribbean to France, from Spanish to French—are regarded as milestones in a long journey to civilization:

> la historia de una familia cubana emigrada a Haití durante las revueltas de fines de siglo contra la dominación de España, asimilados primero a la lengua francesa en los salones de mármol carcomidos por el calor y la sal de Port-au-Prince y luego . . . a la Francia de la primera guerra, . . . ¿parientes del poeta?, ¿cuál poeta?; no, concluyó con un aire de fatiga presuntuosa, habían desterrado el uso de la lengua española, que para ellos traía sólo recuerdos de barbarie, revolución e impaciencia. (49)

> [a tale about a Cuban family that had emigrated to Haiti during the uprising against the Spanish at the end of the century, first assimilated into the French language in the heat- and salt-pocked marble salons of Port-au-Prince and then . . . into the France of the First World War, . . . Relatives of the poet? What poet? {No,} he concluded with an ostentatious air of ennui, they had forbidden the use of Spanish, which for them carried only memories of restlessness, barbarism, and revolution.] (45–46)

In a certain sense, the journey of this Heredia's family reverses that of José-Maria de Heredia, whose ancestors came to Cuba from Saint-Domingue in 1801, after Toussaint Louverture's revolt, and only then emigrated to France. But it also resembles that of José María Heredia, whose father was named José Francisco

Heredia, a name that resembles that of the French Victor's father in the novel, Luis Francisco, who, to confuse the matter even further, marries a French woman, as Domingo de Heredia, José-Maria's father, did. Curiously, in this fictional tale of the Heredias, the biographies and identities of the two real-world poets named Heredia are intertwined to such an extent that they seem to become one and the same. The almost mirror-like quality of the poets' names—whose double figuration resembles that of *El espejo de agua* and *Horizon carré*—further entangles this story that, despite its initial thrust for sense, ultimately refuses to be clear. When Branly asks Victor if his family are relatives of "the poet," Victor's answer is equally vague, for "¿cuál poeta?" may mean "which of the two?" or it may also imply that Victor is unaware of the existence of any of the two poets. Upon Branly's apparent clarification, Victor seems to deny a connection with the Hispanophone Heredia, a denial that also triggers his linkage of the Spanish language with barbarism.

But even as one Heredia is insinuated, the other Heredia appears as a shadow in the text. The narrator's words to describe Victor's gestures—"an ostentatious air of ennui"—as he denies his family's relation to the Hispanophone poet invoke a line from *Les Trophées*, one which focuses on the origins of European migration to the New World. José-Maria de Heredia's sonnet, "Les Conquérants" (1869), presents the Spanish conquest of the New World as the ambivalent undertaking of frenzied men: "Comme un vol de gerfauts hors du charnier natal, / Fatigués de porter leurs misères hautaines, / De Palos de Moguer, routiers et capitaines / Partaient, ivres d'un rêve héroïque et brutal" [As from their native eyries hawks take wing, / Spurred by the miseries they proudly share, / Bravos and chiefs from Palos de Moguer / Sail drunk with dreams that brutal conquests bring].[44] (The sonnet's second line will also reappear, in French, as the epigraph of chapter 14 in the novel.) This allusion, again, underscores the barbarism on which Spanish America was founded and, indirectly, the civilization that France may represent for those who wish to escape from it. Eventually, however, Spanish America takes over France: in the novel's last episode, on an unusually warm evening of November, the swimming pool of the Automobile Club—perhaps the mirror of water missing from the Clos des Renards—is transformed into a jungle of sorts. If the two Heredias seem to fuse into one, so the spaces of Paris and the New World are superimposed on each other. Here, a clue is also to be found in Heredia, this time in "Le Récif de corail" (1882), the sonnet from which the epigraph of chapter 14 is drawn:

> Le soleil sous la mer, mystérieuse aurore,
> Éclaire la forêt des coraux abbysins
> Qui mêle, aux profondeurs de ses tièdes bassins,
> La bête épanouie et la vivante flore. (154)

> [The sun under the sea, mysterious dawn,
> Lights the forest of Abyssinian corals
> Which mixes, in the depths of its warm basins,
> The blossoming beast and the living flora.]

In this submarine vision, things appear in reverse fashion: the sun is now under the sea, plants are like animals, animals are like flowers. In *Una familia lejana,* there is an imagination linked with New and Old World relations that transposes the usual order of things; moreover, the literary bodies of France and Spanish America coalesce because of specific authors and books into one library.

Originating in the fusion of the two Heredias into one vague figure, this Babel-like library also implies an ambivalent interpretation of the continent's practice of writing. Even as it retrieves the distant relations between the two poets, the novel tells a literary story of Spanish America in which authors have uncanny doubles, or in which a European author's unity, as it migrates to the Americas, is divided into two, or into two halves. That Fuentes's fictional Heredias are named either Victor or Hugo, somehow splitting the authorial solidity of the nineteenth-century literary colossus, seems to suggest an essential fissure in the history of the New World, or in the fabric of its people: a cultural breach at the heart of Spanish America. Indeed, the idea of rupture acquires physical concreteness towards the end of *Una familia lejana,* when Hugo Heredia narrates his son Víctor's finding, at the excavation in Xochicalco, of an indescribably beautiful object, "una unidad de tal manera excelente, sin fisuras, como una poderosa gota de oro cóncavo, que no necesitaba adorno, talla o añadido alguno" (174) [a unity so perfect, so seamless, like a potent, concave drop of gold, that it needed no added embellishment, carving or detail] (182). In this sublime instant of archaeology, Víctor's reaction is to break the object in two, throwing both halves away from him, and thus, in a sense, mimicking the various ruptures in the history of Mexico and Spanish America—one of which will be heterolingualism.

But the meaning of Víctor's perfect object must first be read within his father's conception of pre-Hispanic cultures, which he explains to Branly, on the Frenchman's second trip to Xochicalco, as the central lesson of Mexican antiquity: "todo está relacionado, nada está aislado, todas las cosas están acompañadas de la totalidad de sus atributos espaciales, temporales, físicos, oníricos, visibles e invisibles" (176) [all things are related, nothing is isolated; all things are accompanied by the totality of their spatial, temporal, physical, oneiric, visible and invisible attributes] (183–84). In the fantastic tale of *Una familia lejana,* the restoration of the object will also concern the union between Víctor and André at the Clos des Renards, a possibility to which the text alludes vaguely in the two children's sexual coupling inside a Citroën overgrown with vegetation, or in the exchange of a black child for a white one in which Alexandre Dumas *père,* whose father was a Creole from Saint-Domingue, is involved. The French Víctor Heredia convinces Hugo to take his son to Paris so that this union may occur, but what preoccupies the archaeologist most is to *locate* the two pieces of the broken object so that its unity can be restored. In effect, the fragmented, multiplying story that *Una familia lejana* tells concerns the location—in the active sense of the word—of Spanish American culture. The possibility of finding again Hugo's *trouvaille* and reconstituting it pertains to an even larger vision of the continent: "Quisiera que las mitades de ese objeto se reuniesen para que esa unidad no falte en el arte, la historia, el pasado, la cultura, como usted guste" (183) [I {would want} the halves of that object to be rejoined; I wanted their wholeness to become a part of art, of history, of the past, of culture, of anything you can name] (192).

The search for this unity is one of the central themes in Fuentes's narrative, and in *Una familia lejana* it involves the existence of those Spanish Americans—mostly writers, but others too—who have torn themselves from their native countries and emigrated to France. They emerge in this novel as a sign of the continent's fragmented condition. Can their art somehow be incorporated into the culture of Spanish America? Is there a history that can tell their various stories? Besides Heredia's poetry, there are many instances in the novel of intertextuality with the writings of Lautréamont, Jules Laforgue, and, chiefly, Jules Supervielle and his poem "La Chambre voisine" (1930). Other authors, such as Balzac, Lamartine, Musset, and Nerval appear in the text several times, and, at the end of the novel, the narrator invokes some of their names in conjunction with those of still other Spanish American authors who lived in Paris: "desde aquel puente, en el mismo instante en que Nerval escribía *El desdichado,* se contemplaba ya en las aguas incesantes César Vallejo; en el Boulevard de Latour Mabourg oiré la voz de Pablo Neruda, en la rue de Longchamp la de Octavio Paz, cruzaré con mi espectro la Passerelle Debilly" (211) [from that bridge, at the very moment Nerval was writing *El desdichado,* César Vallejo was gazing at his reflection in the rushing water; on the Boulevard La Tour-Mabourg I will hear the voice of Pablo Neruda; on the Rue de Longchamp, that of Octavio Paz; along with my specter I will walk across the footbridge of the Passerelle Debilly] (222). This passage exemplifies well the strange history of literature that *Una familia lejana* seems to tell, one that is both factual and fictional. If Neruda's and Paz's voices are believably linked with the streets mentioned—they are the actual sites of Chile's and Mexico's diplomatic missions in Paris, where both authors served—Nerval and Vallejo were of course not contemporaries, an anachronism that also reflects the many temporal inconsistencies in the novel's plot, which I will examine below. As for "mi espectro," it concerns Carlos Fuentes himself, the first-person narrator: the ghostliness of Fuentes is one more turn of the screw in this tale of duplications and split identities.

In the strange gathering of authors and books that the novel convokes, Fuentes is arguably the strangest. As if mirroring the fate of those Spanish American natives who became something else— French authors, for instance—Fuentes in *Una familia lejana* plays with the idea of his own dormant foreignness: the actual possibility of his having become, had he chosen to write in another tongue, not the Mexican or Spanish American novelist that he is today, but an altogether different creature. Toward the end of the novel, as if exchanging the literary lives of the two poets named Heredia, the character named Fuentes sheds the author's familiar biography and finds a new one that resembles not so much that of José María Heredia, but that of José-Maria de Heredia. The real-world Fuentes, after living in various cities in South America where his father, a diplomat, was stationed, returns to Mexico City and eventually becomes one of the major figures in Spanish America's boom; but the fictional Fuentes remains in Buenos Aires and Montevideo for ten years, then goes to live in Paris, where he becomes, as Branly puts it, "más francés que otra cosa, ¿no es verdad?" (204) [more French than anything else. Isn't that so?] (215). Not only that, but Branly asks Fuentes to imagine what might have happened had he chosen a different path:

> Imagine si hubiese regresado a México al terminar la guerra y se hubiese arraigado en el país de sus padres. Imagine que publica su primer libro de cuentos a los veinticinco años y su primera novela cuatro después; habla usted de México y los mexicanos, las heridas de un cuerpo, la persistencia de unos sueños, la máscara del progreso. Queda para siempre identificado con ese país y su gente. (204–5).

> [Imagine; what would have happened if you had returned to Mexico after the war and put down roots in the land of your parents? Imagine; you publish your first book of stories when you are twenty-five, your first novel four years later. You write about Mexico, about Mexicans, the wounds of a body, the persistence of a few dreams. You remain forever identified with that country and its people.] (215)

Indeed, following closely what Branly asks the fictional Fuentes to imagine, the real Fuentes—born on November 11, just like the novel's narrator—published his first collection of short stories, *Los días enmascarados* (1954), when he was twenty-five, and his first novel, *La región más transparente* (1958), four years later; moreover, the author—this figure in the atrium—is now clearly identified with Mexico and its people, and the themes mentioned by Branly are not only those that lie at the heart of Fuentes's narrative fiction, but also, specifically, of *Una familia lejana*.

That the circumstances surrounding the real Fuentes's life are seen as "imagination," while those attached to the fictional character are called "truth"—Branly's tag question in Spanish, "¿no es verdad?," means literally "isn't it truth?"—concerns not only the status of those two concepts in Fuentes's narrative—indeed, in all fiction—but the story of heterolingualism that *Una familia lejana* obliquely recognizes and tells. Fuentes has often stated that, as a bilingual person—he was raised partially in Washington, D.C.—he could very well have chosen to write in English; the fact that "everything" had already been said in that language made him choose Spanish instead.[45] Moreover, the absence or weakness of civil institutions throughout Spanish America, in Fuentes's eyes, gives literature—and its real-world authors—a very specific role to play.[46] That he now is able to speak about, or for, certain writers disregarded by national and continental literary institutions may be seen an important element of the author's endeavor. The text of *Una familia lejana,* however, goes even further, for it questions not only the linguistic and cultural limits of Spanish America, but also the possibilities of *historia* itself. The confusion surrounding Fuentes's identity is only one element within the text's problematization of culture and storytelling: what is the full story being told?

Like *Terra nostra,* the novel of the Heredias tantalizes the reader by implying the existence of a story that, confusing as it may be, ultimately will make sense; yet, in the end, it becomes apparent that the nature of characters and events will remain mostly unclear, even contradictory. There is a double narrative movement in *Una familia lejana.* On the one hand, it opens almost as a traditional tale of adventures and exoticism, a story that readers can follow with absolute certainty about the events being narrated. In a sense, the text's narration, with its heightening unintelligibility, mirrors the notions of "French classicism" and "Spanish American baroque" on which cultural formulations are initially based. The novel's beginnings are indeed classically simple,[47] but this reassuring transparency soon gives way to a text whose inconsistencies affect the central notions of plot and characterization: after an accident, Branly is forced to stay at the Clos des Renards for a few days and nights, and what he experiences there may soon be described, indeed, as a baroque proliferation of memories, dreams, and omens. Some of the text's difficulty may be attributed to its engagement with mysteries and the fantastic genre, but *Una familia lejana,* like other fictions by Fuentes, recounts a story in which events and characters end up violating not only the codes of realism, but also those of narrative logic, especially the temporal axis. From the room where he is convalescing at the Clos des Renards, Branly overhears Víctor and André play a game of countries and capitals in which the reader soon senses, indeed, an uncanny regression in time: "—Capital de Noruega. —Oslo. —No. —Perdón. Cristiania" (57) ['Capital of Norway.' 'Oslo.' 'No.' 'Sorry. Christiania'] (55). On one level, the boys' game serves to tell the novel's story of imperial relations—there is mention of the Belgian Congo, French Equatorial Africa, Anglo-Egyptian Sudan, etc.—but it ends by frustrating the reader's expectations of final clarity; after all, the novel's initial classicism suggests that some light will be shed, eventually, on any obscurities. Instead, there is only an ironical self-reflecting exposition of the various unanswered questions, most of them concerning the French Heredia's origins and age (145, 169; 150–51, 176), which ultimately contradict all possibilities of verisimilitude and logic that have tantalized the reader throughout the text. Any attempt to solve these and other mysteries can only end in failure— unless, of course, one is reminded of Fuentes's poetics of simultaneity,[48] or if one looks at the puzzle itself as its own solution, a riddle on which other types of stories, including literary history, may ponder.

This is not the place to list or analyze in any length the various inconsistencies of the novel; suffice it to say that the text, on its general meditation on stories and history, engages throughout in the interrogation of its own storytelling. As he listens to Branly tell a story that he himself will retell, Fuentes, the very nonomniscient narrator, admits his "titubeante comprensión del relato" (109) [faltering comprehension of {the} story] (111). Frequently, perhaps because of this absence of sense in the story he has to transmit, Fuentes simply reports verbatim what Branly says—"me dice ahora Branly" (39) [Branly is telling me] (36); "me confiesa ahora" (78) [he confesses now] (77); "me cuenta" (93) [he tells me] (94)— without much of an attempt at interpretation. Branly himself admits that he does not know the full story yet, and that he will not *know* it until he *tells* it (110; 112). This relationship between knowledge and telling obtains until the very end of the text, when Fuentes—at the jungle-covered swimming pool of the Automobile Club, where the bodies of young Víctor and André are united— realizes that the story of the Heredias, these New World transplants in Paris, is very much also about himself: "Heredia. Tú eres Heredia" (214) [Heredia. You are Heredia] (225). In the face of this epiphany, what he understands is the limits of his own knowledge, which he expresses here in terms that invoke memory and the telling of stories: "Nadie recuerda toda la historia" (214) [No one remembers the whole story] (225).

Meaning both "story" and "history"—the text has dealt too obsessively with history to pretend otherwise at this late stage—one may certainly read this last line of the novel both as a comment on the tale that it purports to tell, but also in the more general context of Spanish American history, including that of literature. Almost like an archaeologist, the real-world Fuentes has brought to light heterolingual works that are not well known in the discussions of Spanish American literature; with them, he weaves a new text. The lines of Supervielle's "La Chambre voisine" are quoted in French throughout the novel; it is Branly's favorite poem, and he tells Fuentes: "es de allá, como usted" (28) [he comes from your world] (24). But chapter 16, specifically, is literally written with the lines of the poem translated into Spanish. In a sense, the effect is that of the jungle covering the swimming pool. Supervielle's text is intimate and simple in its mournful images:

> Laissez-le seul sur son lit,
> Le temps le borde et le veille,
> En vue de ces hauts rochers
> Où gémit, toujours caché,
> Le cœur des nuits sans sommeil.
> Qu'on n'entre plus dans la chambre . . .

> [Leave him alone on his bed,
> Time tucks him in, watches over him,
> Within sight of those hidden rocks
> Where, forever hidden, moans
> The heart of sleepless nights.
> Let no one enter the room . . .] (ix)[49]

In a Baroque takeover, Fuentes surrounds those lines with materials that pertain to his own tale of two worlds: "Han salido de las tumbas en las barrancas podridas de manglar y plátano para reunirse en los altos miradores rocosos donde gime, siempre escondido, el corazón de las noches sin sueño. Que nadie entre más a esta recámara, exclama la mujer con el viejo traje del Primer Imperio" (126) [They have emerged from the graves in rotten barrancas of mangrove and plantain to be reunited on the high rock cliffs where moans forever concealed the heart of insomniac nights. Let no one enter that {room} again, exclaims the woman in the outmoded dress of the First Empire] (129).[50] With Supervielle's words amid his own, Fuentes tells the remarkable story of a mother and child who manage to be reunited in spite of death and time. The text makes that clear: it is a feat of memory, love, and imagination. The last words in the chapter express this sense of wonderment: *Reunidos al fin*" (127; emphasis in original) [Reunited at last] (130). If no one remembers the whole story, someone at least does remember this part. Likewise, if no history can exist that will remember all writers and texts, there is one work, *Una familia lejana,* in which the strange heterolinguals are reunited through a novelist's imagining; indeed, this is a space in which the words of all are intertwined into a new whole, the wholeness not of literary history, but that of one novel and of narrative fiction.

The heterolinguals, with their stories of separation from Spanish America, are easily viewed as emblems of the continent's essential fissures. But, as the title of the novel already suggests, despite the wide cultural distances between Spanish America and France, one may still speak about the familial ties that bind the Heredias and their literary kin. In this novel about the telling of tales, all authors from Spanish America, regardless of their tongue, may emerge as part of one household—provided one decides to imagine and narrate them, beyond the logic of linguistic unity, as one literary community. This strange grouping of distant relations may seem an overwhelming or frightening prospect, because it is a clear reminder of the house's possible fragmentation: it is a story that makes little sense. But, then again, to repress these authors who will not go away may be still more dangerous. Here, the novel's epigraph, taken from Proust and opening this tale of a haunted household, may offer the best clue: "Ce qui est affreux, c'est ce qu'on ne peut pas imaginer" [The frightening is that which one cannot imagine]. By openly imagining, instead of repressing, the frightening—such as a haunted house outside of Paris inhabited by a ghostly man named Heredia, or an entire culture whose elements may always seem about to scatter into senselessness—Fuentes's text may be viewed as a site in which the verbal act of exposing one's unhomeliness is already a form of shelter and refuge.

Habitations of the Unhoused: An Afterword

Not long ago and not so far away, at the same university in whose library I found the volumes of Merlin's *La Havane* with which I began this study of heterolingualism, I was a short-lived student of classical Arabic. Having just arrived on that campus, I was unfamiliar with its Semitic Museum, where the course was held. On the first day of school, I became lost for some time among the old stones and sarcophaghi of the museum's collection, but I eventually found the classroom. Sitting around a table, there were ten or twelve students, most of whom spoke our lingua franca, English, with inflections denoting their national origins, I thought, in various parts of Asia and Europe. Right across the table from me sat a woman whose accent I could not quite place; I asked her where she was from, and it was revealed that she and I had been born in the same country. Our families had left when we were children and had gone to live in cities on different continents; we had learned other tongues and picked up other accents, so that even when we switched into Spanish, our mother tongue, we did not speak or sound quite the same. Holders of four or five different passports between the two of us, we had not lived in the one city where most of our compatriots had settled and were now quite at home, so, in a way, we felt doubly detached from our country of origin. Yet I think it was in those degrees of separation from home that we found a common bond; we became good friends and later also took a German class together, where we read Freud.

In a way, this personal story of language and nation may be read against what I defended in these pages, namely, that a country is not a tongue, a tongue is not a nation, and if ever the twain shall meet, it might be, as in the realm of fiction, entirely coincidental. Indeed, what ultimately linked my friend and me was a linguistic sign, yet what mattered most therein was not only what we had in common but also what we did not, elements that variously revealed and concealed our shared birthplace. If, looking back now, I can imagine us as a kind of community, it is because our speech

194

was both familiar and strange: sounds and words that marked us as natives of one land coexisted in the same verbal space with other sounds and words that bespoke our absence from there, our lives elsewhere, our shared foreignness. The uncanny resemblances that at times became overt in our speech were vestiges of a common past, ever more precious because of their rareness and *rareza,* their strange attributes. Yet, our variants, whose origins one could trace to various other countries, various other friends, also united us: in the end, all of our sounds and words, those that were familiar and those that were strange, told one story of unhomeliness, a narrative at whose core, splendidly visible or vaguely out of focus, lay the notion of home, or, more exactly, homes.

Our verbal woods—cultural patterns and forms, as one can read in Fuentes's *Una familia lejana,* do not resemble logically designed gardens—were crisscrossed by paths whose various forks and convergences could also serve to trace a new map of Spanish American literature and its foreign tongues. Or, more in tune with the architectural diction that I have adopted here, one may speak of the blueprints for a new house of Spanish American literature. There, in that fantastic structure, one can envision rooms for the likes of Merlin and Hudson whose doors open into yet other houses in the forests of culture, just as the rooms of Bombal and Cabrera Infante lead to the house's atrium, where they also may stand, a canonical space—but not necessarily a more riveting one. In this house where authors can now be sheltered who were previously unhoused, readers are free to move around freely and visit, as it were, whomever they please, which is, after all, what Spanish American readers unconcerned with institutions—academic, political—have always managed to do.

Why call this the house of Spanish American literature? Why not simply dispense with this linguistically specific term and speak, instead, of Latin American literature, or the increasingly visible literature of the Americas, both of which are polyglot concepts? Or why not adopt, once and for all in the new global village, Goethe's old notion of *Weltliteratur,* and by this mean that literature is supranational? Indeed, new figurations of Steiner's extraterritorial condition abound—in literature, film, and opera—in which several tongues coexist as if to suggest a brave new world without verbal frontiers. A U.S. American text, Guy Davenport's novella "The Dawn in Erewhon" (1974), is daringly written in English interspersed with passages in Dutch, French, German, Latin, even

Greek, while *Trois vies et une seule mort* (1996), by the Chilean filmmaker Raúl Ruiz, is in French—but, in one more turn of the screw, all characters speak that language with an accent. *Marco Polo* (1996), the opera by the Chinese composer Tao Dun, has a multilingual libretto—English, Italian, German, Chinese—by Paul Griffiths, an Englishman; at one point, the chorus sings the word "journey" in ten different tongues. More and more, there is evidence of a veritable world culture; in it, many languages as well as interlingualism function both as elements and emblems of the unstoppable hyphenation among citizens of the world.

Yet, in the case of those authors from Spanish America who write in a language other than Spanish, the venerable concepts of Spanish American literature and its various national traditions ought to be retained, for in what other cultural contexts would the essential unhomeliness of heterolinguals reveal and conceal itself so meaningfully? The same holds true for the concepts of country and continent. Before evicting these notions from the study of literature, one must note that for the unhomely to be identifiable, there have to be houses—not the old structures where authors and texts were valued for the sense of familiar cohesion they instilled, but new spaces where the overt and the secret can be seen to come and go at will. If Cuban literature, for instance, did not exist, we might have to invent it in order to make sense of Merlin's narrative of her journey to her strange birthplace, and the same applies to other heterolinguals. Their oddity may still be visible within other configurations, but not as patently as in the specific categories, such as *costumbrismo* or *literatura gauchesca,* that critics and literary historians long ago designed for the study of Spanish American literature.

But why still focus on the unhomely nature of heterolingual writing? Why not just translate these authors into Spanish for the average reader, and thus resolve to once and for all the problem of nonunderstanding that worries Richard, or Ricardo, Lamb in *The Purple Land?* This, in fact, has happened in multiple cases and the outcome has been positive, in the sense that readership has been increased. Yet, if that is gained in translation, what is lost is, paradoxically, what is gained and should have to some extent remained missing: Spanish, now the language of the text, is no longer a virtual absence, no longer the author's—or the reader's—original loss. New readers emerge, and this is a fortunate turn of events, but one should not hide again the old, dusty books in the other tongues, their strange beauty. In the first sentence of "Das Un-heimliche," Freud situates his discussion clearly within the realm of aesthetics: "It is only rarely that a psycho-analyst feels impelled to investigate the subject of aesthetics, even when aesthetics is un-derstood to mean not merely the theory of beauty but the theory of the qualities of feeling."[1] From the start, then, Freud wants us to feel the *unheimlich* as a part of verbal art. Indeed, it is a fortunate coincidence that, in English, "unhomely" should sound as the ant-onym of plainness, for there is an aesthetic value in the seemingly ruptured fabric of heterolingual texts that may not be found else-where. As one reads the texts of Merlin and Hudson, Bombal and Cabrera Infante, one can see languages and literary systems sur-facing and vanishing intermittently. In a sense, they constitute winding transcultural formations that may yet emerge as more fig-ures in our *barroco de Indias*, just as the house itself of Spanish American literature, with its new habitations, may be regarded not just as a cool postmodern edifice, but as an obscure Baroque abode in whose various chambers one can hear a proliferation of lan-guages, inflections, and silences.

Writing this in the many-tongued city of Los Angeles, this place called L.A. whose two letters are the residue of the older Pueblo de Nuestra Señora la Reina de los Ángeles, I am reminded of Leonard Forster's observation in *The Poet's Tongues* about the passionate sentiments that often surround languages: "Since the Romantics we have all been brought up to believe that each language has its mystery and its soul, and that these are very sacred things, in whose name much blood has been shed in our lifetime and is still being shed."[2] Indeed, in the decades since the publication of For-ster's study, issues of linguistic difference have continued to pro-voke much conflict around the world, not the least in California, whose old name is presently half-concealed, just as the second half of its southern double is also habitually repressed: the various fig-urations of Alta California and Baja California—where houses and fear, the domestic and the foreign, intersect visibly and secretly—may stand to benefit from being seen in the light of Freud's vision of the uncanny as "nothing new or alien, but something which is familiar and old-established in the mind and which has become alienated from it only through the process of repression" (217). But the superimposition of languages in these lands also tells a story that pertains to Spanish America, not only in the old sense of terri-torial loss, but of cultural continuity: the continent's cultural forms, including those of literature, function well beyond political or linguistic borders, and English, for one, cannot be seen as just a foreign language.

Writing this in English, I cannot but lament the absence of my mother tongue, the feeling that this other language in which I have conducted this study may not have been the clearest tool to retrieve, for a mostly monolingual literary culture, the works of those whose own linguistic alterity has led to obscurement. Yet my sense of loss translates itself into a specific gain: the architectural metaphors that I have employed here function best in English, where "home" stands as the opposite of "abroad," "Home Secretary" and "domestic flights" conjure the nation, and another word for one's country is, again, "home." There also seems to be a measure of justice as well as irony in the notion that I, seeking to situate the heterolinguals as unhomely figures, should place myself by virtue of my other tongue—by mirroring, in effect, the alterity of their practice of writing—in an equally unhoused position. Given that Spanish remains the continent's lingua franca, the unhomely habitations I have sought to raise may well house authors who still remain in search of readers.

Yet, my own sense of critical unhomeliness, however, is illusory, because I have an advantage that Spanish American heterolingual authors lack. My situation is not so peripheral, after all. As I finish this study through which I have sought to shift somewhat the linguistic foundations of Spanish American literature, I am also aware that the established discussion of this literary tradition, of which my study seeks to be a part, is hardly a monolingual affair. Critics and literary historians, including those from Spanish America itself, have long written in other tongues, and this practice is, of course, hardly surprising: humanists, after all, are established masters of several languages. The heterolingualism of critics may well serve as another stepping stone in a fuller recognition of that of authors and general readers. In a field where linguistic crossings are numerous, the multilingualism of the discussion may constitute a new angle from which to obtain an insight into the continent's heterolingual body of writing; literary scholars who live, teach, and travel "abroad" are, after all, among those best situated to act as readers of these unhomely texts, as many, indeed, already do.

In José-Maria de Heredia's "Le Lit," there is yet another invocation of houses, this time through the figure of that most intimate of objects, a bed. First published in a book entitled *Le Meuble en France au XVIe siècle* (1887), by Edmond Bonnafé, the sonnet may well be read as an emblem of Heredia's dual stance: at the heart of French cultural institutions, but also in a location of displacement regarding his native land. The speaker focuses on the role that beds play in the lives of humans, as sites of birth, repose, love, and death, and ends on a sense of loss, perhaps the poet's meditation on his own unhomeliness:

> Heureux qui peut dormir sans peur et sans remords
> Dans le lit paternel, massif et vénérable,
> Où tous les siens sont nés aussi bien qu'ils son morts.
>
> [Blessed is he who can sleep without fear or regrets
> In the paternal bed, solid and venerable,
> Where all his loved ones were born and also died.][3]

Once again, the dual motion of heterolingual texts emerges here. Where, in what room, is Heredia's bed? Does it lie in Cuba? Will he lie in France? The poet's *beatus ille* links him with a classical past and, specifically, with Joachim Du Bellay's memorable Sonnet 31 in *Les Regrets* (1558), whose speaker beholds his own exile and hopes to be blessed like Ulysses, who made a voyage but returned to live among his people for the rest of his time. But if Du Bellay refers to one land, his native Anjou, whose language is the language of the text, Heredia has two tongues and, in the end, two Ithacas. While Du Bellay's sonnet ends on an invocation of his native rivers and hills, that of Heredia concludes on a mournful note where birth and death are united. Yet, there might be nothing to fear in these lines, for nothing is concealed—not the strangeness of houses and nations, nor that of one's self. Having imagined a literary habitation for his own unhousedness, Heredia now sleeps in expectation of readers who will find their own horizons in his text.

Notes

INTRODUCTION

1. My focus is not on the categories of Self and Other, which is underscored by many of the essays in *An Other Tongue: Nation and Ethnicity in the Linguistic Borderland*, ed. Alfred Arteaga (Durham: Duke University Press, 1994). Instead, I view linguistic alterity in the context of Freud's "Das Unheimliche," whose flexible interplay between the strange and the familiar, I seek to show, provides a model for reading and speaking about heterolingual writing in the Spanish American context. Also, since I treat individual authors whose other tongue is often only their own, not that of an identifiable social group, I do not speak of "minority language." Yet, since heterolingual works are written in another tongue and, at least when viewed together, constitute a textual family of sorts, some of the power relations analyzed in *An Other Tongue* and in the general discussion of minority language will in effect become apparent here. Distinguishing itself from the broader meanings of Bakhtinian heteroglossia, my own term "heterolingualism" combines a Greek prefix and a Latin root to encapsule the interlingual nature of many Spanish American texts written in foreign languages and, more generally, the landscape that emerges when one looks at a literary tradition in which authors choose to write in various tongues.

2. As will become apparent, I use the term "literature" in a broad sense to encompass not only such modes as the novel, poetry, etc., but also—as it normally happens in the established discussion of Spanish American literature—other forms such as historical and political discourses.

3. For a detailed discussion of Sahagún and his group, specifically the extent to which Book Twelve of the Florentine Codex can be considered "an authentic product and expression of indigenous people, Nahuas, and Nahuatl speakers" (28), see James Lockhart's introduction to *We People Here: Nahuatl Accounts of the Conquest of Mexico*, ed. James Lockhart (Berkeley: University of California Press, 1993), 27–37. Lockhart's splendid edition of Book Twelve includes both the original Nahuatl and Sahagún's translation into Spanish, as well as Lockhart's rendering of both versions into English. See also Walter Mignolo, *The Darker Side of the Renaissance: Literacy, Territoriality, and Colonization* (Ann Arbor: University of Michigan Press, 1997). On the functions of Quechua in Guaman Poma, see Rolena Adorno, *Guaman Poma: Writing and Resistance in Colonial Peru* (Austin: University of Texas Press, 1986).

4. In *Sor Juana Inés de la Cruz o las trampas de la fe* (Mexico City: Fondo de Cultura Económica, 1985), Octavio Paz discusses the relations between Baroque aesthetics and the self-perceived "strangeness" of the criollos in New Spain; see

chapter 2 of my study. The linguistic diversity of New Spain would be part and parcel of the strangeness the criollos could discern in their midst.

5. Rafael Landívar, *Rusticatio mexicana,* ed. Octaviano Valdés (Mexico City: Jus, 1965), 45. Unless otherwise indicated, all translations are my own. José Mata Gavidia views Landívar's choice of Latin in the context of scholarly communications; see 94–96. For Octaviano Valdés's discussion of the poem as an expression of Spanish American *mestizaje,* see 13–14. Also a Jesuit exiled in Bologna, the Chilean Juan Ignacio Molina is the author of *Saggio sulla storia naturale del Chili* (1782), a possible influence in Pablo Neruda's *Canto general* (1950); see Enrico Mario Santí, "*Canto general:* Caligrafía de la historia," in *Por una politeratura* (Mexico City: Ediciones del Equilibrista, 1997), 111–12.

6. See, for instance, Enrique Anderson Imbert, *Historia de la literatura hispanoamericana,* 9th ed. (Mexico City: Fondo de Cultura Económica, 1995), 1:146. Anderson Imbert's history, arguably the most complete in the field, is analyzed in Chapter 2 of this study.

7. Speaking about the "disciplinary division of labor" between literature and anthropology, Andrew Bush contrasts how works by Mariano Melgar (Peru, 1791–1815) and Juan Wallparrimachi Maita (Bolivia, 1793–1814) have been differently read; while Melgar's transposition of the *yaraví,* a native form, into Spanish has secured him a place in the literary canon, Wallparrimachi's adaptation of the Spanish *décima* into Quechua was acknowledged in the established discussion of Spanish American literary culture only recently. "Lyric Poetry of the Eighteenth and Nineteenth Centuries," in *The Cambridge History of Latin American Literature,* ed. Roberto González Echevarría and Enrique Pupo-Walker (Cambridge: Cambridge University Press, 1996), 1:380–81. In the interdisciplinary volume, *Latin American Identity and Constructions of Difference,* ed. Amaryll Chanady (Minneapolis: University of Minnesota Press, 1994), only articles from the field of anthropology deal with minority languages.

8. Rolena Adorno, "Cultures in Contact: Mesoamerica, the Andes, and the European Written Tradition," in *The Cambridge History of Latin American Literature,* 1:33.

9. See Carmen Vásquez, introduction to *Souvenirs et mémoires de Madame la Comtesse Merlin: Souvenirs d'une Créole,* by María de las Mercedes Santa Cruz y Montalvo, comtesse Merlin (Paris: Mercure de France, 1990), 13.

10. See, for instance, William Luis, "Latin American (Hispanic Caribbean) Literature Written in the United States," and Luis Leal and Manuel M. Martin-Rodríguez, "Chicano Literature," in *The Cambridge History of Latin American Literature,* included in the volumes devoted specifically to Spanish America. In the context of one national literature, see *Mexican Literature: A History,* ed. David William Foster (Austin: University of Texas Press, 1994), which contains chapters on pre-Columbian literatures as well as Mexican and Mexican-American literary relations. More common is the stance of James Higgins, who examines works in indigenous languages, but not in European languages other than Spanish; on César Moro, for instance, Higgins states: "with the exception of *La tortuga ecuestre* . . . he chose to write his work in French. It is, however, on the basis of his Spanish verse that his contribution to Peruvian poetry has to be assessed." *A History of Peruvian Literature* (Liverpool: Francis Cairns, 1987), 185.

11. José Donoso, *Historia personal del "boom"* (Barcelona: Seix Barral, 1983), 34.

12. George Steiner, *Extraterritorial: Papers on Literature and the Language Revolution* (New York: Atheneum, 1976). Steiner's adjective, "extraterritorial," used to describe the "linguistic unhousedness" of Beckett, Nabokov, and Borges, enters the critical discussion of Spanish American literature in José Miguel Oviedo, "La excepción y la regla en la literatura de América Latina," in *Escrito al margen* (Mexico City: Premià, 1987). In Oviedo's view, "literary nationalism" has elevated the concept of "representative writer" and ostracized marginal or dissident voices, including those of authors who write in other languages, like César Moro (332–33). See also Oviedo, "Cabrera Infante en el espejo de Nabokov," *Quimera: Revista de Literatura* 78–79 (June 1988): 74–81.

13. Among recent studies, see Roberto González Echevarría, *Myth and Archive: A Theory of Latin American Narrative* (Durham: Duke University Press, 1998), on Merlin and Páez; Efraín Kristal, *The Andes Viewed from the City* (New York: Peter Lang, 1987), on F. García Calderón; Francine Masiello, *Between Civilization and Barbarism* (Lincoln: University of Nebraska Press, 1982), on Mansilla de García; Adriana Méndez Rodenas, *Gender and Nationalism in Colonial Cuba* (Nashville: Vanderbilt University Press, 1998), on Merlin; Sylvia Molloy, *At Face Value: Autobiographical Writing in Spanish America* (Cambridge: Cambridge University Press, 1991), on V. Ocampo and Merlin. The theory of heterolingualism in Spanish American literature that this study seeks to formulate builds upon these critics' observations and analyses.

14. The 1890 Guatemala City edition of Darío's *Azul* includes "Pensée" and "Chanson crepusculaire" as well as a third poem in French, "À Mademoiselle"; they appear under one common title, "Échos." That *Azul*, one of the landmarks of Spanish American literature, contains, if only in one edition, texts in another tongue is another reason for the expediency of reconsidering the linguistic premises of the tradition. See also "France-Amérique" (1914), translated as "Oda a la Francia," or the playful interlingual verse of "Epístola" (1907) dedicated to Leopoldo Lugones's wife: "*Madame Lugones, j'ai commencé ces vers / en écoutant la voix d'un carillon d'Anvers... / ¡Así empecé, en francés, pensando en Rodenbach / cuando hice hacia el Brasil una fuga... de Bach!*" (emphasis in original) [Madame Lugones, I began these lines, listening to the sound of chimes in Antwerp. Thus I began, in French, thinking of Rodenbach, when I enacted toward Brazil a *fuga* {escape, fugue}... by Bach]. *Poesías completas* (Buenos Aires: Ediciones Antonio Zamora, 1967), 629. On Martí's English-language publication, see Carlos Ripoll, *Seis trabajos desconocidos de Martí en "The Hour"* (New York: Eliseo Torres & Sons, 1974), 1–6.

15. For the possible Argentine aspects of Gombrowicz's writing, see Gerardo Fernández, "Reportaje a Laura Yusem," *Teatro* 2.5 (1981): 50–55.

16. See my "Wallace Stevens y el discurso en La Habana: Palabras de José Rodríguez Feo," *Revista Canadiense de Estudios Hispánicos* 22.1 (autumn 1997): 3–18.

17. On its finding at the Library of Congress and possible aesthetic merits, see Enrique Anderson Imbert, "Exhumación de un folleto anónimo de Sarmiento," in *Modernidad y posmodernidad* (Buenos Aires: Torres Agüero, 1997), 91–104.

18. Gastón Baquero, "Introducción a la novela," in *La Enciclopedia de Cuba* (San Juan: Playor, 1975), 3:8.

19. For an analysis of various forms of translation in Cuban culture, see Gus-

tavo Pérez Firmat, *The Cuban Condition: Translation and Identity in Modern Cuban Literature* (Cambridge: Cambridge University Press, 1989).

20. Claudio Guillén, *Literature as System* (Princeton: Princeton University Press, 1971), 21.

21. Ibid.

22. David Perkins, *Is Literary History Possible?* (Baltimore: Johns Hopkins University Press, 1992), 13.

23. Vicente Huidobro, *Altazor / Temblor de cielo*, ed. René de Costa (Madrid: Cátedra, 1981), 57.

24. Joseph Brodsky, "To Please a Shadow," in *Less than One: Selected Essays* (New York: Farrar Straus Giroux, 1988), 357.

25. In this, I follow Julia Kristeva's interimplication of Freud's essay in her analysis of nation and foreignness in *Étrangers à nous-mêmes* (Paris: Seuil, 1988); see chapter 2 of my study. For other invocations of Freud's concept in cultural theory, see Homi Bhabha, *The Location of Culture* (London: Routledge, 1994), 9–18, 164–69. To stress the ideas of "home" and "house"—and also in connection with Steiner's vision of "linguistic unhousedness" in *Extraterritorial*—I follow Bhabha and others in translating *unheimlich* as "unhomely" most of the time. For other uses of *unheimlich* in literary scholarship, see Harold Bloom, *The Anxiety of Influence: A Theory of Poetry* (New York: Oxford University Press, 1997), 77–92; and Marjorie Garber, *Shakespeare's Ghost Writers: Literature as Uncanny Causality* (New York: Routledge, 1987). In the Spanish American literary context, with a focus on the problems of defining the uncanny as a feeling, see Antonio Benítez Rojo, "Bartolomé de las Casas: Entre el infierno y la ficción," *MLN* 103.2 (March 1988): 259–88. For a discussion of the *unheimlich* in the field of architecture, see Anthony Vidler, *The Architectural Uncanny* (Cambridge: MIT Press, 1996), to whose conceptualizations and metaphors about real-world buildings my study is also indebted. In yet another disciplinary context, see Avery F. Gordon, *Ghostly Matters: Haunting and the Sociological Imagination* (Minneapolis: University of Minnesota Press, 1997).

1. The House of Spanish, I

1. Manuel Mujica Lainez, "París: el equilibrio y el vértigo," in *Placeres y fatigas de los viajes* (Buenos Aires: Sudamericana, 1986), 209. Subsequent quotations from this work are cited parenthetically in the text. Similarly, when quoting other primary sources throughout this book, bibliographical references will be provided in an endnote or first reference, and page numbers for subsequent quotations from the same work will be cited parenthetically in the text.

2. Mujica Lainez, "El premio Nobel de Gabriela Mistral," in *Placeres y fatigas de los viajes*, 124.

3. José Martí, "Nuestra América," in *Obras completas* (Havana: Editorial Nacional de Cuba, 1963–66), 6:18; "Our America," in *Our America by José Martí: Writings on Latin America and the Struggle for Cuban Independence*, trans. Elinor Randal et al. (New York: Monthly Review Press, 1977), 88.

4. Jean Franco, *Spanish American Literature since Independence* (London: Ernest Benn, 1973), 53.

5. The Spanish translation of Franco's history expresses the notion of progress even more precisely: "*Habrá que esperar* a José Martí para que un escritor
hispanoamericano intente encontrar virtudes en la barbarie que la civilización europea condenaba sin remisión" (my emphasis) [One will have to wait . . .]. *Historia de la literatura hispanoamericana* (Barcelona: Ariel, 1983), 93. For a most
perceptive analysis of the Latin American dilemma between "native" and "foreign," viewed in the case of Brazil, see Roberto Schwartz, "Nacional por subtração," in *Que horas são?* (São Paulo: Companhia das Letras, 1987), 29–48.

6. Domingo F. Sarmiento, *Facundo*, ed. Roberto Yahni (Madrid: Cátedra,
1993), 372.

7. See Samuel L. Baily, "Sarmiento and Immigration: Changing Views on the
Role of Immigration in the Development of Argentina," in *Sarmiento and His Argentina*, ed. Joseph T. Criscenti (Boulder: Lynne Rienner Publishers, 1993), 131–
42, especially p. 133. On Sarmiento's *gaucho alemán*, see also chapter 2 of this
study.

8. The ideas in Martí's essay itself denote a foreign origin that, as Juan Marichal explains, is not readily apparent: "Tras la lectura de este texto no cabe sos-
pechar que Martí supiera que estaba exponiendo ideas enteramente importadas,
ideas procedentes originariamente de los pensadores conservadores de principios
del siglo XIX, y de una manera general, de la oposición intelectual a la Revolución
Francesa, sobre todo de la alemana" [After reading this essay, one would not suspect that Martí knew that he was exposing entirely imported ideas, stemming originally from the conservative thinkers of the early nineteenth century and,
generally, from the intellectual opposition to the French Revolution, especially
German]. *Cuatro fases de la historia intelectual latinoamericana, 1810–1979* (Madrid: Fundación Juan March, 1978), 77–78. On "Nuestra América" and its role in
the development of "a new, pan-American postcolonial identity" (15), see José
David Saldívar, *The Dialectics of Our America: Genealogy, Cultural Critique, and
Literary History* (Durham: Duke University Press, 1991).

9. Coinciding with Franco's language on the Argentine Romantics, Fernández
Retamar's views on Borges and Carlos Fuentes are based on their perceived status
as "colonial" authors; see *Calibán: Apuntes sobre la cultura en nuestra América*
2nd ed., (Mexico City: Diógenes, 1974), 60–61, 71.

10. María Pilar Donoso, *Los de entonces (Recuerdos)* (Barcelona: Seix Barral,
1987), 189. Donoso's phrase, "ancha y extensa," recalls the title of Ciro Alegría's
novel, *El mundo es ancho y ajeno* (1941); it is significant that, instead of alienation, the prevailing sentiment here should be one of mutual awareness among
the continent's nations and social groups: the continent emerges as one large
house whose inhabitants are in the process of meeting each other.

11. Jorge Luis Borges, review of *La amortajada*, by María Luisa Bombal, *Sur* 8.7
(1938): 80–81.

12. See Peter Winn, *Americas: The Changing Face of Latin America and the Caribbean* (New York: Pantheon, 1992), 20–21.

13. Pablo Neruda, *Confieso que he vivido* (Barcelona: Seix Barral, 1974), 77;
Memoirs, trans. Hardie St. Martin (New York: Farrar, Straus, and Giroux, 1977), 54.

14. Miguel de Unamuno, "La sangre del espíritu," in *Obras completas: Poesía*
(Madrid: Escelicer, 1969), 6:375.

15. Carlos Fuentes, *The Buried Mirror: Reflections on Spain and the New World*
(Boston: Houghton Mifflin, 1992), 15.

16. Himself occasionally a writer in English, Fuentes addresses the complexities of Spanish American heterolingualism in *Una familia lejana*; see chapter 5 of this study. On Ferré's bilingualism and self-translation, see her essay, "On Destiny, Language, and Translation; or, Ophelia Adrift in the C. & O. Canal," in *The Youngest Doll* (Lincoln: University of Nebraska Press, 1991), 153–65.

17. Nicolás Guillén, "Canta el sinsonte en el Turquino," in *Obra poética* (Havana: Arte y Literatura, 1974), 2:101.

18. For the relations among literature, exile, and linguistic change, see Claudio Guillén, *El sol de los desterrados: Literatura y exilio* (Barcelona: Quaderns Crema, 1995), and the essays collected in *Literature in Exile,* ed. John Glad (Durham: Duke University Press, 1990). The relation between exile and heterolingualism also informs my readings of Merlin, Hudson, Bombal, and Cabrera Infante in the chapters that follow.

19. Luis Iñigo Madrigal, introduction to *Summa poética,* by Nicolás Guillén (Madrid: Cátedra, 1983), 17–18.

20. Guillén, "Tú no sabe inglé," in *Obra poética* 1:109.

21. Critics do not agree on the nuances of the speaker's view of Víctor Manuel. For Ángel Augier, the poem ridicules Víctor Manuel for wanting to flirt with a U.S. American tourist without knowing any English. *Nicolás Guillén: Notas para un estudio biográfico-crítico* (Santa Clara, Cuba: Universidad Central de Las Villas, 1965), 1:126. For Keith Ellis, it introduces "a new cause of frustration—the unequal status Vito Manué has with the American woman as evidenced by his extreme embarrassment at not being able to speak English in Cuba." *Cuba's Nicolás Guillén: Poetry and Ideology* (Toronto: University of Toronto Press, 1983), 68–69. In either case, English constitutes a destabilizing element in Cuban culture.

22. A similar artful application of English to reprove the language's influence is Guillén's "Canción puertorriqueña" (1958), which mocks Puerto Rico's political status as a commonwealth of the United States: "¿En qué lengua me entiendes, / en qué lengua por fin te podré hablar, / si en yes, / si en sí, / si en bien, / si en well, / si en mal, / si en bad, si en very bad?" (2:21–22) [In what tongue do you understand me, in what tongue will I finally be able to speak to you: will it be in "yes" or in "sí," in "well" or in "mal," or in "bad", or in "very bad"?]. A similar use of interlingualism to condemn the involvements of one's peers with another language and culture is a short poem from 1929 in Unamuno's *Cancionero: Diario poético*: "—*Vous aimez la France?*—No sé... / es una *cocotte*?... creía... / vamos, *pardon*! *s'il vous plait*... / *mon vieux* ¡qué babosería!" ['*Vous aimez la France?*' 'I don't know... / is she a *cocotte*?... I thought... / come on, *pardon*! *s'il vous plait*... / *mon vieux* what drivel!]. *Obras completas: Poesía* (Madrid: Escelicer, 1969), 6:1169. In another literary context, compare also the use of French in Tolstoy's fiction: the presence of the other tongue in the speech of characters is viewed as a sign of pernicious foreign influence.

23. Ana Lydia Vega, "Pollito chicken," in *Vírgenes y mártires,* by Vega and Carmen Lugo Filippi (Río Piedras: Antillana, 1983), 77.

24. See Gerald Guinness, *Here and Elsewhere: Essays on Caribbean Literature* (Río Piedras: Universidad de Puerto Rico, 1993), 47–50. Compare also Vega's aptly titled "Trabajando pal inglés," a short story in which the language of Cuban exiles in Puerto Rico is parodied, like Suzie's diction in "Tú no sabe inglé." The text's epigraph, by Nicolás Guillén, constitutes an initial sign of ideological filia-

tion: "Ay, yo bien conozco a tu enemigo, el mismo que tenemos por acá..." [Oh, do I know your enemy well: he's the same we have over here]. *Vírgenes y mártires*, 101. Yet, the nation that both of Vega's fictions construe is a site of heterolingualism and heteroglossia that problematizes the epigraph's Manichaean viewpoints.

25. See Efraín Barradas's introduction to his anthology, *Herejes y mitificadores: Muestra de poesía puertorriqueña en los Estados Unidos*, ed. Barradas and Rafael Rodríguez (Río Piedras: Huracán, 1980), especially 11, 15–17, 22–29.

26. Guillermo Cabrera Infante, *Tres tristes tigres* (Barcelona: Biblioteca de Bolsillo, 1983), 15; *Three Trapped Tigers*, trans. Donald Gardner and Suzanne Jill Levine with Cabrera Infante (London: Faber and Faber, 1990).

27. Can one translate French into French? This is in effect what occurs in *Three Trapped Tigers*, where Carpentier's footnote now reads, *"Avis au traducteur: Monsieur, Vous pouvez traduire le titre—'Explosion ex cathedra.'*. S.V.P.—L'Auteur"; the change reflects the fact that *Explosion in the Cathedral* is the title in English of Carpentier's *El siglo de las luces* (1962). *Tres tristes tigres*, 255. The title of the chapter is also understood only in the other literary culture: "Lot's Steps" is a reference to *The Lost Steps*. Because of their location between two literary cultures, problems of this kind involve not only the translation of heterolingual texts, but also their reading; see chapter 4. On Cabrera Infante's collaboration in the translation of his works into English, see Suzanne Jill Levine, *The Subversive Scribe: Translating Latin American Fiction* (Saint Paul: Greywolf Press, 1991).

28. Carlos Fuentes, *La nueva novela hispanoamericana* (Mexico City: Cuadernos de Joaquín Mortiz, 1980), 25.

29. Some statistics: "By 1914 Argentina was overwhelmingly an immigrant country. In each of the ten years before 1914 there had been a net balance of 100,000 immigrants per year. One-third of the nation's population and 50 per cent of that of Buenos Aires was foreign-born, and 80 per cent were descendants of immigrants who had entered since the 1860s. Of this foreign population there were approximately 1 million Italians, 800,000 Spaniards, 94,000 Russians and Poles (many of whom were Jews), 86,000 French, 80,000 'Turcos' (the generic term for anyone from the Middle East), 35,000 Germans and some 40,000 British, making it the largest British community outside of the Empire." Alistair Hennessy, "Argentines, Anglo-Argentines and Others," in *The Land That England Lost: Argentina and Britain, A Special Relationship* ed. by Hennessy and John King (London: British Academy Press, 1992), 9.

30. Jorge Luis Borges, "La señora mayor," in *El informe de Brodie* (Madrid: Alianza Editorial, 1974), 71–82. On Spanish immigration in Argentina, see José C. Moya, *Cousins and Strangers: Spanish Immigrants in Buenos Aires, 1850–1930* (Berkeley: University of California Press, 1998). Other immigrants, or descendants of immigrants, whose language is found peculiar in Borges's fiction include Carlos Argentino Daneri in "El Aleph" and Zimermann in "Guayaquil." Significantly, both of these characters, a poet and a historian, are writers, if rather unskillful ones.

31. Manuel Mujica Lainez, *El gran teatro* (Barcelona: Planeta, 1979), 25.

32. Ernesto Schóó, *El placer desbocado* (Buenos Aires, Emecé, 1988), 17.

33. Victoria Ocampo, "Dette à la France," in *Testimonios: Segunda Serie* (Buenos Aires: Sur, 1941), 166.

34. Victoria Ocampo, "And So I Shall Have Mine," in *Testimonios: Segunda Serie*, 506.

35. See Sylvia Molloy, *At Face Value: Autobiographical Writing in Spanish America* (Cambridge: Cambridge University Press, 1991), 62, 67. On Ocampo's self-translation as an act of repossession, particularly as it pertains to the various volumes of her *Autobiografía,* see ibid., 72–73. Ocampo herself confronts the subject in the preface to *338.171 T.E. (Lawrence d'Arabie)* (1947), written originally in French, but published first in Spanish: "Je n'ai jamais cessé d'écrire en français. Je n'ai jamais publié que des traductions plus ou moins fidèles de ce que j'avais écrit dans cette langue. J'ai cru devoir m'infliger ce supplice et cette déformation parce que je vivais dans un pays—le mien—de langue espagnole et parce que je m'addressais à son public" [I never stopped writing in French. I never published anything except more or less faithful translations of what I had written in that language. I thought I needed to inflict that suffering and deformation on myself because I lived in a country—my own—where Spanish is spoken, and I wanted to address myself to its audience]. Quoted by Laura Ayerza de Castilho and Odile Felgine, *Victoria Ocampo* (Paris: Criterion, 1991), 180.

36. One case in point is the polemics about the Spanish language and the Hispanic cultural legacy in Santiago de Chile in the 1840s; see Efraín Kristal, "Dialogue and Polemics: Sarmiento, Lastarria, and Bello," in *Sarmiento and His Argentina,* ed. Criscenti, 61–70.

37. Borges, "Las alarmas del doctor Américo Castro," in *Otras inquisiciones* (Madrid: Alianza, 1976), 35–40; "Dr. Américo Castro Is Alarmed," in *Other Inquisitions, 1937–1952,* trans. Ruth L. C. Simms (Austin: University of Texas Press, 1995), 26–30. For an analysis of Borges's and Castro's conflicting philosophies, see Richard M. Morse, *New World Soundings: Culture and Ideology in the Americas* (Baltimore: Johns Hopkins University Press, 1989); Efraín Kristal, "Dialogue and Polemics," 61–63; and Verónica Cortínez, "El siglo de Borges" in *Actas de ALFAL,* ed. Víctor Martínez Álvarez (Santiago: Universidad de Santiago de Chile, forthcoming).

38. Juan de Valdés, *Diálogo de la lengua* (Madrid: Espasa-Calpe, 1976), 155.

39. Esteban Echeverría, *El matadero / La cautiva,* ed. Leonor Fleming (Madrid: Cátedra, 1990), 117.

40. Ibid., 101; "The Slaughterhouse," in *The Borzoi Anthology of Latin American Literature,* ed. Emir Rodríguez Monegal (New York: Knopf, 1997), 1:215.

41. See Noé Jitrik, "Forma y significación en *El matadero,* de Esteban Echeverría," in *El fuego de la especie* (Buenos Aires: Siglo XXI, 1971), 63–98.

42. That the tongue of Fuguet's narrator is marked by the presence of English words and constructions is an unexpected form of interlingualism that may be read as one more sign of the unhomely condition of culture in Spanish America. On McOndo, see Fuguet and Sergio Gómez, "Presentación," in *McOndo,* ed. Fuguet and Gómez (Barcelona: Mondadori, 1996), 11–20.

43. José Donoso, *Historia personal del "boom"* (Barcelona: Seix Barral, 1983), 21.

44. In the same essay, Borges identifies nevertheless certain textual markings that may be read as Argentine traits. Speaking of the non-Argentine landscape in Enrique Banchs's poetry, he concludes, "yo diría que en el manejo de estas imágenes convencionales, en esos tejados y en esos ruiseñores anómalos, no estarán desde luego la arquitectura ni la ornitología argentinas, pero están el pudor argentino, la reticencia argentina" [I would say that the use of these conventional images, in these anomalous roofs and nightingales, Argentine architecture and

ornithology are of course absent, but we do find in them the Argentine's reticence, his constraint]. "El escritor argentino y la tradición," in *Discusión* (Buenos Aires: Emecé, 1976), 156; "The Argentine Writer and Tradition," in *Labyrinths: Selected Stories and Other Writings*, trans. James E. Irby (New York: New Directions, 1964), 181. But the question remains whether the absence of *pudor* or *reticencia*, or other traits identifiable with a national style, may affect a work's potential status as an Argentine text in Borges's eyes. On Borges's use of Gibbon and the Koran, see Verónica Cortínez, "El siglo de Borges," in *Actas de ALFAL*.

45. Relating Borges to Sarmiento, whom he sees as the antithesis of Martí, Fernández Retamar states, "si se le reconoce *americanidad* a Sarmiento—lo que es evidente y no significa que represente el polo positivo de esa americanidad—, nunca he podido entender por qué se le niega a Borges: Borges es un típico escritor colonial, representante entre nosotros de una clase ya sin fuerzas, cuyo acto de escritura—como él sabe bien, pues es de una endiablada inteligencia—se parece más a un acto de lectura. Borges no es un escritor europeo: no hay ningún escritor europeo como Borges" [if the "American-ness" of Sarmiento is always taken for granted (although it is obvious in him, this is not to say he represents the positive pole of that "American-ness"), I have never been able to understand why it is denied to Borges. Borges is a typical colonial writer, the representative among us of a now-powerless class for whom the act of writing—and he is aware of this, for he is a man of diaboloical {sic} intelligence—is more like the act of reading. He is not a European writer; there is no European writer like Borges]. *Calibán: Apuntes sobre la cultura en nuestra América* (Mexico City: Diógenes, 1974), 60; *Caliban and Other Essays*, trans. Edward Baker (Minneapolis: University of Minnesota Press, 1997), 28.

46. For an author's insightful differentiation between "national" and "nationalist" literature, see Ernesto Sábato, "Los sofismas de la literatura nacionalista," in *El escritor y sus fantasmas* (Barcelona: Seix Barral, 1987), 61–63.

47. Roberto González Echevarría, *Alejo Carpentier: The Pilgrim at Home* (Austin: University of Texas Press, 1977), 38.

48. Ibid., 154.

49. Martí knew French well, but was less proficient in English, so one may surmise the help of others in his English-language publications. This view is put forth by Carlos Ripoll, who states, "No resulta fácil determinar por dónde anda la pluma de Martí en *The Hour*. Con notable rapidez el idioma, que al principio es algo incorrecto, se hace flexible para acercarse al de los otros colaboradores. Quizás en alguna ocasión logró ayuda de un traductor, como el que vierte al inglés, a partir de julio, los trabajos que empieza a publicar en *The Sun*, otro periódico de Nueva York, de más categoría que aquel semanario de 'artes y salones,' como llamaba Martí a *The Hour*" [It is not easy to determine the place of Martí's pen in *The Hour*. With remarkable speed, his language, which at the beginning was somewhat incorrect, becomes flexible and starts resembling that of other contributors. Perhaps on some occasions he received the help of a translator, as in those articles which, from July on, he started to publish in *The Sun*, another New York periodical, more prestigious than that weekly of "arts and salons," which is how Martí referred to *The Hour*.] *Seis trabajos desconocidos de Martí en "The Hour"* (New York: Eliseo Torres & Sons, 1974), 4.

50. Jorge Mañach, *Martí el apóstol* (Madrid: Espasa-Calpe, 1968), 129–30.

51. Martí, 'Impressions of America," in *Obras completas,* 19:103.
52. Martí, "Modern Spanish Poets," in *Obras completas,* 15:15.
53. Martí, "Centenario de Calderón," in *Obras completas,* 15:110.
54. Martí, "The Bull Fight," in *Obras completas,* 15:15.
55. Cristina Garcia, *Dreaming in Cuban* (New York: Knopf, 1992), *passim.*

2. THE HOUSE OF SPANISH, II

1. Pablo Neruda, *Confieso que he vivido* (Barcelona: Seix Barral, 1974), 175–76; *Memoirs,* trans. Hardie St. Martin (New York: Farrar, Straus, and Giroux, 1977), 126.
2. Roberto González Echevarría observes: "He is a Latin American writer for whom Spanish is as close to being a foreign language as any since Garcilaso de la Vega el Inca." *Alejo Carpentier: The Pilgrim at Home* (Austin: University of Texas Press, 1977), 30. On Carpentier's "Histoire de lunes," a French-language text, see ibid., 89–94. For a first-person account of one Cuban writer's relations with Carpentier, in which the issue of foreignness is addressed, see Guillermo Cabrera Infante, "Carpentier, cubano a la cañona," in *Mea Cuba* (Barcelona: Plaza & Janés, 1993), 370–88.
3. Ángel Rama, "Diez problemas para el novelista hispanoamericano," in *Literatura y arte nuevo en Cuba,* by Miguel Barnet et al. (Barcelona: Laia, 1977), 218.
4. Ibid.
5. In the Spanish American literary context, see Octavio Paz, "Sobre la crítica," in *Corriente alterna* (Mexico City: Siglo XXI, 1981), 39–44.
6. Two insightful surveys of the histories of Spanish American literature are Roberto González Echevarría, "A Brief History of the History of Spanish American Literature," in *The Cambridge History of Latin American Literature,* ed. González Echevarría and Enrique Pupo-Walker (Cambridge: Cambridge University Press, 1996) 1:7–32; and Efraín Kristal, "En torno a la historia del concepto de historia literaria hispanoamericana," *Teoría/Crítica* 1 (1994), 195–209.
7. Enrique Anderson Imbert, *Historia de la literatura hispanoamericana,* 9th ed. (Mexico City: Fondo de Cultura Económica, 1995), 1:9; *Spanish American Literature: A History,* trans. John V. Falconieri (Detroit: Wayne State University Press, 1963), 2. Unless otherwise specified, all volume and page numbers refer to the 1995 printing of the *Historia.* English translations are my own, unless a page number is given; in some cases, I have slightly modified Falconieri's translation, as in the passage just quoted. Here, Falconieri renders "sin experiencia americana" [without American experience] as "did not write of American experiences" (2), but I have modified his version, albeit clumsily, to retrieve Anderson Imbert's biographical, rather than thematical, guidelines; the two, of course, often intersect, but here Anderson Imbert is examining authorial figures rather than texts.
8. In this, Anderson Imbert coincides with his precursor, Pedro Henríquez Ureña, who, discussing José-Maria de Heredia, Lautréamont, Laforgue, and Supervielle in a footnote, states: "todos ellos pertenecen a la literatura francesa" [all of them belong to French literature]. *Las corrientes literarias en la América hispánica* (Mexico City: Fondo de Cultura Económica, 1978), 242. The monolingual principle, of course, is not shared by every literary historian. See, for instance, José Miguel Oviedo's very receptive *Historia de la literatura hispanoamericana*

(Madrid: Alianza, 1995), or Giuseppe Bellini's *Historia de la literatura hispano-americana* (Madrid: Castalia, 1985), which does not include texts in other European tongues, but does begin with an account of literature in indigenous languages (7–47).

9. Also absent from Anderson Imbert's *Historia* are U.S. American authors who write in Spanish, such as José Antonio Villarreal and Tomás Rivera.

10. See David Perkins's discussion of "narrative literary history": "literary history may fulfill the essential criteria of narrative, for it may and very often does describe a transition through time from one state of affairs to a different state of affairs, and a narrator reports this transition to us." *Is Literary History Possible?* (Baltimore: Johns Hopkins University Press, 1992), 29. There are, indeed, a narrative and a narrator in Anderson Imbert's *Historia,* but the story they tell is rather open-ended: no ideological lessons; no clear objectives to be reached.

11. See also Anderson Imbert, *Historia,* 2:200.

12. On Anderson Imbert's continental framework and its debt to Pedro Henríquez Ureña's "pautas americanistas" (205) [Americanist guidelines], see Kristal, "En torno a la historia del concepto de historia literaria hispanoamericana," 205–6.

13. Enrique Anderson Imbert, "Justificación," in *Los domingos del profesor* (Buenos Aires: Gure, 1972), 7.

14. It is perhaps not coincidental that José Miguel Oviedo also places his "La excepción y la regla en la literatura de América Latina," in which he argues for such heterolinguals as César Moro, in a separate section, virtually an appendix, at the end of *Escrito al margen* (Mexico City: Premià, 1987).

15. Enrique Anderson Imbert, "El nacionalismo literario," in *Los domingos del profesor,* 15.

16. See Andrew Bush, "Lyric Poetry of the Eighteenth and Nineteenth Centuries," in *The Cambridge History of Latin American Literature,* 1:357.

17. In chapter 5, I will argue that the Spanish American narrative boom, with the ensuing shift in the general reception of literature from Spanish America, allows for a self-confident reconsideration of the tradition by the authors themselves in which heterolingualism is no longer seen as a threat to unity.

18. José Martí, "Nuestra América," in *Prosa y poesía* (Buenos Aires: Editorial Kapelusz, 1968), 130. "Our America," in *Our America by José Martí: Writings on Latin America and the Struggle for Cuban Independence,* trans. Elinor Randal et al. (New York: Monthly Review Press, 1977), 92.

19. See Kristal, "En torno a la historia del concepto de historia literaria hispanoamericana," 206.

20. In this regard, see Ventura García Calderón's opening remarks to his history of Peruvian literature, with which Efraín Kristal ends his survey of Spanish American literary histories: "Ninguna novela más extravagante que la historia literaria de América. Después de ser el sueño de cien poetas, un soñador inventa un continente como un poema" [no novel is more extravagant than the literary history of America. After being dreamed by a hundred poets, the continent is invented by a dreamer in the form of a poem]. Quoted by Kristal, ibid., 209.

21. For a discussion of Darío's defense of *hispanidad* at this stage of his literary career, see Anderson Imbert, *La originalidad de Rubén Darío* (Buenos Aires: Centro Editor de América Latina, 1967), 117–21.

22. Rubén Darío, "A Roosevelt," in *Poesías completas* (Buenos Aires: Ediciones

Antonio Zamora, 1967), 38; "To Roosevelt," in *Twentienth-Century Latin American Poetry: A Bilingual Anthology.* ed. Stephen Tapscott (Austin: University of Texas Press, 1996), 38–39.

23. Rubén Darío, *Los raros* (Mexico City: Universidad Autónoma Metropolitana, 1985), 21, 23. See also "Los cisnes" (1905), where the speaker's neocolonial anxiety also has a linguistic sign: "¿Seremos entregados a los bárbaros fieros? / ¿Tantos millones de hombres hablaremos inglés?" [Shall we be surrendered to the fierce barbarians? Will so many millions of men speak English?]. *Poesías completas,* 548.

24. Max Henríquez Ureña studies de Armas for his Spanish-language poems, which show the influence of Julián del Casal, but is dismissive of his heterolingual book: "Su libro *Rimes bizantines* . . . lo incorporó a la literatura francesa" [His book *Rimes bizantines* . . . incorporated him into French literature]. *Panorama histórico de la literatura cubana* (Havana: Arte y Cultura, 1978), 2:297.

25. On the origins of the concept of "Latin America" and its subsequent usage as a political discourse, see Enrico Mario Santí, "Latinoamericanismo," in *Por una politeratura: Literatura hispanoamericana e imaginación política* (Mexico City: Ediciones del Equilibrista, 1997), 15–21.

26. On de Armas's poetry, see Max Henríquez Ureña, "Poetas cubanos de expresión francesa," *Revista iberoamericana* 3.6 (May 1941): 325–36. In this early article on Cuban authors who write in French—"lo que ya constituye una tradición" (304) [which already constitutes a tradition], albeit a partially concealed one in the more official spaces of his own history of his Cuban literature—Henríquez Ureña remarks on the possible influence of Darío's "Sonatina" in de Armas's "Gongorine" (333).

27. On the Hispanisms of Lautréamont's style, for instance, see Leyla Perrone-Moisés and Emir Rodríguez Monegal, "Isidoro Ducasse et la rhétorique espagnole," *Poétique* 55 (September 1983): 351–77.

28. On Bello in England, see Antonio Cussen, *Bello and Bolívar* (Cambridge: Cambridge University Press, 1992).

29. On internal colonization and linguistic alterity, see Alfred Arteaga, *Chicano Poetics: Heterotexts and Hybridities* (Cambridge: Cambridge University Press, 1997), 82–90.

30. Paz underscores the links between Baroque singularity and criollo self-perceptions: "la singularidad estética del barroco mexicano corresponde a la singularidad histórica y existencial de los criollos. Entre ellos y el arte barroco había una relación inequívoca, no de causa a efecto, sino de afinidad y coincidencia. Respiraban con naturalidad en el mundo de la extrañeza porque ellos mismos eran y se sabían extraños" [the unique aesthetic of the Mexican baroque corresponded to the historical and existential uniqueness of the criollo. Their relationship was not one of cause and effect, but of affinity and coincidence. The criollo breathed naturally in a world of strangeness because he was, and knew himself to be, a strange being]. *Sor Juana Inés de la Cruz o las trampas de la fe* (Mexico City: Fondo de Cultura Económica, 1985), 86; *Sor Juana; or, The Traps of Faith,* trans. Margaret Sayers Peden (Cambridge: Harvard University Press, 1988), 59.

31. Sor Juana Inés de la Cruz, Loa para el Auto Sacramental de "El divino Narciso," in *Obra selecta,* ed. Luis Sainz de Medrano (Barcelona: Planeta, 1987), 357; Loa to "The Divine Narcissus," in *Poems, Protest, and a Dream,* trans. Margaret Sayers Peden (New York: Penguin, 1997), 213.

32. Domingo F. Sarmiento, *Facundo*, ed. Roberto Yahni (Madrid: Cátedra, 1993), 237.

33. In his edition of *Facundo*, Roberto Yahni summarizes the various possible sources of the phrase, including the possibility that it might even have been invented by Sarmiento as a synthesis of his book; see *Facundo*, 35 n. 1. For an analysis of Sarmiento's misattribution of the epigraph in the context of his "reading, translating, quoting and misquoting, borrowing and adapting, in sum cannibalizing texts written by others" (32), see Sylvia Molloy, *At Face Value: Autobiographical Writing in Spanish America* (Cambridge: Cambridge University Press, 1991), 29–32.

34. Jorge Luis Borges, "Historia del guerrero y de la cautiva," in *El Aleph* (Madrid' Alianza, 1976), 53; "Story of the Warrior and the Captive," in *Labyrinths: Selected Stories and Other Writings* (New York: New Directions, 1964), 130.

35. Lucio V. Mansilla, *Una excursión a los indios ranqueles* (Madrid: Ediciones de Cultura Hispánica, 1993), 659; *An Expedition to the Ranquel Indians*, trans. Mark McCaffrey (Austin: University of Texas Press, 1997), 367.

36. Julio Ramos explains Mansilla's textual quarrel with the president: "En el sentido de su crítica a Sarmiento, *Una excursión* es un *deliberado* viaje al lugar del otro, al territorio excluido de la 'barbarie'. Como deliberado viaje propone, no sólo el encuentro del coronel Mansilla con los ranqueles, sino también la puesta en crisis de la 'naturalidad' del 'nosotros' que entonces determinaba las cualidades propias de lo 'bárbaro' y lo 'civilizado'. En la época de *Una excursión*, ese 'nosotros' era el sujeto que determinaba la política del Estado entonces presidido por Sarmiento" (emphasis in original) [In its critique of Sarmiento, *Una excursión* is a *deliberate* journey to the place of the other, the excluded territory of barbarism. As a deliberate journey, it proposes not only the encounter between Mansilla and the Ranquels, but the enactment of a crisis in the "naturalness" of that "we" which at the time determined the proper qualities of "barbarian" and "civilized." When *Una excursión* was written, that "we" was the subject that determined the policies of the State presided by Sarmiento]. "Entre otros: *Una excursión a los indios ranqueles* de Lucio V. Mansilla," *Filología* 21.1 (1986): 149–50.

37. José Hernández, *Martín Fierro*, ed. Ángel J. Battistessa (Madrid: Cátedra, 1994); parenthetical number indicates first or second part as well as lines. *The Gaucho Martín Fierro*, trans. C. E. Ward (Albany: State University of New York Press, 1967), 203.

38. Nevertheless, words derived from the lexicon of native languages abound in *Martín Fierro*; see, for instance, Domingo A. Bravo, *El quichua en el "Martín Fierro" y en "Don Segundo Sombra"* (Buenos Aires: Instituto Amigos del Libro Argentino, 1968).

39. This is Borges's fictional construction of that "vida feral" [savage life] in "Historia del guerrero y de la cautiva": "los toldos de cuero de caballo, las hogueras de estiércol, los festines de carne chamuscada o de vísceras crudas, las sigilosas marchas al alba; el asalto de los corrales, el alarido y el saqueo, la guerra, el caudaloso arreo de las haciendas por jinetes desnudos, la poligamia, la hediondez y la magia" (53) [the horsehide shelters, the fires made of dry manure, the feasts of scorched meat or raw entrails, the stealthy departures at dawn, the attacks on corrals, the yelling and the pillaging, the wars, the sweeping charges on the haciendas by naked horsemen, the polygamy, the stench and the superstition]

(130). Many of these elements can be traced back directly to Argentine texts of the nineteenth century; "alaridos" [yelling], for instance, is a word used repeatedly in *Martín Fierro*.

40. The author at times views himself as an Indian. On Mansilla's mimicry of the Ranquels, see Julio Ramos, "Entre otros," 152–55; on Mansilla's self-perception as as Indian "de fuera" [from outside] and a possible connection with T. E. Lawrence's sense of duality, see Blas Matamoro's introduction to *Una excursión a los indios ranqueles*, 49.

41. Julia Kristeva, *Étrangers à nous-mêmes* (Paris: Seuil, 1988), 283; *Strangers to Ourselves*, trans. Leon S. Roudiez (New York: Columbia University Press, 1991), 191.

42. Garcilaso de la Vega, *Comentarios reales de los incas*, ed. Carlos Araníbar (Lima: Fondo de Cultura Económica, 1991), 1:38; *Royal Commentaries of the Incas and General History of Peru*, trans. Harold V. Livermore (Austin: University of Texas Press, 1994), 39.

43. Margarita Zamora summarizes it thus: "Garcilaso's task in the *Comentarios reales* was to reconcile the Inca experience of the past with the European world view, in an attempt to restore and ultimately vindicate the indigenous tradition. . . . [He] sought to reconcile the oppositions and contradictions that he perceived in those discourses in order to achieve the Renaissance ideal of *concordia,* or the conciliation of opposites. In the final analysis, his interpretation of Inca civilization strives to demonstrate the fundamental complementarity of New World and Christian histories." *Language, Authority, and Indigenous History in the "Comentarios reales de los incas"* (Cambridge: Cambridge University Press, 1988), 3.

44. Karlheinz Stierle explains: "Renaissance is at the same time the discovery of plurality, perspective, dialogue, polyphony. Culture now means, as Leonid Baktin puts it, the culture of the communications of cultures. This new experience brings about a new aesthetics of plurality." "Translatio Studii and Renaissance: From Vertical to Horizontal Translation," in *The Translatability of Culture: Figurations of the Space Between,* ed. Sanford Budick and Wolfgang Iser (Stanford: Stanford University Press, 1996), 65.

45. Elisabeth Burgos, introduction to *Me llamo Rigoberta Menchú y así me nació la conciencia,* by Rigoberta Menchú (Mexico City: Siglo XXI, 1992), 18; introduction to *I, Rigoberta Menchú: An Indian Woman in Guatemala,* ed. Elisabeth Burgos-Debray, trans. Ann Wright (London: Verso, 1996), xxi.

46. Pablo Neruda, "Alturas de Macchu Picchu," in *Canto general* (Barcelona: Seix Barral, 1982), 42–43; "The Heights of Macchu Picchu," in *Canto General,* trans. Jack Schmitt (Berkeley: University of California Press, 1991), 31–32.

47. This does not mean that in other instances Neruda will not alter Quechua to make the language fit into his own poetic vision; see Enrico Mario Santí, "Canto general: Caligrafía de la historia," in *Por una politeratura,* 126, for an insightful discussion of Neruda's twelve-letter spelling of Machu Picchu. Neruda's epigraph is a transcription from an erroneous source; see Santí, introduction to *Canto general,* by Neruda (Madrid: Cátedra, 1992), 143. It means: "Oh, avenging God, see how my enemies spill my blood!"

48. I am persuaded here by Wolfgang Iser's arguments about "mutuality" in "Coda to the Discussion," the last text in *The Translatability of Cultures: Figurations of the Space Between.* In the words of editor Sanford Budick, the essays col-

lected here "record, or even enact, an assortment of crises in the use of the concept of alterity" (1). For Iser, mutuality comprises all modes of thinking about alterity, such as fusion, conversion, assimilation, appropriation, and syncretism, but also exposes them as "reifications that eliminate difference and pose as an overarching third dimension" (301). Mutuality also "points to the fact that whenever features of culture are translated intra- or cross-culturally, a trace of untranslatability imprints itself on all such endeavors, just as mutual understanding of cultures will encounter a certain incommensurability which, in actual fact, energizes such attempts at comprehension. Therefore, mutuality is marked simultaneously by an insurmountable difference between cultures and an interminable drive to build bridges" (301). I conceive my incorporation of Freud's *unheimlich* into this discussion of literary heterolingualism in Spanish America as a form of "bricolage," which Iser defines as "a set of explanations as to how one can conceive of encounters between cultures," and which operates "by making assertions and simultaneously trying to spotlight what they exclude" (302).

3. MERLIN'S CRAFT

1. For Merlin's biography, see Emilio Bacardí Moreau, *La condesa de Merlin* (Santiago de Cuba: Biblioteca Oriente, 1924); Domingo Figarola-Caneda, *La condesa de Merlin* (Paris: Excelsior, 1928); Adriana Méndez Rodenas, *Gender and Nationalism in Colonial Cuba: The Travels of Santa Cruz y Montalvo, Condesa de Merlin* (Nashville: Vanderbilt University Press, 1998), 19–24.

2. María de las Mercedes Santa Cruz y Montalvo, comtesse Merlin, *La Havane* (Paris: Librairie d'Amyot, 1844), 1:23–24. My English translation does not attempt to represent departures from standard French in the original version. On the difficulty of translating texts marked by any kind of *Sprachmischung*, see Rogelio Reyes, "The Translation of Interlingual Texts," in *Translating Latin America: Culture as Text*, ed. William Luis and Julio Rodríguez-Luis (Binghamton, N.Y.: Center for Research in Translation, 1991), 301–8.

3. Fanny is Fanny Elssler, the dancer, on her way to the New World for a two-year tour. In Nicolás Guillén's *El diario que a diario* (1972), a poetical history of Cuba from the nineteenth century through the Revolution that formally imitates a newspaper, Fanny Elssler's visit to Havana is "advertised" in juxtaposition with announcements of slave auctions and escapes. In this later context, Merlin's onboard association with Elssler can only surface as one more token of foreignness and detachment from Cuban social realities. Nicolás Guillén, *Summa poética* (Madrid: Cátedra, 1983). On the poems in French dedicated to Elssler by the Cuban writer José Jacinto Milanés, who wrote almost exclusively in Spanish, see Max Henríquez Ureña, "Poetas cubanos de expresión francesa," *Revista Iberoamericana* 3.6 (May 1941): 304.

4. That Méndez Rodenas's and Sylvia Molloy's studies should focus mostly on translations of Merlin's texts, such as *Viaje a La Habana* and *Mis doce primeros años*, is entirely justified, because these versions were, and still are, most easily available to Cuban and other Spanish American readers. Adriana Méndez Rodenas, "A Journey to the (Literary) Source: The Invention of Origins in Merlin's *Viaje a La Habana*," *New Literary History* 21.3 (1990): 707–31; "Voyage to *La Havane*:

The Countess of Merlín's Preview of National Identity," *Cuban Studies* 16 (1986): 71–99; *Gender and Nationalism in Colonial Cuba.* Sylvia Molloy, *At Face Value: Autobiographical Writing in Spanish America* (Cambridge: Cambridge University Press, 1991), 79–96. I pay attention to the original texts to stress certain nuances of Merlin's practice of writing that I believe are most patent in French: not only aspects of the interlingual and the interliterary, but also the emerging figure of a reader who may be termed, like Merlin herself, "unhomely."

5. For a vivid depiction of Merlin as the "grande dame" of Paris's musical salons, see William G. Atwood, *The Parisian Worlds of Frédéric Chopin* (New Haven: Yale University Press, 1999). On the various names given to Merlin and her works, see my "Paratextual Snow; or, The Threshold of Mercedes Merlin," *Colby Quarterly* 28.4 (December 1996): 237–54. For a response to this article, see Méndez Rodenas, *Gender and Nationalism in Colonial Cuba*, 245 n. 24.

6. April Fitzlyon, *Maria Malibran: Diva of the Romantic Age* (London: Souvenir Press, 1987), 50; John Rosselli, *The Life of Bellini* (Cambridge: Cambridge University Press, 1996), 13.

7. The debate about the primacy of music or words in opera, ongoing since the genre's inception in Florence around 1600, acquires a particular resonance in Spanish America; since most of the traditional repertoire of opera consists mostly of works in Italian, German, or French, not until the advent of supertitles could the meaning of what was sung on stage have been understood by more than a minority within the audience. For an analysis of the historical controversy between words and music, see Herbert Lindenberger, *Opera: The Extravagant Art* (Ithaca: Cornell University Press, 1984), 108–27; on the growing role of libretto analysis in contemporary operatic criticism and theory, see Arthur Groos's introduction to *Reading Opera*, ed. Groos and Roger Parker (Princeton: Princeton University Press, 1988), 1–11; and David J. Levin's introduction to *Opera through Other Eyes*, ed. Levin (Stanford: Stanford University Press, 1994), 1–18.

8. For an analysis of the ambivalent reviews of Merlin's concerts in Havana, see Méndez Rodenas, *Gender and Nationalism in Colonial Cuba*, 84–87. Méndez Rodenas stresses the tensions between Merlin's talent and Creole anxieties about female creativity: "Merlin's operatic voice is received by the Creole community as an excess, as an overabundance of femininity and female talent that threatened to unsettle not just accepted paradigms of female behavior but, most of all, the limits of creative expression allowed women within the tight circles of Creole society" (84).

9. See, for instance, Rafael Esténger, "El otoño galante de la Condesa de Merlin," in *Los amores de cubanos famosos* (Havana: Alfa, 1939), 9–19.

10. Francine Masiello analyzes the case of Eduarda Mansilla de García, author of *Pablo ou la vie dans les pampas* (1869), viewing the writer's heterolingualism as a "form of empowerment": "As different forces competed for public authority and different sectors of the liberal front assumed the challenge of political power, Eduarda Mansilla inserted herself into national debate through recourse to a literary language of higher international prestige than Spanish." *Between Civilization and Barbarism: Women, Nation, and Literary Culture in Modern Argentina* (Lincoln: University of Nebraska Press, 1982), 43. Indeed, French boasted a higher status than Spanish among many in Latin America, but the fact remains that Mansilla de García, like Merlin, is still excluded from much of the established discussion of Argentine and Spanish American literatures.

216 NOTES

11. For an analysis of the fictional retrieval of Merlin's operatic figure in Reinaldo Arenas's *El color del verano* (1991), see Adriana Méndez Rodenas, *Gender and Nationalism in Colonial Cuba*, 231–40.

12. On the status of the real-world writer in relation to the author's textual figures in recent Spanish American fiction, see Lucille Kerr, *Reclaiming the Author: Figures and Fiction from Spanish America* (Durham: Duke University Press, 1992), 164–70.

13. See Max Henríquez Ureña, "Poetas cubanos de expresión francesa," 303; Rosario Rexach, *El pensamiento de Félix Varela y la formación de la conciencia cubana* (Havana: Lyceum, 1950), 81.

14. José María Heredia, "Niágara," in *Poesías* (Havana: Letras Cubanas, 1980), 54; "Ode to Niagara," in *Hispanic Anthology*, ed. Thomas Walsh (New York: G. P. Putnam's Sons, 1920), 407–8.

15. As Sylvia Molloy states in her analysis of *Mis doce primeros años*, "Mercedes Merlin finds her identity as a writer in exile and because of exile." *At Face Value*, 86.

16. Comtesse Merlin, *Souvenirs et mémoires de Madame la Comtesse Merlin: Souvenirs d'une Créole* (Paris: Mercure de France, 1990), 86. Compare Merlin's vision of winter with that of Heredia in his "Carta sobre los Estados Unidos" (1826): "Bajé a tierra, y vi con horror lo que es invierno. Un río estaba ya helado. Todo el campo parecía consumido por un incendio reciente. Ninguna yerba pudo consolar la vista de esta aridez espantosa" [I stepped on shore and saw with horror what winter is like. A river was already frozen. The whole countryside seemed to have been burned by a recent fire. No blade of grass could palliate the vision of this dreadful barrenness]. *Prosas* (Havana: Letras Cubanas, 1980), 132.

17. Gustavo Pérez Firmat describes thus the bicultural condition of Cuban-Americans: "Unlike acculturation or transculturation, biculturation implies an equilibrium, however tense or precarious, between the two contributing cultures. Cuban-American culture is a balancing act." *Life on the Hyphen: The Cuban-American Way* (Austin: University of Texas Press, 1994), 6. Although it is difficult to determine whether the real-world Merlin could be described as bicultural, one can read in *La Havane* a kind of balancing act—precarious and, at times, tense—that connects with Pérez Firmat's observations of Cuban-American culture.

18. Quoted by Salvador Bueno, "Una escritora habanera de expresión francesa," in *De Merlin a Carpentier: Nuevos temas y personajes de la literatura cubana* (Havana: Unión de Escritores y Artistas de Cuba, 1977), 43.

19. Francisco Calcagno, *Diccionario biográfico cubano* (New York: Imprenta y Librería de N. Ponce de León, 1878), 358.

20. The passage included is taken from Carta II of *Viaje a la Habana* (1844), the abridged Spanish version of *La Havane* published in Madrid. Carta II corresponds to Lettre XIV of *La Havane*, the author's first vision of her native city upon her return, which I examine later in this chapter.

21. In her introduction to the anthology, Mirta Yáñez relates exile with the rise of heterolingualism: "No quiero dejar de comentar la presencia de 'otra orilla' de la cuentística cubana, puesto que los autores del exilio pertenecen a la literatura cubana, quiéranlo o no. . . . Han surgido nuevos nombres y el hecho, entre las más recientes autoras, de escribir en una lengua intermedia, o llanamente en el idioma del país donde se han formado, en inglés. La dilucidación de este complejo

fenómeno sólo ha comenzado por ambas partes hace apenas muy poco" [I do not want to overlook the presence of "another shore" in Cuban short fiction, since the authors of exile belong to Cuban literature, whether they want it or not. . . . New names have emerged as well as the practice, among the newest authors, of writing in an intermediate tongue, or simply in the language of the country where they have been raised, in English. The analysis of this complex phenomenon has begun only very recently on both sides]. "Y entonces la mujer de Lot miró...," introduction to *Estatuas de sal: Cuentistas cubanas contemporáneas*, ed. Mirta Yáñez and Marilyn Bobes (Havana: Unión, 1996), 41 n. 19. The last sentence, if tentative, signals a salutary willingness to delay judgment on linguistic alterity. Interestingly, one phrase in this essay—"quiéranlo o no" ["whether they want it or not"]—remains ambiguous: Is Yáñez referring to exile authors, or other entities? Whose will controls reception?

22. Richard Henry Dana, *To Cuba and Back* (Boston: Ticknor and Fields, 1845), iii.

23. For a reading of *La Havane* as a "mother/daughter" text, see Méndez Rodenas, *Gender and Nationalism in Colonial Cuba*, 25–35.

24. In its journey from Europe to the United States to the tropics, *La Havane* anticipates the route of Rubén Darío's *El viaje a Nicaragua* (1909); both travel narratives also coincide in their intermittently exotic vision of the native land. On Darío's book and its Oriental allusions, see Aníbal González, *La crónica modernista hispanoamericana* (Madrid: José Porrúa Turanzas, 1983), 134–46.

25. I employ the term *crónicas de Indias* rather loosely, to reflect the manner in which Merlin perceives what is really a generically complex group of texts; see Walter Mignolo, "Cartas, crónicas y relaciones del descubrimiento y la conquista," in *Historia de la literatura hispanoamericana: Época colonial*, ed. Luis Iñigo Madrigal (Madrid: Cátedra, 1982), 57–116.

26. Another heterolingual author, José-Maria de Heredia, finds in the history and writings of the Spanish conquest a subject for his own literary endeavors; a section of *Les Trophées* is entitled "Les Conquérants de l'or," and he also translates Bernal Díaz del Castillo's *Historia verdadera de la conquista de la Nueva España* into French.

27. Cintio Vitier, *Lo cubano en la poesía* (Havana: Instituto del Libro, 1970), 84.

28. José Martí, *Ismaelillo / Versos libres / Versos sencillos* (Madrid; Cátedra, 1982), 179.

29. Tzvetan Todorov, *La Conquête de l'Amérique* (Paris: Seuil, 1982), 40; *The Conquest of America*, trans. Richard Howard (New York: Harper and Row, 1984), 34.

30. In one of Merlin's Romantic novels, the narrator places Columbus first on a list of "tous les grands hommes," [all great men] but remarks that these great men "nous ont prouvé qu'il n'y a pas de route facile pour le génie et pour la vertu" [have shown us that there is no easy road for genius and virtue]. *Les Lionnes de Paris* (Paris: Librairie d'Amyot, 1845), 1:159. Merlin stresses both Columbus's achievements and travails, as if to signal that not all discoverers (herself included?) are granted the recognition they deserve.

31. Merlin's sardonic words are only part of a more ambiguous position on slavery. Although she does not favor emancipation, she does oppose continued trade; in *Souvenirs et mémoires*, she underscores the horrors of slavery: "Ces infor-

tunés n'ont qu'une idée fixe, celle de retourner dans leur pays; et souvent on les trouve pendus dans leurs chaumières, à cause de la persuasion où ils sont que ce monde meilleur, qui nous est promis au-delà de celui-ci, doit être pour eux la patrie habitée par leurs familles" (23) [These unfortunate people have only one fixed idea, to return to their country; one often finds them hanged in their cottages because they are persuaded that this better life, promised to us after this one, must be for them the fatherland where their relatives live]. This ambivalence is interpreted by Méndez Rodenas as "a byproduct of Merlin's consciously adopting a feminine position of mediation between metropolis and colony." *Gender and Nationalism in Colonial Cuba*, 146. Claire Emilie Martin views the matter differently: "Merlin appears to be torn between articulating an 'enlightened,' humanitarian, and paternalistic view of slavery and representing the more pragmatic concerns of colonial landowners on the brink of losing the foundation of their wealth through the emancipation of slaves." "Slavery in the Spanish Colonies: The Racial Politics of the Countess of Merlin," in *Reinterpreting the Spanish American Essay: Women Writers of the 19th and 20th Centuries*, ed. Doris Meyer (Austin: University of Texas Press, 1995), 43–44. Molloy also discusses her "ambiguous stance towards slavery" in *Mis doce primeros años*: "What does seem important is the way in which she resorts, perhaps unwittingly but nonetheless systematically, to a group whose place in society was essentially uncertain, whose freedom of movement was nil and whose identity depended on a higher authority, to play out her own basic comedy of origins and make visible its fissures, its contradictory texture." *At Face Value*, 91. In *La loma del Ángel*, Reinaldo Arenas traces a parallel between Merlin's marginality and that of black slaves, which leads, in the novel, to the violent expulsion of both Merlin and the slaves from Cuban society. See my "La habitación contigua: Extraterritorialidad y multilingüismo en la literatura hispanoamericana" (Ph.D. diss., Harvard University, 1991), 150–56; Jorge Olivares, "Otra vez *Cecilia Valdés*: Arenas con(tra) Villaverde," *Hispanic Review* 62.2 (spring 1994): 169–84; Méndez Rodenas, *Gender and Nationalism in Colonial Cuba*, 230–35.

    32. See Méndez Rodenas, "A Journey to the (Literary) Source," 711.

    33. Merlin, *Viaje a la Habana* (Havana: Arte y Literatura, 1974).

    34. José Antonio Portuondo, " 'Períodos' y 'generaciones' en la historiografía literaria hispanoamericana," in *La historia y las generaciones* (Santiago de Cuba: Tipografía Román, 1958), 97.

    35. Salvador Bueno, prologue to *Costumbristas cubanos del siglo XIX*, ed. Bueno (Caracas: Biblioteca Ayacucho, 1985), xiv.

    36. José María de Cárdenas y Rodríguez, "¡Educado afuera!" in *Costumbristas cubanos del siglo XIX*, ed. Bueno, 77–78. Emphasis in original indicates departure from standard Spanish.

    37. The title of the short section on Merlin in Max Henríquez Ureña's history of Cuban literature is blunt: "La Condesa de Merlín y su adaptación de 'Una pascua en San Marcos' " [The Countess Merlin and her adaptation of "Una pascua en San Marcos"]. *Panorama histórico de la literatura cubana* (Havana: Arte y Cultura, 1978), 1:289. That it directly follows the section devoted to Ramón de Palma can only enhance this tale of Merlin as a falsifier.

    38. Méndez Rodenas, "A Journey to the (Literary) Source," 712.

    39. Christopher L. Miller, "Orientalism, Colonialism," in *A New History of*

French Literature, ed. Dennis Hollier et al. (Cambridge: Harvard University Press, 1989), 700.

40. M. Henríquez Ureña, *Panorama histórico de la literatura cubana,* 1:289.

41. In Amalia Bacardí's rendering of this passage, Merlin's quirky spelling is normalized: "—¿Lo viste, Pepilla, cómo lo miró? —Ya lo vi, ya— ¿Y con qué furia rompió el abanico cuando lo condenaron a darme un beso? —Y él, ¡qué colorado se puso!" Comtesse Merlin, *La Habana,* trans. Amalia E. Bacardí (Madrid: Crono-color, 1981), 200. However, the change of "Pepiya" (the spelling "Pepyia" being very likely a typographical error) into "Pepilla" forfeits Merlin's skillful depiction of Cuban Spanish, where the two Castilian phonemes represented by the conso-nants "ll" and "y" merge into one.

4. Hudson's and Bombal's Lost Horizon

1. I transcribe Hudson's peculiar diacritics: "Orientál," "Paquíta," etc. Some of these orthographic quirks—especially the accent on "Orientál"—are, as we shall see, meaningful elements in Hudson's unhomely practice of writing.

2. W. H. Hudson, *The Purple Land* (New York: AMS Press, 1968), 330.

3. On the historical events to which this first title alludes, see Elizabeth Ham-psten, "Revisiting a Land That England Lost," *North Dakota Quarterly* 61.2 (spring 1993): 93–94.

4. By speaking of emotions, I seek to preserve the initial thrust of Freud's "Das Unheimliche," whose first sentence reads: "It is only rarely that a psycho-analyst feels impelled to investigate the subject of aesthetics, even when aesthet-ics is understood to mean not merely the theory of beauty but the theory of the qualities of feeling." "The Uncanny," in *Writings on Art and Literature* (Stanford: Stanford University Press, 1997), 193. The German original is even more per-sonal, speaking of feelings in the first-person plural: "sonders sie als Lehre von den Qualitäten unseres Fühlens beschreibt." "Das Unheimliche," in *Der Moses des Michelangelo: Schriften über Kunst und Künstler* (Frankfurt: Fischer, 1993), 137. If Freud sees feelings in verbal art, my discussion of heterolingualism, as will become more evident in this chapter, also finds an aesthetic quality in the un-homeliness of these texts.

5. H. S. Ferns, *Britain and Argentina in the Nineteenth Century* (New York: Arno Press, 1977), 423.

6. Quoted by David Miller, *W. H. Hudson and the Elusive Paradise* (New York: St. Martin's Press, 1990), 4.

7. Nevertheless, some have expressed a measure of irritation about the influ-ence of Spanish in Hudson's rhythm and syntax, especially early in his career; see Alicia Jurado, *Vida y obra de W. H. Hudson* (Buenos Aires: Fondo Nacional de las Artes, 1971), 94. Exploring the author's family tree, Irish and U.S. Ameri-can critics have occasionally engaged in readings of Hudson that underscore his vague ties with their own countries; see ibid., 12.

8. Jorge Luis Borges, "Sobre *The Purple Land,*" in *Otras inquisiciones* (Madrid: Alianza, 1976), 140; "About *The Purple Land,*" in *Other Inquisitions, 1937–1952* (Austin: University of Texas Press, 1995), 143.

9. See John Walker, " 'Home Thoughts from Abroad': W. H. Hudson's Argen-

tine Fiction," *Canadian Review of Comparative Literature* 10.3 (September 1983): 334.

10. Luis Leal, *Breve historia de la literatura hispanoamericana* (New York: Knopf, 1971), 163.

11. Jean Franco, *Spanish American Literature since Independence* (London: Ernest Benn, 1973), 39.

12. This citation from Borges also appears as an epigraph to a chapter in Roberto González Echeverría's *Myth and Archive*, a critical act that, though it perpetuates Hudson's status as a traveler, does reevaluate the contributions of travel writing to Spanish American fiction. *Myth and Archive: A Theory of Latin American Narrative* (Durham: Duke University Press, 1998), 100.

13. As Walker explains, compared with the English travelers who visited the River Plate region from England and recorded their impressions, "the fact is that in chronological and geographical terms almost the reverse process is true of Hudson." " 'Home Thoughts from Abroad,' " 333. In an early essay on *The Purple Land* collected in *El tamaño de mi esperanza* (1926), Borges sees in the English, but not in others, the capacity to become something else: "un desinglesamiento despacito, instintivo, que los americaniza, los asiatiza, los africaniza y los salva" [a slow, instinctive un-Englishment that makes them American, Asian, and African, a process whereby they are redeemed]. He then calls Hudson "inglés chascomusero" [an English from Chascomús], a phrase that recalls the duality, perhaps the strangeness, of Mansilla's "Argentine Indians." "*La tierra cárdena*," in *El tamaño de mi esperanza* (Barcelona: Seix Barral, 1993), 33–34.

14. On Hudson's connections with British literature, Jurado states, "Estoy convencida . . . de que nadie puede estudiar con seriedad la obra de Hudson sin saber el inglés como lo supo él—es decir, como su lengua materna—y sin conocer la literatura de ese idioma lo bastante como para percibir hasta qué punto su prosa está entretejida de alusiones, a veces distorsionadas o insinuadas apenas, a versos de Shakespeare, Milton, Blake, Coleridge, Pope y tantos otros" [I am convinced that Hudson's work cannot be studied seriously by anyone who does not know English as he did—that is, as a mother tongue—or the literature of that language well enough to perceive the extent to which his prose is interwoven with allusions, at times distorted or vaguely insinuated, to lines by Shakespeare, Milton, Blake, Coleridge, Pope, and so many others]. *Vida y obra de Hudson*, 11. Jurado's point is well taken, but here I intend to make a case as well for a reader who also knows the literary systems of the River Plate reader, vague but determining signs of which appear through *The Purple Land*.

15. Nicolas Shumway, *The Invention of Argentina* (Berkeley: University of California Press, 1993), 68.

16. See Borges, "La poesía gauchesca," in *Discusión* (Buenos Aires: Emecé, 1976), 11–38; Ángel Rama, "El sistema literario de la poesía gauchesca," in *Literatura y clase social* (Mexico City: Folios, 1983).

17. Johan Huizinga, *Homo Ludens: A Study of the Play Element in Culture* (Boston: Beacon Press, 1955). On the *payada*, or song contest, in *Martín Fierro*, see Jean Franco, *Spanish American Literature since Independence*, 53.

18. An analogous yet different stance exists in Rudyard Kipling's fiction, in which Ali Behdad observes: "The inclusion of Orientals as storytellers or speakers of dramatic monologues addressed to sahibs . . . expresses a narrative desire for

the Other—a desire that 'dialogizes' the monolithic (authorial) discourse—while it points to a hegemonic impulse to appropriate the native voice." *Belated Travelers: Orientalism in the Age of Colonial Dissolution* (Durham: Duke University Press, 1994), 85. In *The Purple Land,* however, Lamb's patent failure complicates the imperial relations that Behdad sees at work so clearly in Kipling, where "the Oriental storyteller, often reduced to a rhetorical or narrative device, is thus appropriated by the colonialist writer to provide an exotic flavor for his familiar tale while showing his mastery in imitating the Other's speech. In this sense, the inclusion of the native as a narrative frame reaffirms his exteriority in relation to the story's actual interlocutionary situation, which is that of 'white' writing for 'white' readers." Ibid., 85. Yet, as Behdad points out, the presence of this other discourse is still an instance of heteroglossia, even if at the end there subsists in Kipling a colonial relationship: oral stories serving as "raw material" for the "white" literary culture. Ibid. 90.

19. An exception would be Alejo Carpentier's *La consagración de la primavera* (1978), whose second epigraph is an excerpt from Stravinsky's *Rite of Spring;* see Gérard Genette, *Seuils* (Paris: Seuil, 1987), 140.

20. Hudson, *La tierra purpúrea,* trans. Eduardo Hillman (Montevideo: Ministerio de Instrucción Pública y Previsión Social, 1965), 38, n.1. Hillman's confusion of author and narrator is not surprising given the widespread tendency to read *The Purple Land* as autobiographical; on these readings, see Jurado, *Vida y obra de Hudson,* 91, Walker, " 'Home Thoughts from Abroad,' " 342.

21. For another unhomely rendering of a classical Spanish stanza, see my reading of Nicolás Guillén's "Tú no sabe inglé" in chapter 1.

22. For an insightful discussion of Hudson's own conflictive relation with England, especially as it concerns his reading of Darwin's *The Voyage of the Beagle,* see Jason Wilson, "W. H. Hudson: The Colonial's Revenge," *Review: Latin American Literature and Arts* 31 (January–April 1982): 53–59.

23. See Borges, "Sobre *The Purple Land,*" 139; "About *The Purple Land.*"

24. Doris Sommer, *Foundational Fictions: The National Romances of Latin America* (Berkeley: University of California Press), 1991.

25. María Luisa Bombal, *House of Mist / The Shrouded Woman* (Austin: University of Texas Press, 1995), 3.

26. The two works are *La última niebla* and *La amortajada.* In Bombal's Spanish-language fiction, Alicia Borinsky observes that "trabajar a contracorriente de lo que el lector espera, significa también que la lectura resultante está formada por elementos de *resistencia* al texto" (emphasis in original) ["working against what the reader expects has as its outcome an act of reading made up of elements of resistance to the text"]. "El paisaje de la apatía," in *María Luisa Bombal: Apreciaciones críticas,* ed. Marjorie Agosín et al. (Tempe: Bilingual Press/Editorial Bilingüe, 1987), 31–32.

27. Although *La última niebla* is often described as a novel, its length and closely constructed plot point more clearly to the genre of the novella.

28. See Ágata Gligo, *María Luisa (Sobre la vida de María Luisa Bombal)* (Santiago de Chile: Andrés Bello, 1985), 125.

29. On the interior movement of *La última niebla,* see Celeste Kostopulos-Cooperman, *The Lyrical Vision of María Luisa Bombal* (London: Tamesis, 1988), 8–20.

30. Amado Alonso writes, "Una novelista que en su primera obra nos da una

construcción poética con tan artística realización y con tan sobrios y eficaces elementos de estilo bien merece ser saludada y presentada por la crítica con especial atención" [A novelist who in her first work gives us such a poetical construction, with such artistic realization and sober and efficient elements of style, deserves to be saluted and introduced by critics with particular attention.] "Aparición de una novelista," foreword to *La última niebla,* by María Luisa Bombal (Buenos Aires: Andina, 1978), 34.

31. Gligo, *María Luisa,* 124–25. U.S. American reviewers were not overly enthusiastic about *House of Mist,* faulting Bombal for "her unwise decision to write directly in English" (Anthony Boucher, *San Francisco Chronicle*) and for the fact that "Miss Bombal's heroine dwells far too steadily on her raptures—and her fears" (Richard Sullivan, *New York Times*). Quoted by Gloria Gálvez Lira, *María Luisa Bombal: Realidad y fantasía* (Potomac, Md.: Scripta Humanistica, 1986), 8. Writing between languages and literary contexts, the author seems to have abandoned her old readers and not quite reached new ones—except those, arguably, with unhomely aesthetics of their own.

32. See María Luisa Bombal, *New Islands and Other Stories,* trans. Richard and Lucía Cunningham (Ithaca: Cornell University Press, 1988).

33. Quoted by Gligo, *María Luisa,* 124.

34. Gligo recounts that having expanded the text of *La amortajada* for an English translation to be published by Knopf, Bombal feels that the all the poetry of the original is gone. Since the book is already printed and about to come out, a friend of the family decides to purchase all copies of the edition. A new version of *The Shrouded Woman* by Bombal, but this time closer to the original, is published in London in 1948. *María Luisa,* 128–29.

35. Cf. also Victoria Ocampo's introduction to reading and writing in foreign tongues in "Dette à la France" and "And So I Shall Have Mine"; see chapter 1.

36. On the connections between Bombal's style in Spanish and folk literature, see Inés Dölz-Blackburn, "Elementos narrativos tradicionales en la obra de María Luisa Bombal y su relación con motivos folklóricos universales," in *María Luisa Bombal: Apreciaciones críticas,* ed. Agosín et al. 51–71. On the relations between *La última niebla* and Joseph Campbell's writings, see Marjorie Agosín, *Las desterradas del paraíso: Protagonistas en la narrativa de María Luisa Bombal* (New York: Senda Nueva de Ediciones, 1983), 25–48.

5. BABEL; OR, EXPLOSION IN THE LIBRARY

1. Guillermo Cabrera Infante, *Holy Smoke* (London: Faber and Faber, 1985), 155.

2. In fact, Enrique Anderson Imbert, for one, does exclude Vicente Huidobro's and César Moro's French-language poetry from his literary history. *Historia de la literatura hispanoamericana,* 9th ed. (Mexico City: Fondo de Cultura Económica, 1995), 2:55, 2:184.

3. Guillermo Cabrera Infante, *Puro humo,* trans. Cabrera Infante and Íñigo García Ureta (Madrid: Alfaguara, 2000).

4. See Verónica Cortínez, "La parroquia y el universo: *Historia personal del "boom"* de José Donoso," *Revista Chilena de Literatura* 48 (April 1996): 13–22.

5. In the preface to the second edition of *Myth and Archive,* Roberto González Echevarría comments explicitly on the habit of Latin American writers "all too often to fashion themselves as critics" (just as many critics have indulged in literary genres): "I wrote *Myth and Archive* spurred by the intemperate ambition to explain to Latin American novelists what they were doing and why. By writing a critical construct about theirs, I hoped to pry away the layers of deceit and self-deceit accumulated over years of pontificating about their own works. I wanted to create a role for the critic's voice in Latin American literature distinct from those of the writers, an urge incited not only by the intellectual challenge, but also by a historical condition known to all but largely unspoken because of the many vested interests involved: the complicity between literature and criticism in Latin America." *Myth and Archive: A Theory of Latin American Narrative* (Durham: Duke University Press, 1998), ix. But if González Echevarría views criticism and literature as two poles, he is also cognizant of the intermediate spaces—for example, "the polymorphous nature of the novel as genre" (xi)—and he even confesses that "I do at least *feel* that I absorb more from the sweetness of literature than from the usefulness of theory, to echo Horace" (x; emphasis in original). In this chapter, I seek to read the works of two novelists for what they may say about the relative silence of criticism, specifically as it concerns the history of writing by one strange kind of Spanish American author. In this sense, my critical gesture follows González Echevarría's belief in sweet literature as a source of useful critical knowledge, which is also what Lucille Kerr, in a different theoretical context, examines in her study of authorial figures in Spanish American fiction: "Spanish American narratives suggest that the apparently discreet doing of literature is also always a way of talking about it." *Reclaiming the Author: Figures and Fiction from Spanish America* (Durham: Duke University Press, 1992), viii.

6. Cabrera Infante, "Guillermo Cabrera Infante: An Interview in a Summer Manner," interview by Jason Wilson, in *On Modern Latin American Fiction,* ed. John King (New York: Noonday Press, 1987), 314.

7. Cabrera Infante states, "The only Cuban book that comes close to my Havana books is a novel by Carpentier called *El acoso (Manhunt).* Like many novels it is actually a thriller. . . . But it is also a driller, what with the rehearsing and the purple patches." Cabrera Infante, interview by Jason Wilson, 315–16.

8. Cabrera Infante, "Utopía termina en Etiopía," interview by Sergio Marras, in *América Latina: Marca registrada* (Buenos Aires: Zeta, 1992), 75.

9. Cabrera Infante, interview by Wilson, 316. Previously, in a well-known lecture, Cabrera Infante had stated, "El Boom Club era una exclusiva sociedad de bombos mutuos en que cada uno de sus miembros se dedicaba a elogiar, a veces desmesuradamente y con contraproducencia, al miembro que tenía al lado, preferiblemente a la siniestra" [The Boom Club was a mutual admiration society in which every member was devoted to praising, in a boundless and counterproductive manner, whomever was sitting next to him, preferably to the left]. Cabrera Infante, "Include Me Out," in *Requiem for the "Boom"—Premature?: A Symposium,* ed. Rose S. Minc and Marilyn R. Frankenthaler (Montclair, N.J.: Montclair State College, 1980), 16. For an insightful reading of *Tres tristes tigres* as both center and negation of the boom, see Enrico Mario Santí, "El boom en Cuba: Guillermo Cabrera Infante," in *Por una politeratura: Literatura hispanoamericana e imaginación política* (Mexico City: Ediciones del Equilibrista, 1997), 272–78.

10. Quoted by Antonio Prieto Taboada, "Idioma y ciudadanía literaria en *Holy Smoke* de Guillermo Cabrera Infante," *Revista Iberoamericana* 57.154 (1991): 260.

11. On Kozer's choice of Spanish as a "spiritual habitat" (157), see Gustavo Pérez Firmat, *Life on the Hyphen: The Cuban-American Way* (Austin: University of Texas Press, 1994), 156–62.

12. That Heredia also translated Bernal Díaz del Castillo's *Historia verdadera de la conquista de la Nueva España* into French may be read as one more token of his enduring ties with a Hispanic literary legacy of some kind. See Simone Szertics, *L'Héritage espagnol de Heredia* (Paris: Klincksieck, 1975).

13. See Souza, *Guillermo Cabrera Infante: Two Islands, Many Worlds* (Austin: University of Texas Press, 1996), 27.

14. See Suzanne Jill Levine, *The Subversive Scribe: Translating Latin American Fiction* (Saint Paul: Greywolf Press, 1991).

15. See Souza, *Guillermo Cabrera Infante*, 60, 73–74, 113.

16. On the relation between fiction and autobiographical discourse in *La Habana para un infante difunto*, see Roberto González Echevarría, "Autobiography and Representation in *La Habana para un Infante difunto*," *World Literature Today* 61.4 (1987): 568–74; José Miguel Oviedo, "Cabrera Infante en el espejo de Nabokov," *Quimera: Revista de Literatura* 78–79 (June 1988): 74–81.

17. The first two books, in the minds of some critics, achieve a precise recovery of time. Souza, for instance, states: "*La Habana para un Infante difunto* ends with the words 'This is where we came in,' an indication that the city that is evoked in the novel will continue to exist in the eternal return of the reels of memory, a process that is reactivated each time a reader enters the text." "Yes, We Have No Havana(s): Requiem for a Lost City," *World Literature Today* 61.4 (1987): 583.

18. "I was born in Cuba, and I hope to die in England." This is the epigraph of Cabrera Infante's contribution to *Literature in Exile*, ed. John Glad (Durham: Duke University Press, 1990), 34.

19. Significantly, the epigraph of Cristina Garcia's *Dreaming in Cuban* is taken from Stevens's poetry in English: "These casual exfoliations are / Of the tropic of resemblances . . ." On Stevens and Cuba, see my "Wallace Stevens y el discurso en La Habana: Palabras de José Rodríguez Feo," *Revista Canadiense de Estudios Hispánicos* 22.1 (autumn 1997): 3–18.

20. Consuelo Hermes and Marjorie May, "What to Wear," in *Havana*, ed. John Miller and Susannah Clark (San Francisco: Chronicle Books, 1996), 73; Graham Green, *Our Man in Havana* (New York: Viking, 1958), 3; Randy Wayne White, *North of Havana* (New York: Berkley Prime Crime, 1998), xi; Wendy Gimbel, *Havana Dreams: A Story of Cuba* (New York: Knopf, 1998), 173.

21. Bertolt Brecht, libretto of *Aufstieg und Fall der Stadt Mahagonny*, music by Kurt Weill, with Lotte Lenya and Heinz Sauerbaum, North German Radio Chorus and Orchestra, Wilhelm Brückner-Rüggeberg, CBS Records compact disc, MK2 77341, 1958, 46–47.

22. Henri Meilhac and Ludovic Halévy, libretto of *Carmen*, music by Georges Bizet, with Leontyne Price and Franco Corelli, Vienna Philharmonic Orchestra, Herbert von Karajan, RCA Victor Opera Series compact disc 6199–2-RG, 1964, 30. On Bizet's "Habanera" as Carmen's *ars erotica*, see Nelly Furman, "The Languages of Love in *Carmen*, in *Reading Opera*, ed. Arthur Groos and Roger Parker (Princeton: Princeton University Press, 1988), especially 176–78; on issues of al-

terity, see Susan McClary, "Structures of Identity and Difference in Bizet's *Carmen*," in *The Work of Opera: Genre, Nationhood, and Sexual Difference*, ed. Richard Dellamora and Daniel Fischlin (New York: Columbia University Press, 1997), 115–29.

23. Cabrera Infante, interview by Marras, 73.

24. For a summary of and response to these polemics, see Rodolfo A. Borello, "¿Es Borges un escritor hispanoamericano?" in *Identidad cultural de Iberoamérica en su literatura*, ed. Saúl Yurkievich (Madrid: Alhambra, 1986), 240–46.

25. Cabrera Infante's English, as Ardis L. Nelson observes, does not conceal its foreign connections: "*Holy Smoke*'s syntax carries over a distinctly Latinate quality from Spanish, and Cabrera Infante continues his practice of sprinkling untranslatable words and phrases in Spanish, French, Latin, and even Catalan throughout the text, along with offering numerous etymologies. Multilingualism is explicit proof that there is more than one view." "*Holy Smoke*: Anatomy of a Vice." *World Literature Today* 61.4 (1987): 599.

26. See Fernando Ortiz, *Contrapunteo cubano del tabaco y el azúcar* (Havana: Jesús Montero, 1940).

27. I am thinking especially of Borges's "Mutaciones," in *El hacedor* (1960), in which signs of arrows and crosses are only vague reminders of the original uses of those objects.

28. Roberto G. Fernández, *Raining Backwards* (Houston: Arte Público Press, 1988), 11.

29. On the connections between *Holy Smoke* and Victorian and Edwardian cultural figures, including Wilde, see Kenneth E. Hall, "Dandyism and *Holy Smoke*," *Hispanófila* 111 (May 1994): 73–82.

30. Cabrera Infante, "El ave del paraíso perdido," in *Mea Cuba* (Barcelona: Plaza & Janés, 1993), 483.

31. Marcel Proust, *À la recherche du temps perdu* (Paris: Pléiade, 1987), 1:27; *Swann's Way*, trans. C. K. Scott Moncrieff and Terence Kilmartin (New York: Vintage, 1989), 29.

32. Luis de Góngora, *Poesía* (Zaragoza: Ebro, 1965), 49.

33. Stéphane Mallarmé, *Poésies* (Paris: Gallimard, 1992), 164; *Collected Poems*, trans. Henry Weinfield (Berkeley: University of California Press, 1994), 77.

34. Quoted by Salvador Bueno, "Una escritora habanera de expresión francesa," in *De Merlin a Carpentier* (Havana: Unión de Escritores y Artistas de Cuba, 1977), 43; see chapter 3.

35. Kristine Ibsen also remarks on other suggestions of the name "Heredia": *herencia* (inheritance), *heredero* (heir). *Author, Text and Reader in the Novels of Carlos Fuentes* (New York: Peter Lang, 1993), 91. On the interplay between inheritance and disinheritance in *Una familia lejana*, see Maarten van Delden, *Carlos Fuentes, Mexico, and Modernity* (Nashville: Vanderbilt University Press, 1998), 161–65.

36. For instance, in Max Henríquez Ureña's *Panorama histórico de la literatura cubana*, José-Maria de Heredia is mentioned several times—as "el de *Los trofeos*" [the one who wrote *Les Trophées*], to distinguish him from the other Heredia—but his works are not studied formally. Yet, in a less official setting, Henríquez Ureña analyzes the Francophone Heredia's poetry from the viewpoint of Hispanic let-

ters; see "Poetas cubanos de expresión francesa," *Revista Iberoamericana* 3.6 (May 1941): 305–17. In this article, he also studies a third Heredia: Severiano de Heredia, who wrote in French. In 1903, on the centennial of José María Heredia, José-Maria de Heredia composes in a somewhat inexpert Spanish a poignant homage to his older cousin: "Y abandonando el habla de la Francia / En que dije el valor de los mayores, / Al evocar los Conquistadores / En su viril, magnífica arrogancia; / Hoy recuerdo la lengua de mi infancia / Y sueño con sus ritmos y colores, / Para hacerte corona con sus flores / Y envolver tu sepulcro en su fragancia" [And forsaking the speech of France, in which I pronounced the courage of our elders upon evoking the conquistadors in their virile, magnificent arrogance, today I remember my childhood tongue, and I dream of its rhythms and colors, to make you a crown with its flowers, and shroud your sepulcher with their fragrance]. *Œuvres poétiques complètes* (Paris: Les Belles Lettres, 1984) 2:195. In a gesture not unlike that of Eduardo Hillman, who searches for the Spanish-language original of a verse "rendered" in English in Hudson's *The Purple Land*, Henríquez Ureña undertakes his own translation of Heredia's poem "back" into French! See "Poetas cubanos de expresión francesa," 340–41.

   37. Margo Glantz writes about José María Heredia's imprint in *Una familia lejana*: "La constante relación entre Europa y América se marca en el cubano Heredia, heredero de ese otro Heredia, prerromántico, que también naciera en Cuba y escribiera en el *teocalli* de Cholula, confrontado, como Fuentes, a las dos culturas: la civilizada y precisa y la selvática y sangrienta" [The constant relation between Europe and America is marked in the Cuban Heredia, a pre-Romantic, who was also born in Cuba and wrote at Cholula's *teocalli*, facing, like Fuentes, both cultures: the civilized and precise one, and the jungle-like and bloody one]. "Fantasmas y jardines: *Una familia lejana,*" *Revista Iberoamericana* 48.118–19 (January–June 1982): 401–2. Archaeology also concerns José-Maria de Heredia, a student at the École des Chartes and an exacting craftsman of historical reconstructions in his sonnets.

   38. José María Heredia, *Poesías* (Havana: Letras Cubanas, 1980), 51. On the Cholula pyramid in Fuentes's *Cambio de piel*, see Chalene Helmuth, *The Postmodern Fuentes* (Lewisburg, Pa.: Bucknell University Press, 1997), 38–39.

   39. Carlos Fuentes, *Una familia lejana* (Mexico City: Biblioteca Era, 1992), 29; *Distant Relations,* trans. Margaret Sayers Peden (New York: Farrar, Straus, and Giroux, 1990), 25.

   40. Ibsen establishes a parallel between *Terra nostra* and *Una familia lejana* based on their use of intertextuality: "While *Terra Nostra* focuses on the texts of the Spanish language literature, in *Una familia lejana* the primary texts which are activated are drawn from French literature and, particularly, those authors who are in some way associated with both France and Latin America." *Author, Text and Reader in the Novels of Carlos Fuentes,* 91. On Fuentes's discussion of Spain in *Terra nostra,* see Roberto González Echevarría, "*Terra Nostra*: Theory and Practice," in *Carlos Fuentes: A Critical View,* ed. Robert Brody and Charles Rossman (Austin: University of Texas Press, 1982), 132–45; Raymond Leslie Williams, *The Writings of Carlos Fuentes* (Austin: University of Texas Press, 1996), 48–107.

   41. On the challenges to the mimetic function of literature in *Una familia lejana,* see Helmuth, *The Postmodern Fuentes,* 65–68.

   42. See René de Costa, *Vicente Huidobro: The Careers of a Poet* (Oxford: Clarendon Press, 1984), 43–56.

43. On Borges and mirrors, see Jaime Alazraki, *Versiones, inversiones, reversiones: El espejo como modelo estructural del relato en los cuentos de Borges* (Madrid: Gredos, 1977).

44. José-Maria de Heredia, *Les Trophées* (Paris: Gallimard, 1981), 135; *The Trophies*, trans. John Myers O'Hara and John Hervey (Westport, Conn.: Hyperion, 1929), 117.

45. Writing in English about language and literary identity, Fuentes states, "The English language, after all, did not need another writer. The English language has always been alive and kicking, and if it ever becomes drowsy, there will always be an Irishman. . . ." "How I Started to Write," in *Myself with Others* (New York: Noonday Press, 1988), 12.

46. See, for instance, this pronouncement from the 1960s: "No quiero generalizar, pero en la mayoría de nuestros países, donde no hay periódicos dignos de ese nombre, donde no hay Congresos dignos de ese nombre, o partidos políticos o sindicatos, y el cine, la televisión y la radio están en manos de los más catastróficos mercaderes que uno pueda imaginar, corresponde finalmente al escritor decir lo que la historia no dice, lo que los medios de comunicación de masa no dicen. En América Latina el escritor se enfrenta con este desafío permanente" [I don't want to generalize, but in most of our countries, where there are no newspapers worthy of the name, nor congresses worthy of the name, nor political parties nor unions, and where film, television, and radio are in the hands of the most catastrophic merchants one can imagine, it is ultimately the task of the writer to say what history does not say, what the media don't say. In Latin America, the writer must always face this permanent challenge]. "Papel del escritor en América Latina," round table discussion with Homero Aridjis et al., *Mundo Nuevo* 5 (November 1966): 28. Beyond this public role, however, it is to this author's credit that in his narrative fiction—despite his search for a coherent whole—polysemy ultimately reigns. On Fuentes's vision of his entire œuvre conceptualized in fourteen cycles entitled "La Edad del Tiempo," see Williams, *The Writings of Carlos Fuentes*, 110–45. On how one text, *Terra nostra*, plays out several themes linked with an author's authority, see Kerr, *Reclaiming the Author*, 65–88.

47. Although this is deceitfully so; as Margaret Sayers Peden observes, already in the first chapter there appear some minor inconsistencies; see "Forking Paths, Infinite Novels, Ultimate Narrators," in *Carlos Fuentes: A Critical View*, ed. Brody and Rossman, 157–58.

48. See Lilvia Soto-Duggan, "La poética de la simultaneidad en Carlos Fuentes," (Ph.D. diss., State University of New York at Stony Brook, 1980).

49. Jules Supervielle, "La Chambre voisine," in *Le Forçat innocent* (Paris: Gallimard, 1987), 58. English translation in Fuentes, *Distant Relations*, ix.

50. Peden demonstrates how "La Chambre voisine" also functions to structure the whole novel: events in the plot coincide with the lines of the poem. "Forking Paths, Infinite Novels, Ultimate Narrators," 166–68.

HABITATIONS OF THE UNHOUSED

1. Sigmund Freud, "The Uncanny," in *Writings on Art and Literature* (Stanford: Stanford University Press, 1997), 193.

2. Leonard Forster, *The Poet's Tongues: Multilingualism in Literature* (Cambridge: Cambridge University Press, 1970), 7.

3. José-Maria de Heredia, *Les Trophées* (Paris: Gallimard, 1981), 174.

Bibliography

Adorno, Rolena. "Cultures in Contact: Mesoamerica, the Andes, and the European Written Tradition." In *The Cambridge History of Latin American Literature,* edited by Roberto González Echevarría and Enrique Pupo-Walker, vol. 1, 33–57. Cambridge: Cambridge University Press, 1996.

———. *Guaman Poma: Writing and Resistance in Colonial Peru.* Austin: University of Texas Press, 1986.

Agosín, Marjorie. *Las desterradas del paraíso: Protagonistas en la narrativa de María Luisa Bombal.* New York: Senda Nueva de Ediciones, 1983.

Alonso, Amado. "Aparición de una novelista." Foreword to *La última niebla,* by María Luisa Bombal, 7–34. Buenos Aires: Andina, 1978.

Anderson Imbert, Enrique. *Los domingos del profesor.* Buenos Aires: Gure, 1972.

———. "Exhumación de un folleto anónimo de Sarmiento." In *Modernidad y posmodernidad,* 91–104. Buenos Aires: Torres Agüero, 1997.

———. *Historia de la literatura hispanoamericana.* 6th ed. Mexico City: Fondo de Cultura Económica, 1974.

———. *Historia de la literatura hispanoamericana.* 9th ed. Mexico City: Fondo de Cultura Económica, 1995.

———. *La originalidad de Rubén Darío.* Buenos Aires: Centro Editor de América Latina, 1967.

———. *Spanish American Literature: A History.* Translated by John V. Falconieri. Detroit: Wayne State University Press, 1963.

Arteaga, Alfred. *Chicano Poetics: Heterotexts and Hybridities.* Cambridge: Cambridge University Press, 1997.

———, ed. *An Other Tongue: Nation and Ethnicity in the Linguistic Borderland.* Durham: Duke University Press, 1994.

Augier, Ángel. *Nicolás Guillén: Notas para un estudio biográfico-crítico.* 2 vols. Santa Clara, Cuba: Universidad Central de Las Villas, 1965.

Ayerza de Castilho, Laura, and Odile Felgine. *Victoria Ocampo.* Paris: Criterion, 1991.

Bacardí Moreau, Emilio. *La Condesa de Merlin.* Santiago de Cuba: Biblioteca Oriente, 1924.

Baily, Samuel L. "Sarmiento and Immigration: Changing Views on the Role of Immigration in the Development of Argentina." In *Sarmiento and His Argentina,* edited by Joseph T. Criscenti, 131–42. Boulder: Lynne Rienner Publishers, 1993.

Behdad, Ali. *Belated Travelers: Orientalism in the Age of Colonial Dissolution*. Durham: Duke University Press, 1994.

Bellini, Giuseppe. *Historia de la literatura hispanoamericana*. Madrid: Castalia, 1985.

Benítez Rojo, Antonio. "Bartolomé de las Casas: Entre el infierno y la ficción." *MLN* 103.2 (March 1988): 259–88.

Bhabha, Homi K. *The Location of Culture*. London: Routledge, 1994.

Bloom, Harold. *The Anxiety of Influence: A Theory of Poetry*. New York: Oxford University Press, 1997.

Bombal, María Luisa. *House of Mist / The Shrouded Woman*. Austin: University of Texas Press, 1995.

———. *New Islands and Other Stories*. Translated by Richard and Lucía Cunningham. Ithaca: Cornell University Press, 1988.

———. *La última niebla / La amortajada*. Barcelona: Biblioteca de Bolsillo, 1994.

Borges, Jorge Luis. "About *The Purple Land*." In *Other Inquisitions, 1937–1952*, 131–45. Austin: University of Texas Press, 1995.

———. "Las alarmas del doctor Américo Castro." In *Otras inquisiciones*, 35–40. Madrid: Alianza, 1976.

———. "*La amortajada*." Review of *La amortajada*, by María Luisa Bombal. *Sur* 8.7 (1938): 80–81.

———. "The Argentine Writer and Tradition." In *Labyrinths: Selected Stories and Other Writings*, translated by James E. Irby, 177–85. New York: New Directions, 1964.

———. "Dr. Américo Castro Is Alarmed." In *Other Inquisitions 1937–1952*, translated by Ruth L. C. Simms, 26–30. Austin: University of Texas Press, 1995.

———. "El escritor argentino y la tradición." In *Discusión*, 151–62. Buenos Aires: Emecé, 1976.

———. "Historia del guerrero y de la cautiva." In *El Aleph*, 49–54. Madrid: Alianza, 1976.

———. "La poesía gauchesca." In *Discusión*, 11–38. Buenos Aires: Emecé, 1976.

———. "Sobre *The Purple Land*." In *Otras inquisiciones*, 138–42. Madrid: Alianza, 1976.

———. "Story of the Warrior and the Captive." In *Labyrinths: Selected Stories and Other Writings*, 127–31. New York: New Directions, 1964.

———. "La tierra cárdena." In *El tamaño de mi esperanza*, 33–37. Barcelona: Seix Barral, 1993.

Borinsky, Alicia. "El paisaje de la apatía." In *María Luisa Bombal: Apreciaciones críticas*, edited by Marjorie Agasín et al. 31–42. Tempe: Bilingual Press/Editorial Bilingüe, 1987.

Bravo, Domingo A. *El quichua en el "Martín Fierro" y en "Don Segundo Sombra."* Buenos Aires: Instituto Amigos del Libro Argentino, 1968.

Brodsky, Joseph. "To Please a Shadow." In *Less than One: Selected Essays*, 357–83. New York: Farrar, Straus, and Giroux, 1988.

Budick, Sanford, and Wolfgang Iser, eds. *The Translatability of Cultures: Figurations of the Space Between*. Stanford: Stanford University Press, 1996.

Bueno, Salvador, "Una escritora habanera de expresión francesa." In *De Merlin a Carpentier: Nuevos temas y personajes de la literatura cubana*, 9–55. Havana: Unión de Escritores y Artistas de Cuba, 1977.

———, ed. *Costumbristas cubanos del siglo XIX*. Caracas: Biblioteca Ayacucho, 1985.

Bush, Andrew. "Lyric Poetry of the Eighteenth and Nineteenth Centuries." In *The Cambridge History of Latin American Literature*, edited by Roberto González Echevarría and Enrique Pupo-Walker, vol. 1, 375–400. Cambridge: Cambridge University Press, 1996.

Cabrera Infante, Guillermo. "Guillermo Cabrera Infante: An Interview in a Summer Manner." Interview by Jason Wilson. In *On Modern Latin American Fiction*, edited by John King, 305–25. New York: Noonday Press, 1987.

———. *Holy Smoke*. London: Faber and Faber, 1985.

———. "Include Me Out." In *Requiem for the "Boom"—Premature?: A Symposium*. edited by Rose S. Minc and Marilyn R. Frankenthaler, 9–20. Montclair, N.J.: Montclair State College, 1980.

———. *Mea Cuba*. Barcelona: Plaza & Janés, 1993.

———. "Nest, Door, Neighbours." In *Writes of Passage*, 62–75. London: Faber and Faber, 1993.

———. "The Phantom of the Essoldo." In *A Hammock beneath the Mangoes: Stories from Latin America*, edited by Thomas Colchie, 382–415. New York: Plume, 1992.

———. *Puro humo*. Translated by Cabrera Infante and Íñigo García Ureta. Madrid: Alfaguara, 2000.

———. *Three Trapped Tigers*. Translated by Donald Gardner and Suzanne Jill Levine with Cabrera Infante. London: Faber and Faber, 1990.

———. *Tres tristes tigres*. Barcelona: Biblioteca de Bolsillo, 1983.

———. "Utopía termina en Etiopía." Interview by Sergio Marras. In *América Latina: Marca registrada*, 67–95. Buenos Aires: Zeta, 1992.

Cárdenas y Rodríguez, José María de. "¡Educado afuera!" In *Costumbristas cubanos del siglo XIX*, edited by Salvador Bueno, 75–79. Caracas: Biblioteca Ayacucho, 1985.

Chanady, Amaryll, ed. *Latin American Identity and Constructions of Difference*. Minneapolis: University of Minnesota Press, 1994.

Cortínez, Verónica. "El siglo de Borges." In *Actas de ALFAL*, edited by Víctor Martínez Alvarez. Santiago: Universidad de Santiago de Chile, forthcoming.

Costa, René de. *Vicente Huidobro: The Careers of a Poet*. Oxford: Clarendon Press, 1984.

Criscenti, Joseph T., ed. *Sarmiento and His Argentina*. Boulder: Lynne Rienner Publishers, 1993.

Cussen, Antonio. *Bello and Bolívar: Poetry and Politics in the Spanish American Revolution*. Cambridge: Cambridge University Press, 1992.

Dana, Richard Henry. *To Cuba and Back*. Boston: Ticknor and Fields, 1845.

Darío, Rubén. *Poesías completas*. Buenos Aires: Ediciones Antonio Zamora, 1967.

———. *Los raros*. Mexico City: Universidad Autónoma Metropolitana, 1985.

———. "To Roosevelt." In *Twentienth-Century Latin American Poetry: A Bilingual Anthology*, edited by Stephen Tapscott, 38–39. Austin: University of Texas Press, 1996.

Díaz, Roberto Ignacio. "La habitación contigua: Extraterritorialidad y multilingüismo en la literatura hispanoamericana." Ph.D. diss., Harvard University, 1991.

———. "Paratextual Snow; or, The Threshold of Mercedes Merlin." *Colby Quarterly* 38.4 (December 1996): 237–54.

———. "Wallace Stevens y el discurso en La Habana: Palabras de José Rodríguez Feo." *Revista Canadiense de Estudios Hispánicos* 22.1 (autumn 1997): 3–18.

Dölz-Blackburn, Inés. "Elementos narrativos tradicionales en la obra de María Luisa Bombal y su relación con motivos folklóricos universales." In *María Luisa Bombal: Apreciaciones críticas*, edited by Marjorie Agosín et al. 51–71. Tempe: Bilingual Press/Editorial Bilingüe, 1987.

Donoso, José. *Historia personal del "boom."* Barcelona: Seix Barral, 1983.

Donoso, María Pilar. *Los de entonces (Recuerdos)*. Barcelona: Seix Barral, 1987.

Echeverría, Esteban. *El matadero / La cautiva*. Edited by Leonor Fleming. Madrid: Cátedra, 1990.

———. "The Slaughterhouse." In *The Borzoi Anthology of Latin American Literature*, edited by Emir Rodríguez Monegal, vol. 1, 209–22. New York: Knopf, 1997.

Ellis, Keith. *Cuba's Nicolás Guillén: Poetry and Ideology*. Toronto: University of Toronto Press, 1983.

Esténger, Rafael. "El otoño galante de la Condesa de Merlin." In *Los amores de cubanos famosos*, 9–19. Havana: Alfa, 1939.

Fernández Retamar, Roberto. *Caliban and Other Essays*. Translated by Edward Baker. 2nd ed. Minneapolis: University of Minnesota Press, 1997.

———. *Calibán: Apuntes sobre la cultura en nuestra América*. Mexico City: Diógenes, 1974.

Ferns, H. S. *Britain and Argentina in the Nineteenth Century*. New York: Arno Press, 1977.

Ferré, Rosario. "On Destiny, Language, and Translation; or, Ophelia Adrift in the C. & O. Canal." In *The Youngest Doll*, 153–65. Lincoln: University of Nebraska Press, 1991.

Figarola-Caneda, Domingo. *La condesa de Merlin*. Paris: Excelsior, 1928.

Forster, Leonard. *The Poet's Tongues: Multilingualism in Literature*. Cambridge: Cambridge University Press, 1970.

Franco, Jean. *Historia de la literatura hispanoamericana*. Barcelona: Ariel, 1983.

———. Introduction to *La tierra purpúrea / Allá lejos y hace tiempo*, by W. H. Hudson, ix–xlv. Caracas: Ayacucho, 1980.

———. *Spanish American Literature since Independence*. London: Ernest Benn, 1973.

Freud, Sigmund. "The Uncanny." In *Writings on Art and Literature*, 193–233. Stanford: Stanford University Press, 1997.

———. "Das Unheimliche." In *Der Moses des Michelangelo: Schriften über Kunst und Künstler*, 135–72. Frankfurt: Fischer, 1993.

Fuentes, Carlos. *The Buried Mirror: Reflections on Spain and the New World*. Boston: Houghton Mifflin, 1992.

———. *Distant Relations*. Translated by Margaret Sayers Peden. New York: Farrar, Straus, and Giroux, 1990.

———. *Una familia lejana*. Mexico City: Biblioteca Era, 1992.

———. "How I Started to Write." In *Myself with Others*, 3–27. New York: Noonday Press, 1988.

———. *La nueva novela hispanoamericana*. Mexico City: Cuadernos de Joaquín Mortiz, 1980.

Gálvez Lira, Gloria. *María Luisa Bombal: Realidad y fantasía*. Potomac, Md.: Scripta Humanistica, 1986.

Garber, Marjorie. *Shakespeare's Ghost Writers: Literature as Uncanny Causality*. New York: Routledge, 1987.

Garcia, Cristina. *Dreaming in Cuban*. New York: Knopf, 1992.

Gelabert, Francisco de Paula. "El puesto de frutas." In *Costumbristas cubanos del siglo XIX*, edited by Salvador Bueno, 453–58. Caracas: Ayacucho, 1985.

Genette, Gérard. *Palimpsestes: La littérature au second degré*. Paris: Seuil, 1982.

———. *Seuils*. Paris: Seuil, 1987.

Glad, John, ed. *Literature in Exile*. Durham: Duke University Press, 1990.

Glantz, Margo. "Fantasmas y jardines: *Una familia lejana*." *Revista Iberoamericana* 48.118–19 (January–June 1982): 397–402.

Gligo, Ágata. *María Luisa (Sobre la vida de María Luisa Bombal)*. Santiago de Chile: Andrés Bello, 1985.

Góngora, Luis de. *Poesía*. Zaragoza: Ebro, 1965.

González, Aníbal. *La crónica modernista hispanoamericana*. Madrid: José Porrúa Turanzas, 1983.

González Echevarría, Roberto. *Alejo Carpentier: The Pilgrim at Home*. Austin: University of Texas Press, 1977.

———. "Autobiography and Representation in *La Habana para un Infante difunto*." *World Literature Today* 61.4 (1987): 568–74.

———. "A Brief History of the Histories of Spanish American Literature." In *The Cambridge History of Latin American Literature*, edited by Roberto González Echevarría and Enrique Pupo-Walker, vol. 1, 7–32. Cambridge: Cambridge University Press, 1996.

———. *Myth and Archive: A Theory of Latin American Narrative*. Durham: Duke University Press, 1998.

———. "*Terra Nostra*: Theory and Practice." In *Carlos Fuentes: A Critical View*, edited by Robert Brody and Charles Rossman, 132–45. Austin: University of Texas Press, 1982.

González Echevarría, Roberto, and Enrique Pupo-Walker, eds. *The Cambridge History of Latin American Literature*. 3 vols. Cambridge: Cambridge University Press, 1996.

Guillén, Claudio. *Entre lo uno y lo diverso: Introducción a la literatura comparada.* Barcelona: Crítica, 1985.

———. *Literature as System.* Princeton: Princeton University Press, 1971.

———. *El sol de los desterrados: Literatura y exilio.* Barcelona: Quaderns Crema, 1995.

Guillén, Nicolás. *Obra poética.* 2 vols. Havana: Arte y Literatura, 1974.

Hall, Kenneth E. "Dandyism and *Holy Smoke.*" *Hispanófila* 111 (May 1994): 73–82.

Hampsten, Elizabeth. "Revisiting a Land That England Lost." *North Dakota Quarterly* 61.2 (spring 1993): 92–107.

Helmuth, Chalene. *The Postmodern Fuentes.* Lewisburg, Pa.: Bucknell University Press, 1997.

Hennessy, Alistair. "Argentines, Anglo-Argentines and Others." In *The Land That England Lost: Argentina and Britain, A Special Relationship,* 9–48. London: British Academy Press, 1992.

Henríquez Ureña, Max. *Panorama histórico de la literatura cubana.* 2 vols. Havana: Arte y Cultura, 1978.

———. "Poetas cubanos de expresión francesa." *Revista iberoamericana* 3.6 (May 1941): 301–44.

Henríquez Ureña, Pedro. *Las corrientes literarias en la América hispánica.* Mexico City: Fondo de Cultura Económica, 1978.

Heredia, José María. *Poesías.* Havana: Letras Cubanas, 1980.

———. *Prosas.* Havana: Letras Cubanas, 1980.

Heredia, José-Maria de. *Œuvres poétiques complètes.* 2 vols. Paris: Les Belles Lettres, 1984.

———. *Les Trophées.* Paris: Gallimard, 1981.

———. *The Trophies.* Translated by John Myers O'Hara and John Hervey. Westport, Conn.: Hyperion, 1929.

Hernández, José. *The Gaucho Martín Fierro.* Translated by C. E. Ward. Albany: State University of New York Press, 1967.

———. *Martín Fierro.* Edited by Ángel J. Battistessa. Madrid: Cátedra, 1994.

Higgins, James. *A History of Peruvian Literature.* Liverpool: Francis Cairns, 1987.

Hudson, W. H. *The Purple Land.* New York: AMS Press, 1968.

———. *La tierra purpúrea.* Translated by Eduardo Hillman. Montevideo: Ministerio de Instrucción Pública y Previsión Social, 1965.

———. *La tierra purpúrea / Allá lejos y hace tiempo.* Translated by Idea Vilariño. Caracas: Ayacucho, 1980.

Huidobro, Vicente. *Altazor / Temblor de cielo.* Edited by René de Costa. Madrid: Cátedra, 1981.

Ibsen, Kristine. *Author, Text and Reader in the Novels of Carlos Fuentes.* New York: Peter Lang, 1993.

Iñigo Madrigal, Luis. Introduction to *Summa poética,* by Nicolás Guillén, 13–45. Madrid: Cátedra, 1983.

Jitrik, Noé. "Forma y significación en *El matadero,* de Esteban Echeverría." In *El fuego de la especie,* 63–98. Buenos Aires: Siglo XXI, 1971.

———. *Poems, Protest, and a Dream.* Translated by Margaret Sayers Peden. New York: Penguin, 1997.

Jurado, Alicia. *Vida y obra de W. H. Hudson.* Buenos Aires: Fondo Nacional de las Artes, 1971.

Kerr, Lucille. *Reclaiming the Author: Figures and Fiction from Spanish America.* Durham: Duke University Press, 1992.

Kostopulos-Cooperman, Celeste. *The Lyrical Vision of María Luisa Bombal.* London: Tamesis, 1988.

Kristal, Efraín. *The Andes Viewed from the City: Literary and Political Discourse on the Indian in Peru, 1848–1930.* New York: Peter Lang, 1987.

———. "Dialogues and Polemics: Sarmiento, Lastarria, and Bello." In *Sarmiento and His Argentina,* edited by Joseph T. Criscenti, 61–70. Boulder: Lynne Rienner Publishers, 1993.

———. "En torno a la historia del concepto de historia literaria hispanoamericana." *Teoría/Crítica* 1 (1994): 195–209.

Kristeva, Julia. *Étrangers à nous-mêmes.* Paris: Seuil, 1988.

———. *Strangers to Ourselves.* Translated by Leon S. Roudiez. New York: Columbia University Press, 1991.

Landívar, Rafael. *Rusticatio mexicana.* Edited by Octaviano Valdés. Mexico City: Jus, 1965.

Leal, Luis. *Breve historia de la literatura hispanoamericana.* New York: Knopf, 1971.

Leal, Luis, and Manuel M. Martin-Rodríguez. "Chicano Literature." In *The Cambridge History of Latin American Literature,* edited by Roberto González Echevarría and Enrique Pupo-Walker, vol. 2, 557–86. Cambridge: Cambridge University Press, 1996.

Levine, Suzanne Jill. *The Subversive Scribe: Translating Latin American Fiction.* Saint Paul: Greywolf Press, 1991.

Lockhart, James, ed. *We People Here: Nahuatl Accounts of the Conquest of Mexico.* Berkeley: University of California Press, 1993.

Luis, William. "Latin American (Hispanic Caribbean) Literature Written in the United States." In *The Cambridge History of Latin American Literature,* edited by Roberto González Echevarría and Enrique Pupo-Walker, vol. 2, 526–56. Cambridge: Cambridge University Press, 1996.

Mallarmé, Stéphane. *Collected Poems.* Translated by Henry Weinfield. Berkeley: University of California Press, 1994.

———. *Poésies.* Paris: Gallimard, 1992.

Mañach, Jorge. *Martí el apóstol.* Madrid: Espasa-Calpe, 1968.

Mansilla, Lucio V. *Una excursión a los indios ranqueles.* Madrid: Ediciones de Cultura Hispánica, 1993.

———. *An Expedition to the Ranquel Indians.* Translated by Mark McCaffrey. Austin: University of Texas Press, 1997.

Marichal, Juan. *Cuatro fases de la historia intelectual latinoamericana, 1810–1979*. Madrid: Fundación Juan March, 1978.

Martí, José. *Obras completas*. 27 vols. Havana: Editorial Nacional de Cuba, 1963–66.

———. "Our America." In *Our America by José Martí: Writings on Latin America and the Struggle for Cuban Independence*, translated by Elinor Randal et al., 84–94. New York: Monthly Review Press, 1977.

Martin, Claire Emilie. "Slavery in the Spanish Colonies: The Racial Politics of the Countess of Merlin." In *Reinterpreting the Spanish American Essay: Women Writers of the 19th and 20th Centuries*, edited by Doris Meyer, 37–45. Austin: University of Texas Press, 1995.

Martínez Estrada, Ezequiel. *El mundo maravilloso de Guillermo Enrique Hudson*. Mexico City: Fondo de Cultura Económica, 1951.

Masiello, Francine. *Between Civilization and Barbarism: Women, Nation, and Literary Culture in Modern Argentina*. Lincoln: University of Nebraska Press, 1982.

Mata Gavidia, José. Introduction to *Rusticatio mexicana*, by Rafael Landívar. Guatemala: Imprenta Universitaria, 1950.

Menchú, Rigoberta. *I, Rigoberta Menchú: An Indian Woman in Guatemala*. Edited by Elisabeth Burgos-Debray. Translated by Ann Wright. London: Verso, 1996.

———. *Me llamo Rigoberta Menchú y así me nació la conciencia*. Mexico City: Siglo XXI, 1992.

Méndez Rodenas, Adriana. *Gender and Nationalism in Colonial Cuba: The Travels of Santa Cruz y Montalvo, Condesa de Merlin*. Nashville: Vanderbilt University Press, 1998.

———. "A Journey to the (Literary) Source: The Invention of Origins in Merlin's *Viaje a La Habana*." *New Literary History* 21.3 (1990): 707–31.

———. "Voyage to *La Havane*: The Countess of Merlín's Preview of National Identity." *Cuban Studies* 16 (1986): 71–99.

Merlin, María de las Mercedes Santa Cruz y Montalvo, comtesse. *La Habana*. Translated by Amalia E. Bacardí. Madrid: Cronocolor, 1981.

———. *La Havane*. 3 vols. Paris: Librarie d'Amyot, 1844.

———. *Les Lionnes de Paris*. 2 vols. Paris: Librairie d'Amyot, 1845.

———. *Souvenirs et mémoires de Madame la Comtesse Merlin: Souvenirs d'une Créole*. Paris: Mercure de France, 1990.

———. *Viaje a la Habana*. Havana: Arte y Literatura, 1974.

Miller, Christopher L. "Orientalism, Colonialism." In *A New History of French Literature*, edited by Dennis Hollier et al., 698–705. Cambridge: Harvard University Press, 1989.

Miller, David. *W. H. Hudson and the Elusive Paradise*. New York: St. Martin's Press, 1990.

Molloy, Sylvia. *At Face Value: Autobiographical Writing in Spanish America*. Cambridge: Cambridge University Press, 1991.

Morse, Richard M. *New World Soundings: Culture and Ideology in the Americas*. Baltimore: Johns Hopkins University Press, 1989.

Moya, José C. *Cousins and Strangers: Spanish Immigrants in Buenos Aires, 1850–1930.* Berkeley: University of California Press, 1998.

Mujica Lainez, Manuel. *El gran teatro.* Barcelona: Planeta, 1979.

———. *Placeres y fatigas de los viajes.* Buenos Aires: Sudamericana, 1986.

Nelson, Ardis L. "*Holy Smoke*: Anatomy of a Vice." *World Literature Today* 61.4 (1987): 590–93.

Neruda, Pablo. *Canto general.* Barcelona: Seix Barral, 1982.

———. *Canto General.* Translated by Jack Schmitt. Berkeley: University of California Press, 1991.

———. *Confieso que he vivido.* Barcelona: Seix Barral, 1974.

———. *Memoirs.* Translated by Hardie St. Martin. New York: Farrar, Straus, and Giroux, 1977.

Ocampo, Victoria. *Testimonios: Segunda Serie.* Buenos Aires: Sur, 1941.

Olivares, Jorge. "Otra vez *Cecilia Valdés*: Arenas con(tra) Villaverde." *Hispanic Review* 62.2 (spring 1994): 169–84.

Oviedo, José Miguel. "Cabrera Infante en el espejo de Nabokov." *Quimera: Revista de Literatura* 78–79 (June 1988): 74–81.

———. "La excepción y la regla en la literatura de América Latina." In *Escrito al margen.* Mexico City: Premià, 1987.

Paz, Octavio. "Sobre la crítica." In *Corriente alterna,* 39–44. Mexico City: Siglo XXI, 1981.

———. *Sor Juana Inés de la Cruz o las trampas de la fe.* 1982. Mexico City: Fondo de Cultura Económica, 1985.

———. *Sor Juana; or, The Traps of Faith.* Translated by Margaret Sayers Peden. Cambridge: Harvard University Press, 1988.

Paz, Octavio, et al. *Renga: Poème.* Paris: Gallimard, 1971.

Peden, Margaret Sayers. "Forking Paths, Infinite Novels, Ultimate Narrators." In *Carlos Fuentes: A Critical View,* edited by Robert Brody and Charles Rossman, 156–72. Austin: University of Texas Press, 1982.

Pérez Firmat, Gustavo. *The Cuban Condition: Translation and Identity in Modern Cuban Literature.* Cambridge: Cambridge University Press, 1989.

———. *Life on the Hyphen: The Cuban-American Way.* Austin: University of Texas Press, 1994.

Perkins, David. *Is Literary History Possible?* Baltimore: Johns Hopkins University Press, 1992.

Perrone-Moisés, Leyla, and Emir Rodríguez Monegal. "Isidoro Ducasse et la rhétorique espagnole." *Poétique* 55 (September 1983): 351–77.

Pizarro, Ana, ed. *Hacia una historia de la literatura hispanoamericana.* Mexico City: El Colegio de México, 1987.

Portuondo, José Antonio. " 'Períodos' y 'generaciones' en la historiografía literaria hispanoamericana." In *La historia y las generaciones.* Santiago de Cuba: Tipografía Román, 1958.

Prieto Taboada, Antonio. "Idioma y ciudadanía literaria en *Holy Smoke* de Guillermo Cabrera Infante." *Revista Iberoamericana* 57.154 (1991): 257–64.

Rama, Ángel. "Diez problemas para el novelista hispanoamericano." In *Literatura y arte nuevo en Cuba,* by Miguel Barnet et al., 195–259. Barcelona: Laia, 1977.

———. "El sistema literario de la poesía gauchesca." In *Literatura y clase social.* Mexico City: Folios, 1983.

Ramos, Julio. "Entre otros: *Una excursión a los indios ranqueles* de Lucio V. Mansilla." *Filología* 21.1 (1986): 143–71.

Reyes, Rogelio. "The Translation of Interlingual Texts." In *Translating Latin America: Culture as Text,* edited by William Luis and Julio Rodríguez-Luis, 301–8. Binghamton, N.Y.: Center for Research in Translation, 1991.

Sábato, Ernesto. "Los sofismas de la literatura nacionalista." In *El escritor y sus fantasmas,* 61–63. Barcelona: Seix Barral, 1987.

Saldívar, José David. *The Dialectics of Our America: Genealogy, Cultural Critique, and Literary History.* Durham: Duke University Press, 1991.

Santí, Enrico Mario. *Por una politeratura: Literatura hispanoamericana e imaginación política.* Mexico City: Ediciones del Equilibrista, 1997.

Sarmiento, Domingo Faustino. *Facundo.* Edited by Roberto Yahni. Madrid: Cátedra, 1993.

Schwartz, Roberto. "Nacional por subtração." In *Que horas são?* 29–48. São Paulo: Companhia das Letras, 1987.

Shumway, Nicolas. *The Invention of Argentina.* Berkeley: University of California Press, 1993.

Sommer, Doris. *Foundational Fictions: The National Romances of Latin America.* Berkeley: University of California Press, 1991.

Soto-Duggan, Lilvia. "La poética de la simultaneidad en Carlos Fuentes." Ph.D. diss., State University of New York at Stony Brook, 1980.

Souza, Raymond D. *Guillermo Cabrera Infante: Two Islands, Many Worlds.* Austin: University of Texas Press, 1996.

———. "Yes, We Have No Havana(s): Requiem for a Lost City." *World Literature Today* 61.4 (1987): 579–83.

Steiner, George. *Extraterritorial: Papers on Literature and the Language Revolution.* New York: Atheneum, 1976.

Stierle, Karlheinz. "Translatio Studii and Renaissance: From Vertical to Horizontal Translation." In *The Translatability of Culture: Figurations of the Space Between,* edited by Sanford Budick and Wolfgang Iser, 55–67. Stanford: Stanford University Press, 1996.

Szertics, Simone. *L'Héritage espagnol de Heredia.* Paris: Klincksieck, 1975.

Todorov, Tzvetan. *The Conquest of America.* Translated by Richard Howard. New York: Harper and Row, 1984.

———. *La Conquête de l'Amérique.* Paris: Seuil, 1982.

Unamuno, Miguel de. *Obras completas: Poesía.* Vol. 6. Madrid: Escelicer, 1969.

Valdés, Juan de. *Diálogo de la lengua.* Madrid: Espasa-Calpe, 1976.

van Delden, Maarten. *Carlos Fuentes, Mexico, and Modernity.* Nashville: Vanderbilt University Press, 1998.

Vásquez, Carmen. Introduction to *Souvenirs et mémoires de Madame la Comtesse Merlin,* by the Comtesse Merlin, 7–14. Paris: Mercure de France, 1990.

Vega, Ana Lydia, and Carmen Lugo Filippi. *Vírgenes y mártires*. Río Piedras: Antillana, 1983.

Vega, Garcilaso de la. *Comentarios reales de los incas*. 2 vols. Edited by Carlos Araníbar. Lima: Fondo de Cultura Económica, 1991.

———. *Royal Commentaries of the Incas and General History of Peru*. Translated by Harold V. Livermore. Austin: University of Texas Press, 1994.

Vidler, Anthony. *The Architectural Uncanny: Essays in the Modern Unhomely*. Cambridge: MIT Press, 1996.

Vitier, Cintio. *Lo cubano en la poesía*. Havana: Instituto del Libro, 1970.

Walker, John. " 'Home Thoughts from Abroad': W. H. Hudson's Argentine Fiction." *Canadian Review of Comparative Literature* 10.3 (September 1983): 333–76.

Williams, Raymond Leslie. *The Writings of Carlos Fuentes*. Austin: University of Texas Press, 1996.

Wilson, Jason. "W. H. Hudson: The Colonial's Revenge." *Review: Latin American Literature and Arts* 31 (January–April 1982): 53–59.

Winn, Peter. *Americas: The Changing Face of Latin America and the Caribbean*. New York: Pantheon, 1992.

Yáñez, Mirta. "Y entonces la mujer de Lot miró . . ." Introduction to *Estatuas de sal: Cuentistas cubanas contemporáneas*, edited by Mirta Yáñez and Marilyn Bobes, 9–43. Havana: Unión, 1996.

Zamora, Margarita. *Language, Authority, and Indigenous History in the "Comentarios reales de los incas."* Cambridge: Cambridge University Press, 1988.

Index

quino," 39, 41; *El diario que a diario*, 214 n. 3; *Motivos de son*, 40; "Tú no sabe inglé," 38, 40–41, 43, 45
Guinness, Gerald, 205 n. 24
Güiraldes, Ricardo: *Don Segundo Sombra*, 132–33, 136

Hahn, Reynaldo, 21
Halévy, Ludovic, 167
Hampsten, Elizabeth, 219 n. 3
Havana: foreign uses of, 166–67; in Cabrera Infante, 158–59, 163–78, 224 n. 17; in Merlin, 103–5, 111–12
Hebrew, 26
heimlich. *See* uncanny; unhomely
Hemingway, Ernest: *The Old Man and the Sea*, 23
Hennessy, Alastair, 206 n. 29
Henríquez Ureña, Max, 119, 211 n. 24 and 26, 214 n. 3, 216 n. 13, 225 n. 36
Henríquez Ureña, Pedro, 209 n. 8, 210 n. 12
Heredia, José María, 96, 113, 180, 188, 225 n. 36, 226 n. 37. Works: "Carta sobre los Estados Unidos," 216 n. 16; "En el teocalli de Cholula," 181; "Niágara," 97, 109
Heredia, José-Maria de, 20, 21, 160, 180, 184, 188, 209 n. 8, 225 n. 36. Works: "Le Lit," 198–99; *Les Trophées*, 76, 162, 181, 185–86, 217 n. 26
Heredia, Severiano de, 226 n. 36
Hermer, Consuelo, 166
Hernández, José, 132; *Martín Fierro*, 84–86, 134, 137, 220 n. 17
heteroglossia, 44, 200 n. 1, 206 n. 24, 220 n. 18
heterolingual authors, 19–23, 192–93; assertions of kinship to Spanish America, 17–18; critical and literary-historical status of, 13, 14, 62–64, 100, 216 n. 21; in Spanish translation, 14; influence of Spanish in, 26. *See also* heterolingualism
heterolingualism, 20–23, 35, 46, 48–49; and authorship, 92–123; and the Baroque, 16; and canonical au-

thors, 16, 21–22; and Freud's uncanny, 27, 79–90; and identity-thinking, 14; and Hispanic authors in the United States, 22, 52–58; and migration, 16, 44–45; and reading, 18, 55, 124–56; and Spanish American literary history, 15, 18, 25; and theory of literary history, 25; as critical concept, 15–16, 18; as dissonance or fragmentation, 24, 28, 30, 62–63; as elitism, 29–30; as self-imposed exile, 18; European versus indigenous, 19; in colonial Spanish America, 16; in Darío's *Los raros*, 74–78; in post-colonial Spanish America, 21–22; in Spain, 26; literature as a meditation on, 20, 157–99; reasons for, 16, 17, 27. *See also* heterolingual authors
Higgins, James, 201 n. 10
Hijuelos, Oscar, 162
Hillman, Eduardo: translation of *The Purple Land*, 137–39, 145, 225 n. 36
Hispanic authors in the United States, 39–41, 52–58, 77; and José Martí, 22; and Spanish American literary history, 14, 17, 22, 210 n. 9. *See also* Cuban-American authors; interlingualism; multilingualism in the United States
Hitchcock, Alfred: *Rebecca*, 147, 149
Hoffmann, E. T. A.: "Der Sandmann," 43
Hudson, William Henry, 20, 21, 34, 49, 51, 62, 76, 144, 158, 177, 197; as an "English traveler," 50, 129; in Anderson Imbert's *Los domingos del profesor*, 67–69; uses of *literatura gauchesca* by, 133–43. Works: *Afoot in England*, 51; *Birds and Men*, 132; *Birds of La Plata*, 127; *British Birds*, 127: *Far Away and Long Ago*, 98, 172; *Green Mansions*, 129, 131; *The Purple Land*, 19, 50, 51, 124–42, 151, 154, 172–73, 196
Hughes, Langston: "Havana Dreams," 166–67
Hugo, Victor, 80, 186